CCNP Quick Reference

Denise Donohue, CCIE No. 9566
Brent Stewart
Jerold Swan, CCIE No. 17783

Cisco Press
800 East 96th Street
Indianapolis, Indiana 46240 USA

CCNP Quick Reference

Denise Donohue, Brent Stewart, Jerold Swan

Published by:
Cisco Press
800 East 96th Street
Indianapolis, IN 46240 USA

Printed in the United States of America

First Printing June 2008

Library of Congress Cataloging-in-Publication Date available upon request

ISBN-13: 978-1-58720-236-0

ISBN-10: 1-58720-236-0

Publisher
Paul Boger

Associate Publisher
Dave Dusthimer

Cisco Press Program Manager
Jeff Brady

Executive Editor
Brett Bartow

Managing Editor
Patrick Kanouse

Editorial Assistant
Vanessa Evans

Designer
Louisa Adair

Warning and Disclaimer

This book is designed to provide information about networking. Every effort has been made to make this book as complete and as accurate as possible, but no warranty or fitness is implied.

The information is provided on an "as is" basis. The authors, Cisco Press, and Cisco Systems, Inc. shall have neither liability nor responsibility to any person or entity with respect to any loss or damages arising from the information contained in this book or from the use of the discs or programs that may accompany it.

The opinions expressed in this book belong to the author and are not necessarily those of Cisco Systems, Inc.

Trademark Acknowledgments

All terms mentioned in this book that are known to be trademarks or service marks have been appropriately capitalized. Cisco Press or Cisco Systems, Inc., cannot attest to the accuracy of this information. Use of a term in this book should not be regarded as affecting the validity of any trademark or service mark.

Corporate and Government Sales

The publisher offers excellent discounts on this book when ordered in quantity for bulk purchases or special sales, which may include electronic versions and/or custom covers and content particular to your business, training goals, marketing focus, and branding interests. For more information, please contact:

U.S. Corporate and Government Sales 1-800-382-3419
corpsales@pearsontechgroup.com

For sales outside the United States please contact:
International Sales international@pearsoned.com

Feedback Information

At Cisco Press, our goal is to create in-depth technical books of the highest quality and value. Each book is crafted with care and precision, undergoing rigorous development that involves the unique expertise of members from the professional technical community.

Readers' feedback is a natural continuation of this process. If you have any comments regarding how we could improve the quality of this book, or otherwise alter it to better suit your needs, you can contact us through email at feedback@ciscopress.com. Please make sure to include the book title and ISBN in your message.

We greatly appreciate your assistance.

Americas Headquarters
Cisco Systems, Inc.
170 West Tasman Drive
San Jose, CA 95134-1706
USA
www.cisco.com
Tel: 408 526-4000
800 553-NETS (6387)
Fax: 408 527-0883

Asia Pacific Headquarters
Cisco Systems, Inc.
168 Robinson Road
#28-01 Capital Tower
Singapore 068912
www.cisco.com
Tel: +65 6317 7777
Fax: +65 6317 7799

Europe Headquarters
Cisco Systems International BV
Haarlerbergpark
Haarlerbergweg 13-19
1101 CH Amsterdam
The Netherlands
www-europe.cisco.com
Tel: +31 0 800 020 0791
Fax: +31 0 20 357 1100

Cisco has more than 200 offices worldwide. Addresses, phone numbers, and fax numbers are listed on the Cisco Website at **www.cisco.com/go/offices.**

About the Authors

Denise Donohue, CCIE No. 9566, is manager of Solutions Engineering for ePlus Technology in Maryland. She is responsible for designing and implementing data and VoIP networks, supporting companies based in the National Capital region. Prior to this role, she was a systems engineer for the data consulting arm of SBC/AT&T. Denise was a Cisco instructor and course director for Global Knowledge and did network consulting for many years.

Brent Stewart, CCNP, CCDP, CCSI, MCSE, is a network administrator for CommScope. He is responsible for designing and managing a large-scale worldwide IP network. He participated in the development of BSCI with Cisco and has written and taught extensively on CCNA and CCNP.

Jerold Swan, CCIE No. 17783, is a senior network engineer for the Southern Ute Indian Tribe Growth Fund in Ignacio, CO. Prior to that he was a Cisco instructor and course director for Global Knowledge. He has also worked in IT in the higher education and service provider fields. He holds CCNP and CCSP certifications.

About the Technical Editors

Rus Healy, CCIE No. 15025, works as a senior engineer for Annese & Associates, a Cisco partner in upstate New York. He also holds CCNP and CCDP certifications. His other interests include bicycling, skiing, and camping with his family, as well as competitive amateur radio events.

John Mistichelli, CCIE No. 7536, CCSI No. 20000, CCNP, CCDP, CCIP, MCSE, CNE, is a self employed Cisco consultant and trainer. He provides network-consulting services for businesses and government organizations throughout the United States. John is also a world-class technical trainer for Convergent Communications where he teaches service provider courses for Cisco Advanced Services Education. John is a coauthor of the book *Cisco Routers 24Seven* (ISBN: 0782126464).

Contents at a Glance

Contents

Icons Used in This Book

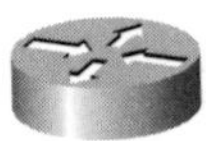
Router

Wireless Router

Multilayer Switch

Switch

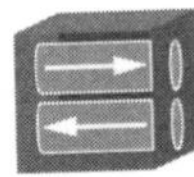
VPN Concentrator

File Server

PC

Laptop

Relational Database

IP Phone

Access Server

PIX Firewall

Network Cloud, White

Serial Line Connection

Ethernet Connection

Command Syntax Conventions

The conventions used to present command syntax in this book are the same conventions used in the IOS Command Reference. The Command Reference describes these conventions as follows:

- **Boldface** indicates commands and keywords that are entered literally as shown. In actual configuration examples and output (not general command syntax), boldface indicates commands that are manually input by the user (such as a **show** command).
- *Italic* indicates arguments for which you supply actual values.
- Vertical bars (|) separate alternative, mutually exclusive elements.
- Square brackets ([ ]) indicate an optional element.
- Braces ({ }) indicate a required choice.
- Braces within brackets ([{ }]) indicate a required choice within an optional element.

PART I

BSCI

CHAPTER 1

The Evolving Network Model

The Hierarchical Design Model

Cisco used the three-level *Hierarchical Design Model* for years. This older model provided a high-level idea of how a reliable network might be conceived, but it was largely conceptual because it didn't provide specific guidance. Figure 1-1 shows the Hierarchical Design Model.

Figure 1-1 Hierarchical Design Model

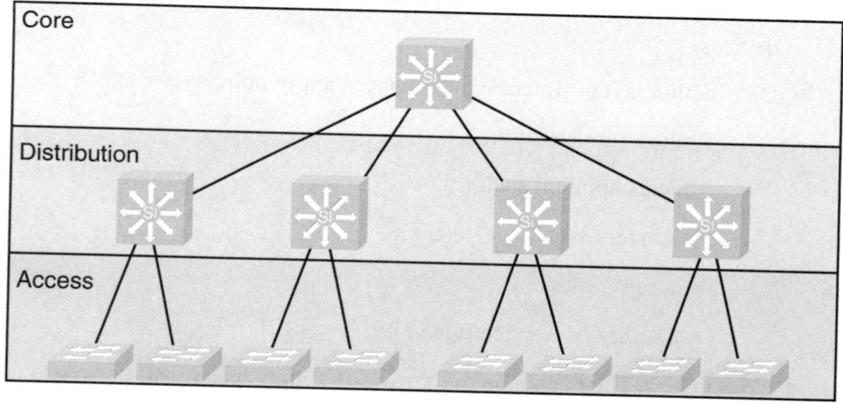

Figure 1-2 is a simple drawing of how the three-layer model might have been built out. A distribution layer-3 switch is used for each building on campus, tying together the access switches on the floors. The core switches link the various buildings together.

This same three-layer hierarchy can be used in the WAN with a central headquarters, division headquarters, and units.

Figure 1-2 Three-Layer Network Design

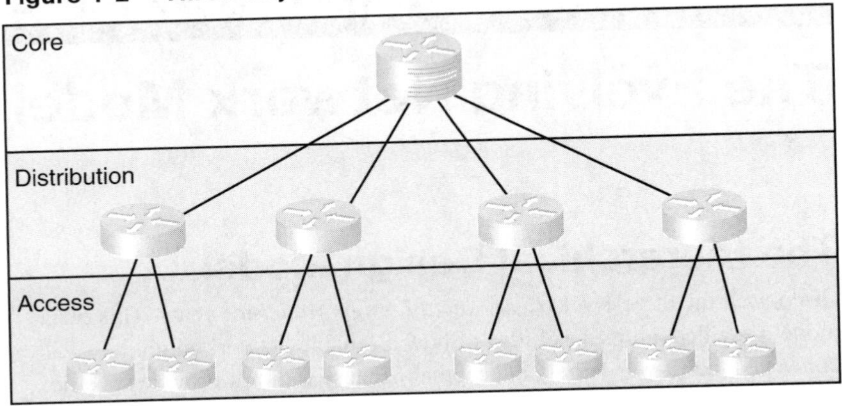

The layers break a network in the following way:

- Access layer—End stations attach to the network using low-cost devices.
- Distribution layer—Intermediate devices apply policies.
  - Route summarization
  - Policies applied, such as:
    - Route selection
    - Access lists
    - Quality of Service (QoS)
- Core layer—The backbone that provides a high-speed path between distribution elements.
  - Distribution devices are interconnected.
  - High speed (there is a lot of traffic).
  - No policies (it is tough enough to keep up).

Later versions of this model include redundant distribution, core devices, and connections, which make the model more fault-tolerant.

Problems with the Hierarchical Design Model

This early model was a good starting point, but it failed to address key issues, such as:

- Where do wireless devices fit in?
- How should Internet access and security be provisioned?
- How do you account for remote access, such as dial-up or VPN?
- Where should workgroup and enterprise services be located?

Enterprise Composite Network Model

The newer Cisco model—the Enterprise Composite Model—is significantly more complex and attempts to address the shortcomings of the Hierarchical Design Model by expanding the older version and making specific recommendations about how and where certain network functions should be implemented. This model is based on the principles described in the Cisco Architecture for Voice, Video, and Integrated Data (AVVID).

The Enterprise Composite Model (see Figure 1-3) is broken into three large sections:

- Enterprise Campus—Switches that make up a LAN
- Enterprise Edge—The portion of the enterprise network connected to the larger world.
- Service Provider Edge—The different public networks that are attached

The first section, the Enterprise Campus, looks like the old Hierarchical Design Model with added details. It features six sections:

- Campus Backbone—The core of the LAN
- Building Distribution—Links subnets/VLANs and applies policy
- Building Access—Connects users to network
- Management
- Edge Distribution—A distribution layer out to the WAN
- Server Farm—For Enterprise services

Figure 1-3 The Enterprise Composite Model

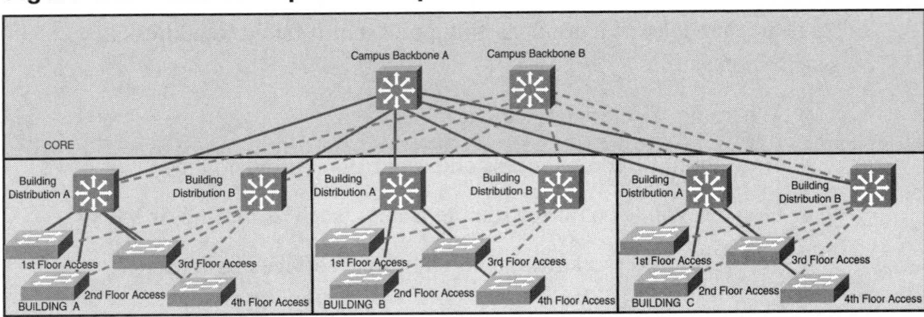

The Enterprise Edge, shown in Figure 1-4, details the connections from the campus to the WAN and includes:

- E-commerce
- Internet connectivity
- Remote access
- WAN

Figure 1-4 The Enterprise Edge

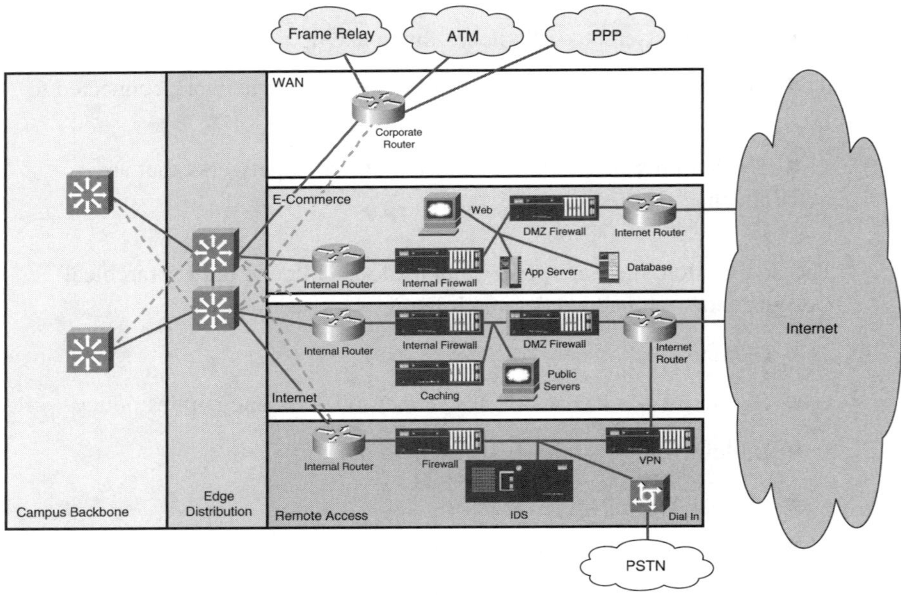

The Service Provider Edge is just a list of the public networks that facilitate wide-area connectivity and include:

- Internet service provider (ISP)
- Public switched telephone network (PSTN)
- Frame Relay, ATM, and PPP

Figure 1-5 puts together the various pieces: Campus, Enterprise Edge, and Service Provider Edge. Security implemented on this model is described in the Cisco SAFE (Security Architecture for Enterprise) blueprint.

Figure 1-5 The Enterprise Composite Model

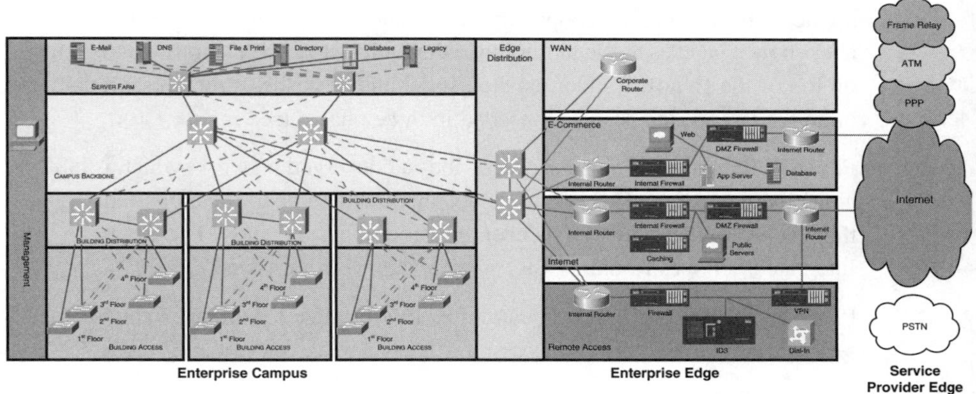

SONA and IIN

Modern converged networks include different traffic types, each with unique requirements for security, QoS, transmission capacity, and delay. These include:

- Voice signaling and bearer
- Core application traffic, such as Enterprise Resource Planning (ERP) or Customer Relationship Management (CRM)
- Database transactions
- Multicast multimedia
- Network management
- Other traffic, such as web pages, e-mail, and file transfer

Cisco routers are able to implement filtering, compression, prioritization, and policing. Except for filtering, these capabilities are referred to collectively as QoS.

Note

The best way to meet capacity requirements is to have twice as much bandwidth as needed. Financial reality, however, usually requires QoS instead.

Although QoS is wonderful, it is not the only way to address bandwidth shortage. Cisco espouses an idea called the Intelligent Information Network (IIN).

IIN describes an evolutionary vision of a network that integrates network and application functionality cooperatively and allows the network to be smart about how it handles traffic to minimize the footprint of applications. IIN is built on top of the Enterprise Composite Model and describes structures overlaid on to the Composite design as needed in three phases (see Figure 1-6).

Phase 1, "Integrated Transport," describes a converged network, which is built along the lines of the Composite model and based on open standards. This is the phase that the industry has been transitioning to recently. The Cisco Integrated Services Routers (ISR) are an example of this trend.

Phase 2, "Integrated Services," attempts to virtualize resources, such as servers, storage, and network access. It is a move to an "on-demand" model.

By "virtualize," Cisco means that the services are not associated with a particular device or location. Instead, many services can reside in one device to ease management, or many devices can provide one service that is more reliable.

An ISR brings together routing, switching, voice, security, and wireless. It is an example of many services existing on one device. A load balancer, which makes many servers look like one, is an example of one service residing on many devices.

VRFs are an example of taking one resource and making it look like many. Some versions of IOS are capable of having a router present itself as many virtual router (VRF) instances, allowing your company to deliver different logical topologies on the same physical infrastructure. Server virtualization is another example. The classic example of taking one resource and making it appear to be many resources is the use of a virtual LAN (VLAN) and a virtual storage area network (VSAN).

Virtualization provides flexibility in configuration and management.

Phase 3, "Integrated Applications," uses application-oriented networking (AON) to make the network application-aware and to allow the network to actively participate in service delivery.

An example of this Phase 3 IIN systems approach to service delivery is Network Admission Control (NAC). Before NAC, authentication, VLAN assignment, and anti-virus updates were separately managed. With NAC in place, the network is able to check the policy stance of a client and admit, deny, or remediate based on policies.

IIN allows the network to deconstruct packets, parse fields, and take actions based on the values it finds. An ISR equipped with an AON blade might be set up to route traffic from a business partner. The AON blade can examine traffic, recognize the application, and rebuild XML files in memory. Corrupted XML fields might represent an attack (called *schema poisoning*), so the AON blade can react by blocking that source from further communication. In this example, routing, an awareness of the application data flow, and security are combined to allow the network to contribute to the success of the application.

Services-Oriented Network Architecture (SONA) applies the IIN ideal to Enterprise networks. SONA breaks down the IIN functions into three layers:

- Network Infrastructure—Hierarchical converged network and attached end systems.
- Interactive Services—Resources allocated to applications.
- Applications—Includes business policy and logic.

Figure 1-6 IIN and SONA

IIN Phases

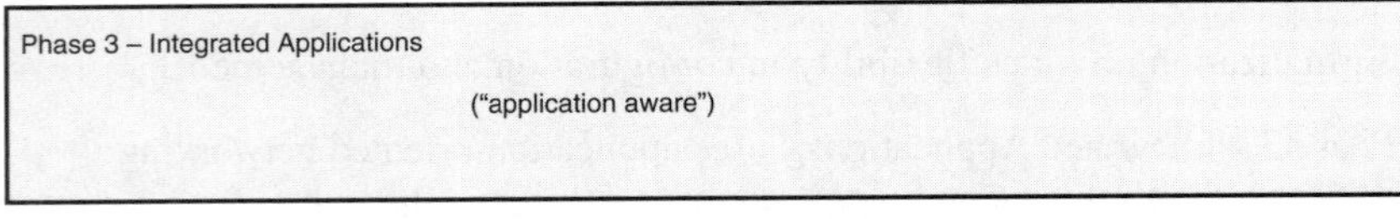

Phase 2 – Integrated Services (virtualized resources)

Phase 1 – Integrated Transport (converged network)

SONA Framework Layers

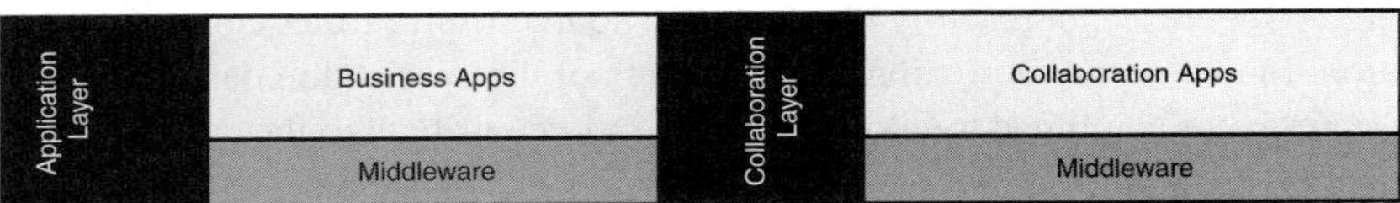

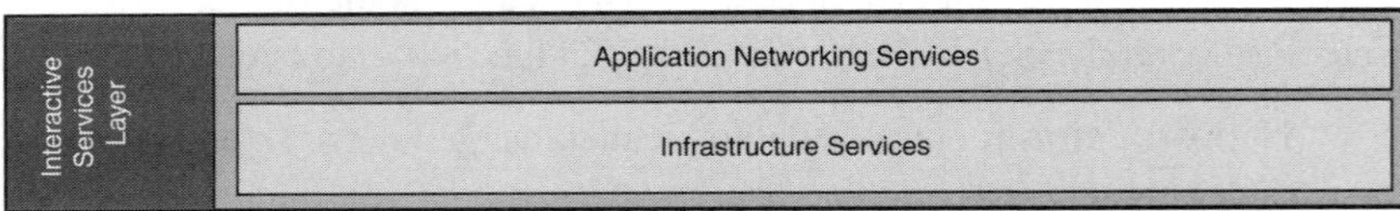

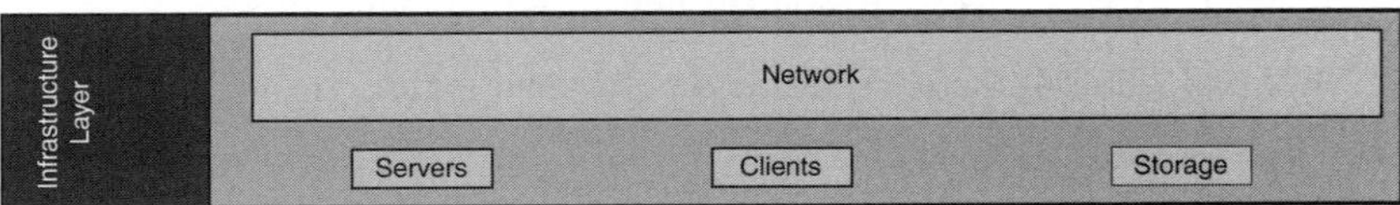

IP Routing Protocols

Routing protocols are used to pass information about the structure of the network between routers. Cisco routers support the following IP routing protocols RIP (versions 1 and 2), IGRP, EIGRP, IS-IS, OSPF, and BGP. This section compares routing protocols and calls out key differences between them.

Administrative Distance

Cisco routers are capable of supporting several IP routing protocols concurrently. When identical prefixes are discovered from two or more separate sources, Administrative Distance (AD) is used to discriminate between the paths. AD is a poor choice of words; *trustworthiness* is a better name. Routers use paths with the lower AD.

Table 1-1 lists the default values for various routing protocols. Of course, there are several ways to change AD for a routing protocol or for a specific route.

Table 1-1 Routing Protocols and Their Default Administrative Distance

Information Source	AD
Connected	0
Static	1
External BGP (Border Gateway Protocol)	20
Internal EIGRP (Enhanced IGRP)	90
IGRP (Internet Gateway Routing Protocol)	100
OSPF (Open Shortest Path First)	110
IS-IS (Intermediate System to Intermediate System)	115
RIP (Routing Information Protocol)	120
ODR (On Demand Routing)	160
External EIGRP	170
Internal BGP	200
Unknown	255

Building the Routing Table

The router builds a routing table by ruling out invalid routes and considering the remaining advertisements. The procedure is:

1. For each route received, verify the next hop. If invalid, discard the route.
2. If multiple, valid routes are advertised by a routing protocol, choose the lowest metric.
3. Routes are identical if they advertise the same prefix and mask, so 192.168.0.0/16 and 192.168.0.0/24 are separate paths and are each placed into the routing table.
4. If more than one specific valid route is advertised by different routing protocols, choose the path with the lowest AD.

Comparing Routing Protocols

Two things should always be considered in choosing a routing protocol: fast convergence speed and support for VLSM. EIGRP, OSPF, and IS-IS meet these criteria. Although all three meet the minimum, there are still important distinctions, as described below:

- EIGRP is proprietary, but it is simple to configure and support.
- OSPF is an open standard, but it is difficult to implement and support.
- There are few books on IS-IS and even fewer engineers with experience who use it. IS-IS is therefore uncommon.

Table 1-2 compares routing protocols.

Table 1-2 Comparison of Routing Protocols

Property	EIGRP	OSPF	IS-IS	BGP
Method	Advanced distance vector	Link state	Link state	Path vector
Summary	Auto and arbitrary	Arbitrary	Arbitrary	Auto and arbitrary
VLSM	Yes	Yes	Yes	Yes
Converge	Seconds	Seconds	Seconds	Minutes
Timers: Update (hello/ dead)	Triggered (LAN 5/15, WAN 60/180)	Triggered, but LSA refreshes every 30 minutes (NBMA 30/120, LAN 10/40)	Triggered (10/30)	Triggered (60/180)

CHAPTER 2

EIGRP

Enhanced Interior Gateway Routing Protocol (EIGRP) is a Cisco proprietary classless routing protocol that uses a complex metric based on bandwidth and delay. The following are some features of EIGRP:

- Fast convergence
- Support for VLSM
- Partial updates conserve network bandwidth
- Support for IP, AppleTalk, and IPX
- Support for all layer 2 (data link layer) protocols and topologies
- Sophisticated metric that supports unequal-metric proportional load-balancing
- Use of multicasts (and unicasts where appropriate) instead of broadcasts
- Support for authentication

EIGRP Overview

EIGRP's function is controlled by four key technologies:

- Neighbor discovery and maintenance—Uses periodic hello messages
- The Reliable Transport Protocol (RTP)—Controls sending, tracking, and acknowledging EIGRP messages
- Diffusing Update Algorithm (DUAL)—Determines the best loop-free route
- Protocol-independent modules (PDM)—Modules are "plug-ins" for IP, IPX, and AppleTalk versions of EIGRP

EIGRP uses three tables:

- The neighbor table is built from EIGRP hellos and used for reliable delivery.
- The topology table contains EIGRP routing information for best paths and loop-free alternatives.
- EIGRP places best routes from its topology table into the common routing table.

EIGRP Messages

EIGRP uses various message types to initiate and maintain neighbor relationships, and to maintain an accurate routing table. It is designed to conserve bandwidth and router resources by sending messages only when needed, and only to those neighbors that need to receive them.

Packet Types

EIGRP uses five packet types:

- Hello—Identifies neighbors and serves as a keepalive mechanism
- Update—Reliably sends route information
- Query—Reliably requests specific route information
- Reply—Reliably responds to a query
- ACK—Acknowledgment

EIGRP is reliable, but hellos and ACKs are not acknowledged. The acknowledgement to a query is a reply.

If a reliable packet is not acknowledged, EIGRP periodically retransmits the packet to the nonresponding neighbor as a unicast. EIGRP has a window size of one, so no other traffic is sent to this neighbor until it responds. After 16 unacknowledged retransmissions, the neighbor is removed from the neighbor table.

Neighbor Discovery and Route Exchange

When EIGRP first starts, it uses hellos to build a neighbor table. Neighbors are directly attached routers that have a matching AS number and k values (the timers don't have to agree). The process of neighbor discovery and route exchange between two EIGRP routers is as follows:

Step 1. Router A sends out a hello.

Step 2. Router B sends back a hello and an update. The update contains routing information.

Step 3. Router A acknowledges the update.

Step 4. Router A sends its update.

Step 5. Router B acknowledges.

Once two routers are EIGRP neighbors, they use hellos between them as keepalives. Additional route information is sent only if a route is lost or a new route is discovered. A neighbor is considered lost if no hello is received within three hello periods (called the *hold time*). The default hello/hold timers are as follows:

- 5 seconds/15 seconds for multipoint circuits with bandwidth greater than T1 and for point-to-point media
- 60 seconds/180 seconds for multipoint circuits with bandwidth less than or equal to T1

The exchange process can be viewed using **debug ip eigrp packets**, and the update process can be seen using **debug ip eigrp**. The neighbor table can be seen with the command **show ip eigrp neighbors**.

EIGRP Route Selection

An EIGRP router receives advertisements from each neighbor that lists the advertised distance (AD) and feasible distance (FD) to a route. The *AD* is the metric from the neighbor to the network. *FD* is the metric from this router, through the neighbor, to the network.

EIGRP Metric

The EIGRP metric is shown in Figure 2-1.

Figure 2-1 EIGRP Metric

$$metric = 256(k1 \times \frac{10^7}{BW_{\min}} + \frac{k2 \times BW_{\min}}{256 - load} + k3 \times \sum delays)(\frac{k5}{reliability + k4})$$

The k values are constants. Their default values are:
k1 = 1, k2 = 0, k3 = 1, k4 = 0, and k5 = 0. If k5 = 0, the final part of the equation (k5 / [rel + k4]) is ignored.

BW^{min} is the minimum bandwidth along the path—the choke point bandwidth.

Delay values are associated with each interface. The sum of the delays (in tens of microseconds) is used in the equation.

Taking the default k values into account, the equation simplifies to the one shown in Figure 2-2.

Figure 2-2 EIGRP Metric Simplified

$$metric = 256(\frac{10^7}{BW_{\min}} + \sum delays)$$

If default k values are used, this works out to be 256 (BW + cumulative delay).

Bandwidth is the largest contributor to the metric. The delay value allows us to choose a more direct path when bandwidth is equivalent.

The EIGRP metric is 256 times the IGRP metric. The two automatically redistribute and algorithmically adjust metrics if they are configured on the same router for the same autonomous system.

Diffusing Update Algorithm (DUAL)

DUAL is the algorithm used by EIGRP to choose best paths by looking at AD and FD. The path with the lowest metric is called the *successor* path. EIGRP paths with a lower AD than the FD of the successor path are guaranteed loop-free and called *feasible successors*. If the successor path is lost, the router can use the feasible successor immediately without risk of loops.

After the router has chosen a path to a network, it is *passive* for that route. If a successor path is lost and no feasible successor is identified, the router sends out queries on all interfaces in an attempt to identify an alternate path. It is *active* for that route. No successor can be chosen until the router receives a reply to all queries. If a reply is missing for three minutes, the router becomes *stuck in active (SIA)*. In that case, it resets the neighbor relationship with the neighbor that did not reply.

Route Selection Example

The following diagrams show EIGRP advertisements to R3 and R5 about a destination network connected to R1. In Figure 2-3, R5 chooses R4 as the successor path because it offers the lowest feasible distance. The AD from R3 indicates that passing traffic through R3 will not loop, so R3 is a feasible successor.

Figure 2-3 EIGRP Path Selection, Part One

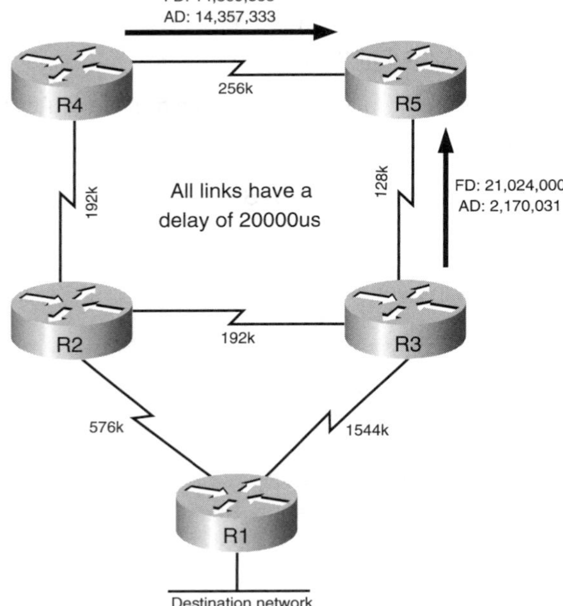

How does R3 choose its path? Figure 2-4 shows the path selection process for R3.

Figure 2-4 EIGRP Path Selection, Part Two

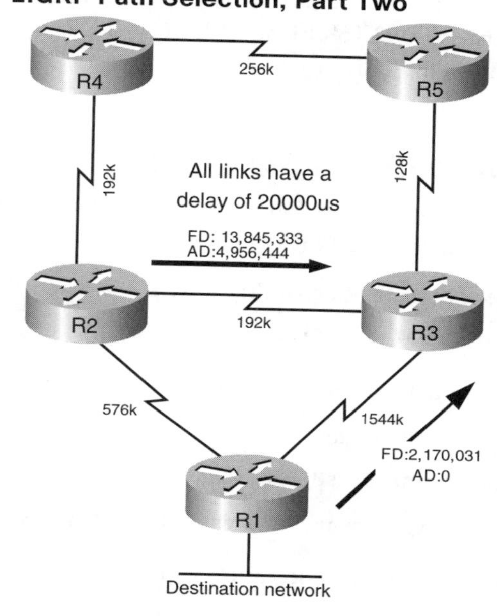

R1 will be its successor because it has the lowest metric. However, no feasible successor exists because R2's AD is greater than the successor path metric. If the direct path to R1 is lost, then R3 has to query its neighbors to discover an alternative path. It must wait to hear back from R2 and R5, and will ultimately decide that R2 is the new successor.

Basic EIGRP Configuration

EIGRP is configured by entering router configuration mode and identifying the networks within which it should run. When setting up EIGRP, an autonomous system number must be used (7 is used in the example). Autonomous system numbers must agree for two routers to form a neighbor relationship and to exchange routes.

```
Router(config)#router eigrp 7
Router(config-router)#network 192.168.1.0
```

The wildcard mask option can be used with the network command to more precisely identify EIGRP interfaces. For instance, if a router has two interfaces—fa0/0 (192.168.1.1/27) and fa0/1 (192.168.1.33/27)—and needs to run only EIGRP on fa0/0, the following command can be used:

```
Router(config-router)#network 192.168.1.0 0.0.0.1
```

In this command, a wildcard mask of 0.0.0.1 matches only two IP addresses in network 192.168.1.0–192.168.1.0 and 192.168.1.1. Therefore, only interface fa0/0 is included in EIGRP routing.

Creating an EIGRP Default Route

Figure 2-5 shows a simple two-router network. You can configure EIGRP on R1 to advertise a default route to R3 in three ways:

- R1 can specify a default network:

  ```
  R1(config)#ip default-network 10.0.0.0
  ```

  R3 now sees a default network with a next hop of R1.

- Produce a summary route:

  ```
  R1(config)#interface s0/0/0
  R1(config-if)#ip summary-address eigrp 7 0.0.0.0 0.0.0.0
  ```

  This passes a default route from R1 out its serial0 interface toward R3.

- Create a static default route and then include network 0.0.0.0 in EIGRP:

  ```
  R1(config)#ip route 0.0.0.0 0.0.0.0 10.1.1.2
  R1(config)#router eigrp 7
  R1(config-router)#network 0.0.0.0
  ```

Figure 2-5 EIGRP Default Route

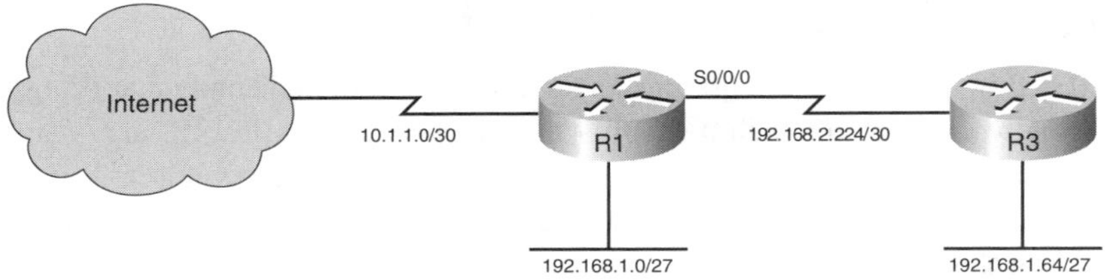

Troubleshooting EIGRP

The most straightforward way to troubleshoot EIGRP is to inspect the routing table—**show ip route**. To filter the routing table and show only the routes learned from EIGRP, use the **show ip route eigrp** command. The **show ip protocols** command verifies autonomous system, timer values, identified networks, and EIGRP neighbors (routing information sources).

The command **show ip eigrp topology** shows the EIGRP topology table and identifies successors and feasible successors. Use **show ip eigrp neighbors** to verify that the correct routers are neighbors, and use **show ip eigrp traffic** to show the amount and types of EIGRP messages.

Advanced EIGRP Configuration

EIGRP provides some ways to customize its operation, such as route summarization, unequal-metric load balancing, controlling the percent of interface bandwidth used, and authentication. This section describes how to configure these.

Summarization

EIGRP defaults to automatically summarizing at classful network boundaries. Automatic summarization is usually disabled using the following command:

```
Router(config-router)#no auto-summary
```

Summaries can be produced manually on any interface. When a summary is produced, a matching route to null0 also becomes active as a loop prevention mechanism. Configure a summary route out a particular interface using the **ip summary-address eigrp** *autonomous_system* command. The following example advertises a default route out FastEthernet0/1 and the summary route 172.16.104.0/22 out Serial0/0/0 for EIGRP AS 7.

```
Router(config)#int fa0/1
Router(config-if)#ip summary-address eigrp 7 0.0.0.0 0.0.0.0
!
Router(config)#int s0/0/0
Router(config-if)#ip summary-address eigrp 7 172.16.104.0
 255.255.252.0
```

Load Balancing

EIGRP, like most IP routing protocols, automatically load balances over equal metric paths. What makes EIGRP unique is that you can configure it to proportionally load balance over *unequal* metric paths. The **variance** command is used to configure load balancing over up to six loop-free paths with a metric lower than the product of the variance and the best metric. Figure 2-3, in the "Route Selection Example" section, shows routers advertising a path to the network connected to R1.

By default, R5 uses the path through R4 because it offers the lowest metric (14,869,333). To set up unequal cost load balancing, assign a variance of 2 under the EIGRP process on R5. R5 multiplies the best metric of 14,869,333 by 2, to get 29,738,666. R5 then uses all loop-free paths with a metric less than 29,738,666, which includes the path through R3. By default, R5 load balances over these paths, sending traffic along each path in proportion to its metric.

```
R5(config)#router eigrp 7
R5(config-router)#variance 2
```

WAN Bandwidth

By default, EIGRP limits itself to bursting to half the link bandwidth. This limit is configurable per interface using the **ip bandwidth-percent** command. The following example assumes EIGRP AS 7 and limits EIGRP to one quarter of the link bandwidth:

```
Router(config)#int s0/0/0
Router(config-if)#ip bandwidth-percent eigrp 7 25
```

The real issue with WAN links is that the router assumes that each link has 1544 kbps bandwidth. If interface Serial0/0/0 is attached to a 128 k fractional T1, EIGRP assumes it can burst to 768 k and could overwhelm the line. This is rectified by correctly identifying link bandwidth.

```
Router (config)#int serial 0/0/0
Router (config-if)#bandwidth 128
```

Figure 2-6 shows a situation in which these techniques can be combined—Frame Relay.

Figure 2-6 EIGRP with Frame Relay

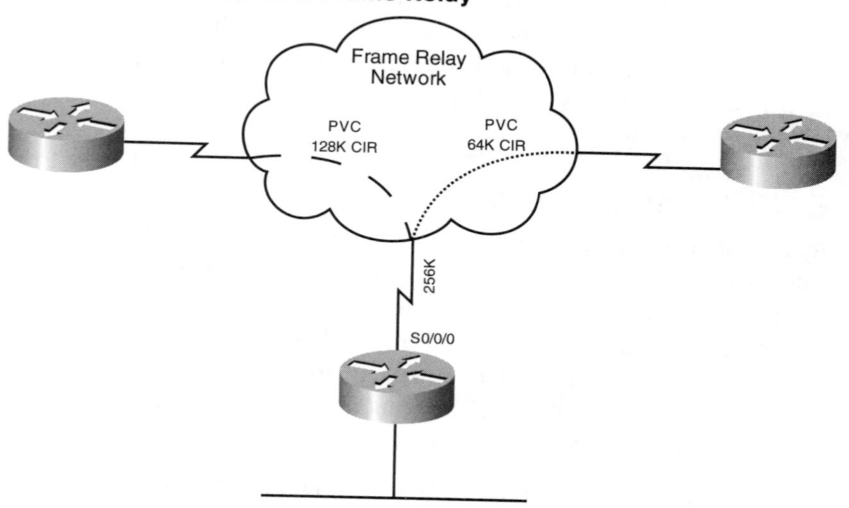

In this example, R1 has a 256 kbps connection to the Frame Relay network and two permanent virtual circuits (PVCs) with committed information rates (CIR) of 128 Kpbs and 64 Kbps. EIGRP divides the interface bandwidth evenly between the number of neighbors on that interface. What value should be used for the interface bandwidth in this case? The usual suggestion is to use the CIR, but the two PVCs have different CIRs. You could use the bandwidth-percent command to allow SNMP reporting of the true bandwidth value, while adjusting the interface burst rate to 25 percent, or 64 kbps.

```
R1(config)#int serial 0/0/0
R1 (config-if)#bandwidth 256
R1 (config-if)#ip bandwidth-percent eigrp 7 25
```

A better solution is to use subinterfaces and identify bandwidth separately. In the following example, s0/0/0.1 bursts to 64 k, and s0/0/0.2 bursts to 32 k, using EIGRP's default value of half the bandwidth.

```
R1(config)#int serial 0/0/0.1
R1 (config-if)#bandwidth 128
!
R1(config)#int serial 0/0/0.2
R1 (config-if)#bandwidth 64
```

In cases where the hub interface bandwidth is oversubscribed, it may be necessary to set bandwidth for each subinterface arbitrarily low, and then specify an EIGRP bandwidth percent value over 100 in order to allow EIGRP to use half the PVC bandwidth.

EIGRP Authentication

By default, no authentication is used for any routing protocol. Some protocols, such as RIPv2, IS-IS, and OSPF, can be configured to do simple password authentication between neighboring routers. In this type of authentication, a clear-text password is used. EIGRP does not support simple authentication. However, it can be configured to authenticate each packet exchanged, using an MD5 hash. This is more secure than clear text, as only the message digest is exchanged, not the password.

EIGRP authenticates each of its packets by including the hash in each one. This helps verify the source of each routing update.

To configure EIGRP authentication, follow these steps:

Step 1. Configure a key chain to group the keys.

Step 2. Configure a key within that key chain.

Step 3. Configure the password or authentication string for that key. Repeat Steps 2 and 3 to add more keys if desired.

Step 4. Optionally configure a lifetime for the keys within that key chain. If you do this, be sure that the time is synchronized between the two routers.

Step 5. Enable authentication and assign a key chain to an interface.

Step 6. Designate MD5 as the type of authentication.

Example 2-1 shows a router configured with EIGRP authentication. It shows configuring a lifetime for packets sent using key 1 that starts at 10:15 and lasts for 300 seconds. It also shows configuring a lifetime for packets received using key 1 that starts at 10:00 and lasts until 10:05.

Example 2-1 Configuring EIGRP Authentication

```
Router(config)#key chain RTR_Auth
Router(config-keychain)#key 1
Router(config-keychain-key)#key-string mykey
Router(config-keychain-key)#send-lifetime 10:15:00 300
Router(config-keychain-key)#accept-lifetime 10:00:00 10:05:00
!
```

```
Router(config)#interface s0/0/0
Router(config-if)#ip authentication mode eigrp 10 md5
Router(config-if)#ip authentication key-chain eigrp 10 RTR_Auth
```

Verify your configuration with the **show ip eigrp neighbors** command, as no neighbor relationship will be formed if authentication fails. Using the **debug eigrp packets** command should show packets containing authentication information sent and received, and it will allow you to troubleshoot configuration issues.

EIGRP Scalability

Four factors influence EIGRP's scalability:

- The number of routes that must be exchanged
- The number of routers that must know of a topology change
- The number of alternate routes to a network
- The number of hops from one end of the network to the other

To improve scalability, summarize routes when possible, try to have a network depth of no more than seven hops, and limit the scope of EIGRP queries.

Stub routing is one way to limit queries. A stub router is one that is connected to no more than two neighbors and should never be a transit router. When a router is configured as an EIGRP stub, it notifies its neighbors. The neighbors then do not query that router for a lost route. Under router configuration mode, use the command **eigrp stub [receive-only|connected|static|summary]**. An EIGRP stub router still receives all routes from its neighbors by default.

Routers use *SIA-Queries* and *SIA-Replies* to prevent loss of a neighbor unnecessarily during SIA conditions. A router sends its neighbor a SIA-Query after no reply to a normal query. If the neighbor responds with a SIA-Reply, then the router does not terminate the neighbor relationship after three minutes, because it knows the neighbor is available.

Graceful shutdown is another feature that speeds network convergence. Whenever the EIGRP process is shut down, the router sends a "goodbye" message to its neighbors. The neighbors can then immediately recalculate any paths that used the router as the next hop, rather than waiting for the hold timer to expire.

CHAPTER 3
OSPF

OSPF Overview

OSPF is an open-standard, classless routing protocol that converges quickly and uses cost as a metric (Cisco IOS automatically associates cost with bandwidth).

OSPF is a link-state routing protocol and uses Dijkstra's Shortest Path First (SPF) algorithm to determine its best path to each network. The first responsibility of a link-state router is to create a database that reflects the structure of the network. Link state routing protocols learn more information on the structure of the network than other routing protocols, and thus are able to make more informed routing decisions.

OSPF routers exchange hellos with each neighbor, learning Router ID (RID) and cost. Neighbor information is kept in the adjacency database.

The router then constructs the appropriate Link State Advertisements (LSA), which include information such as the RIDs of, and cost to, each neighbor. Each router in the routing domain shares its LSAs with all other routers. Each router keeps the complete set of LSAs in a table—the Link State Database (LSDB).

Each router runs the SPF algorithm to compute best paths. It then submits these paths for inclusion in the routing table, or forwarding database.

OSPF Network Structure

OSPF routing domains are broken up into areas. An OSPF network must contain an area 0, and may contain other areas. The SPF algorithm runs within an area, and inter-area routes are passed between areas. A two-level hierarchy to OSPF areas exists; area 0 is designed as a transit area, and other areas should be attached directly to area 0 and only to area 0. The link-state database must be identical for each router in an area. OSPF areas typically contain a maximum of 50–100 routers, depending on network volatility. Figure 3-1 shows a network of five routers that has been divided into three areas: area 0, area 1, and area 2.

Figure 3-1 OSPF Areas

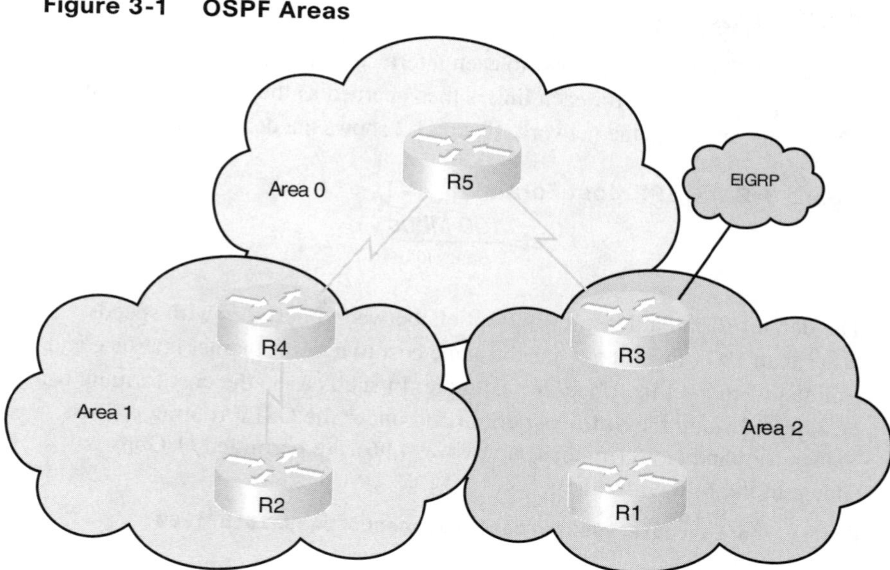

Dividing an OSPF network into areas does the following:

- Minimizes the number of routing table entries.
- Contains LSA flooding to a reasonable area.
- Minimizes the impact of a topology change.
- Enforces the concept of a hierarchical network design.

OSPF defines router roles as well. One router can have multiple roles.

- An internal router has all interfaces in one area. In Figure 3-1, R1, R2, and R5 are all internal area routers.
- Backbone routers have at least one interface assigned to area 0. R3, R4, and R5 are backbone routers.
- An Area Border Router (ABR) has interfaces in two or more areas. In Figure 3-1, R3 and R4 are ABRs.
- An Autonomous System Boundary Router (ASBR) has interfaces inside and outside the OSPF routing domain. In Figure 3-1, R3 also functions as an ASBR because it has an interface in an EIGRP routing domain.

OSPF Metric

By default, Cisco assigns a cost to each interface that is inversely proportional to 100 Mbps. The cost for each link is then accrued as the route advertisement for that link traverses the network. Figure 3-2 shows the default OSPF formula.

Figure 3-2 OSPF Cost Formula

$$Cost=\frac{100\ Mbps}{Bandwidth}$$

The default formula doesn't differentiate between interfaces with speeds faster than 100 Mbps. It assigns the same cost to a Fast Ethernet interface and a Gigabit Ethernet interface, for example. In such cases, the cost formula can be adjusted using the **auto-cost** command under the OSPF routing process. Values for bandwidth (in kbps) up to 4,294,967 are permitted (1 Gbps is shown in the following line):

```
Router(config-router)#auto-cost reference-bandwidth 1000
```

The cost can also be manually assigned under the interface configuration mode. The cost is a 16-bit number, so it can be any value from 1 to 65,535.

```
Router(config-router)#ip ospf cost 27
```

LSAs

Each router maintains a database of the latest received LSAs. Each LSA is numbered with a sequence number, and a timer is run to age out old LSAs.

When a LSA is received, it's compared to the LSDB. If it is new, it is added to the database and the SPF algorithm is run. If it is from a Router ID that is already in the database, then the sequence number is compared, and older LSAs are discarded. If it is a new LSA, it is incorporated in the database, and the SPF algorithm is run. If it is an older LSA, the newer LSA in memory is sent back to whoever sent the old one.

OSPF sequence numbers are 32 bits. The first legal sequence number is 0x80000001. Larger numbers are more recent. The sequence number changes only under two conditions:

- The LSA changes because a route is added or deleted.
- The LSA ages out (LSAs are updated every half hour, even if nothing changes).

The command **show ip ospf database** shows the age (in seconds) and sequence number for each RID.

LSDB Overload Protection

Because each router sends an LSA for each link, routers in large networks may receive—and must process—numerous LSAs. This can tax the router's CPU and memory resources, and adversely affect its other functions. You can protect your router by configuring OSPF LSDB overload protection. LDSB overload protection monitors the number of LSAs received and placed into the LSDB. If the specified threshold is exceeded for one minute, the router enters the "ignore" state by dropping all adjacencies and clearing the OSPF database. The router resumes OSPF operations after things have been normal for a specified period. Be careful when using this command, as it disrupts routing when invoked.

Configure LSDB overload protection with the OSPF router process command **max-lsa** *maximum-number* [*threshold-percentage*] [**warningonly**][**ignore-time** *minutes*] [**ignore-count** *number*] [**reset-time** *minutes*]. The meaning of the keywords of this command are:

- *Maximum-number*—The threshold. This is the most nonlocal LSAs that the router can maintain in its LSDB.
- *Threshold-percentage*—A warning message is sent when this percentage of the threshold number is reached. The default is 75 percent.
- **Warningonly**—This causes the router to send only a warning; it does not enter the ignore state.
- **Ignore-time** *minutes*—Specifies the length of time to stay in the ignore state. The default is five minutes.
- **Ignore-count** *number*—Specifies the maximum number of times a router can go into the ignore state. When this number is exceeded, OSPF processing stays down and must be manually restarted. The default is five times.
- **Reset-time** *minutes*—The length of time to stay in the ignore state. The default is ten minutes.

LSA Types

OSPF uses different types of LSAs to advertise different types of routes, such as internal area or external routing domain. Many of these are represented in the routing table with a distinctive prefix. Table 3-1 describes these LSA types.

Table 3-1 OSPF LSA Types

Type	Description	Routing Table Symbol
1	Router LSA. Advertises intra-area routes. Generated by each OSPF router. Flooded only within the area.	O
2	Network LSA. Advertises routers on a multi-access link. Generated by a DR. Flooded only within the area.	O
3	Summary LSA. Advertises inter-area routes. Generated by an ABR. Flooded to adjacent areas.	O IA
4	Summary LSA. Advertises the route to an ASBR. Generated by an ABR. Flooded to adjacent areas.	O IA
5	External LSA. Advertises routes in another routing domain. Generated by an ASBR. Flooded to adjacent areas.	O E1—The metric increases as it is passed through the network.
		O E2—The metric does not increase (default).
6	Multicast LSA. Used in multicast OSPF operations.	
7	Not-so-stubby area (NSSA) LSA. Advertises routes in another routing domain. Generated by an ASBR within a not-so-stubby area.	O N1—The metric increases as it is passed through the network.
		O N2—The metric does not increase (default).
8	External attributes LSA. Used in OSPF and BGP interworking.	
9, 10, 11	Opaque LSAs. Used for specific applications, such as OSPF and MPLS interworking.	

OSPF Operation

OSPF uses several different message types to establish and maintain its neighbor relationships, and to maintain correct routing information. When preparing for the exam, be sure you understand each OSPF packet type, and the OSPF neighbor establishment procedure.

OSPF Packets

OSPF uses five packet types. It does not use UDP or TCP for transmitting its packets. Instead, it runs directly over IP (IP protocol 89) using an OSPF header. One field in this header identifies the type of packet being carried. The five OSPF packet types are:

- **Hello**—Identifies neighbors and serves as a keepalive.
- **Link State Request (LSR)**—A request for an Link State Update (LSU). Contains the type of LSU requested and the ID of the router requesting it.
- **Database Description (DBD)**—A summary of the LSDB, including the RID and sequence number of each LSA in the LSDB.
- **Link State Update (LSU)**—Contains a full LSA entry. An LSA includes topology information; for example, the RID of this router and the RID and cost to each neighbor. One LSU can contain multiple LSAs.
- **Link State Acknowledgment (LSAck)**—Acknowledges all other OSPF packets (except hellos).

OSPF traffic is multicast to either of two addresses: 224.0.0.5 for all OSPF routers or 224.0.0.6 for all OSPF DRs.

OSPF Neighbor Relationships

OSPF routers send out periodic multicast packets to introduce themselves to other routers on a link. They become neighbors when they see their own router ID included in the Neighbor field of the hello from another router. Seeing this tells each router that they have bidirectional communication. In addition, two routers must be on a common subnet for a neighbor relationship to be formed. (Virtual links are sometimes an exception to this rule.)

Certain parameters within the OSPF hellos must also match in order for two routers to become neighbors. They include:

- Hello/dead timers
- Area ID
- Authentication type and password
- Stub area flag

OSPF routers can be neighbors without being adjacent. Only adjacent neighbors exchange routing updates and synchronize their databases. On a point-to-point link, an adjacency is established between the two routers when they can communicate. On a multiaccess link, each router establishes an adjacency only with the DR and the backup DR (BDR).

Hellos also serve as keepalives. A neighbor is considered lost if no Hello is received within four Hello periods (called the dead time). The default hello/dead timers are as follows:

- 10 seconds/40 seconds for LAN and point-to-point interfaces
- 30 seconds/120 seconds for nonbroadcast multiaccess (NBMA) interfaces

Establishing Neighbors and Exchanging Routes

The process of neighbor establishment and route exchange between two OSPF routers is as follows:

Step 1. **Down state**—OSPF process not yet started, so no hellos sent.

Step 2. **Init state**—Router sends hello packets out all OSPF interfaces.

Step 3. **Two-way state**—Router receives a hello from another router that contains its own router ID in the neighbor list. All other required elements match, so routers can become neighbors.

Step 4. **Exstart state**—If routers become adjacent (exchange routes), they determine who will start the exchange process.

Step 5. **Exchange state**—Routers exchange DBDs listing the LSAs in their LSD by RID and sequence number.

Step 6. **Loading state**—Each router compares the DBD received to the contents of its LS database. It then sends a LSR for missing or outdated LSAs. Each router responds to its neighbor's LSR with a Link State Update. Each LSU is acknowledged.

Step 7. **Full state**—The LSDB has been synchronized with the adjacent neighbor.

Basic OSPF Configuration

OSPF is configured by entering router configuration mode and identifying the range of interface addresses on which it should run and the areas they are in. When setting up OSPF, a process ID must be used (8 is used in the example), but the process ID does not have to agree on different OSPF devices for them to exchange information. The network statement uses a wildcard mask and can specify any range from a single address to all addresses. Unlike EIGRP, the wildcard mask is not optional. The following example shows a router configured as an ABR. Interfaces falling with the 192.168.1.0 network are placed in area 0, and interfaces falling within the 172.16.1.0 network are placed in area 1.

```
Router(config)#router ospf 8
Router(config-router)#network 192.168.1.0 0.0.0.255 area 0
Router(config-router)#network 172.16.1.0 0.0.0.255 area 1
```

Router ID

The SPF algorithm is used to map the shortest path between a series of nodes. This causes an issue with IP, because an IP router is not identified by a single IP address—its interfaces are. For this reason, a single IP address is designated as the "name" of the router—the RID.

By default, the RID is the highest loopback IP address. If no loopback addresses are configured, the RID is the highest IP address on an active interface when the OSPF process is started. The RID is selected when OSPF starts and—for reasons of stability—is not changed until OSPF restarts. The OSPF process can be restarted by rebooting or by using the command **clear ip ospf process**. Either choice affects routing in your network for a period of time and should be used only with caution.

A loopback interface is a virtual interface, so it is more stable than a physical interface for RID use. A loopback address is configured by creating an interface and assigning an IP address.

```
Router(config)#interface loopback0
Router(config-if)#ip address 10.0.0.1 255.255.255.255
```

The loopback address does not have to be included in the OSPF routing process, but if you advertise it, you are able to ping or trace to it. This can help in troubleshooting.

A way to override the default RID selection is to statically assign it using the OSPF **router-id** command.

```
Router(config)#router ospf 8
Router(config-router)#router-id 10.0.0.1
```

Troubleshooting OSPF

The neighbor initialization process can be viewed using the **debug ip ospf adjacencies** command. The neighbor table can be seen with **show ip ospf neighbors**, which also identifies adjacency status, and reveals the designated router and backup designated router. Use the **debug ip ospf packet** command to view all OSPF packets in real time.

Often, the first place OSPF issues are noticed is when inspecting the routing table—**show ip route**. To filter the routing table and show only the routes learned from OSPF, use **show ip route ospf**.

The command **show ip protocols** offers a wealth of information for any routing protocol issue. Use this command to verify parameters, timer values, identified networks, and OSPF neighbors (routing information sources).

Use **show ip ospf** to verify the RID, timers, and counters. Because wildcard masks sometimes incorrectly group interfaces to areas, another good place to check is **show ip ospf interface**. This shows the interfaces on which OSPF runs and their current correct assigned area.

OSPF Network Types

The SPF algorithm builds a directed graph—paths made up of a series of points connected by direct links. One of the consequences of this directed-graph approach is that the algorithm has no way to handle a multiaccess network, such as an Ethernet VLAN. The solution used by OSPF is to elect one router, called the Designated Router (DR), to represent the entire segment. Point-to-point links fit the SPF model perfectly and don't need any special modeling method. On a point-to-point link, no DR is elected and all traffic is multicast to 224.0.0.5.

OSPF supports five network types:

- **NBMA**—Default for multipoint serial interfaces. RFC-compliant mode that uses DRs and requires manual neighbor configuration.
- **Point-to–multipoint (P2MP)**—Doesn't use DRs so adjacencies increase logarithmically with routers. Resilient RFC compliant mode that automatically discovers neighbors.

- **Point-to-multipoint nonbroadcast (P2MNB)**—Proprietary mode that is used on Layer 2 facilities where dynamic neighbor discovery is not supported. Requires manual neighbor configuration.
- **Broadcast**—Default mode for LANs. Uses DRs and automatic neighbor discovery. Proprietary when used on WAN interface.
- **Point-to–point (P2P)**—Proprietary mode that discovers neighbors and doesn't require a DR.

If the default interface type is unsatisfactory, you can statically configure it with the command **ip ospf network** under interface configuration mode:

```
Router(config-if)#ip ospf network point-to-multipoint
```

When using the NBMA or P2MP nonbroadcast mode, neighbors must be manually defined under the routing process:

```
Router(config-router)#neighbor 172.16.0.1
```

Designated Routers

On a multiaccess link, one of the routers is elected as a DR and another as a backup DR (BDR). All other routers on that link become adjacent only to the DR and BDR, not to each other (they stop at the two-way state). The DR is responsible for creating and flooding a network LSA (type 2) advertising the multiaccess link. NonDR (DROTHER) routers communicate with DRs using the IP address 224.0.0.6. The DRs use IP address 224.0.0.5 to pass information to other routers.

The DR and BDR are elected as follows:

Step 1. A router starting the OSPF process listens for OSPF hellos. If none are heard within the dead time, it declares itself the DR.

Step 2. If hellos from any other routers are heard, the router with the highest OSPF priority is elected DR, and the election process starts again for BDR. A priority of zero removes a router from the election.

Step 3. If two or more routers have the same OSPF priority, the router with the highest RID is elected DR, and the election process starts again for BDR.

After a DR is elected, elections do not take place again unless the DR or BDR are lost. Because of this, the DR is sometimes the first device that comes online with a nonzero priority.

The best way to control DR election is to set OSPF priority for the DR and BDR for other routers. The default priority is one. A priority of zero means that a router cannot act as DR or BDR; it can be a DROTHER only. Priority can be set with the **ip ospf priority** command in interface configuration mode.

```
Router(config)#int fa 0/1
Router(config-if)#ip ospf priority 2
```

Nonbroadcast Multiaccess (NBMA) Networks

Routing protocols assume that multiaccess links support broadcast and have full-mesh connectivity from any device to any device. In terms of OSPF, this means the following:

- All Frame Relay or ATM maps should include the broadcast attribute.
- The DR and BDR should have full virtual circuit connectivity to all other devices.
- Hub-and-spoke environments should either configure the DR as the hub or use point-to-point subinterfaces, which require no DR.
- Partial-mesh environments should be configured using point-to-point subinterfaces, especially when no single device has full connectivity to all other devices. If there is a subset of the topology with full connectivity, then that subset can use a multipoint subinterface.
- Full-mesh environments can be configured using the physical interface, but often logical interfaces are used to take advantage of the other benefits of subinterfaces.
- It may be necessary to statically identify neighbor IP addresses.

Advanced OSPF Configuration

OSPF provides many different ways to customize its operation to fit your network needs. This section discusses route summarization, default routes, stub areas, and virtual links.

OSPF Summarization

Summarization helps all routing protocols scale to larger networks, but OSPF especially benefits because its processes tax the memory and CPU resources of the routers. The SPF algorithm consumes all CPU resources when it runs. Summarization prevents topology changes from being passed outside an area and thus saves routers in other areas from having to run the SPF algorithm. OSPF's multiple databases use more memory the larger they are. Summarization decreases the number of routes exchanged, and thus the size of the databases. OSPF can produce summaries within a classful network (VLSM) or summaries of blocks of classful networks (CIDR). There are two types of summarizations:

- **Inter-area route summarizations** are created on the ABR under the OSPF routing process using the **area range** command. The following command advertises 172.16.0.0/12 from area 1:

  ```
  Router(config-router)#area 1 range 172.16.0.0 255.240.0.0
  ```

- **External route summarization** is done on an ASBR using the summary-address command under the OSPF routing process. The following example summarizes a range of external routes to 192.168.0.0/16 and injects a single route into OSPF:

  ```
  Router(config-router)#summary-address 192.168.0.0
  255.255.0.0
  ```

Creating a Default Route

The default route is a special type of summarization; it summarizes all networks down to one route announcement. This provides the ultimate benefit of summarization by reducing routing information to a minimum. There are several ways to use the router IOS to place a default route into OSPF.

The best-known way to produce an OSPF default is to use the **default-information** command under the OSPF routing process. This command, without the keyword **always**, readvertises a default route learned from another source into OSPF. If the **always** keyword is present, OSPF advertises a default even if one does not already exist in the routing table. The **metric** keyword sets the starting metric for this route.

```
Router(config-router)#default-information originate [always]
 [metric metric]
```

Alternatively, a default summary route can also be produced using the **summary-address** command or the **area range** command. These commands cause the router to advertise a default route pointing to itself.

Reducing routing information in non-backbone areas is a common requirement because these routers are typically the most vulnerable in terms of processor and speed, and the links that connect them usually have the least bandwidth. A specific concern is that an area will be overwhelmed by external routing information.

Stub and Not-So-Stubby Areas

Another way to reduce the route information advertised is to make an area a stub area. Configuring an area as a stub area forces its ABR to drop all external (type 5) routes and replaces them with a default route. To limit routing information even more, an area can be made totally stubby using the **no-summary** keyword on the ABR only. In that case, all interarea and external routes are dropped by the ABR and replaced by a default route. The default route starts with a cost of 1; to change it, use the **area default-cost** command. The example that follows shows area 2 configured as a totally stubby area, and the default route injected with a cost of 5:

```
Router(config-router)#area 2 stub no-summary
Router(config-router)#area 2 default-cost 5
```

Stub areas are attractive because of their low overhead. They do have some limitations, including the following:

- Stub areas can't include a virtual link.
- Stub areas can't include an ASBR.
- Stubbiness must be configured on all routers in the area.

Another kind of stub area is a not-so-stubby area (NSSA). NSSA is like a stub or totally stub area, but allows an ASBR within the area. External routes are advertised as type 7 routes by the ASBR. The ABR converts them to type 5 external routes when it advertises them into adjacent areas. NSSA is configured with the **area nssa** command under the OSPF routing process. The **no-summary** keyword on the ABR configures the area as a totally NSSA area; this is a Cisco proprietary feature. By default, the ABR does not inject a default route back into an NSSA area. Use the **default-information-originate** keyword on the ABR or ABR to create this route.

```
Router(config-router)#area 7 nssa [no-summary] [default-
  information-originate]
```

Configuring Virtual Links

OSPF requires that all areas be connected to area 0 and that area 0 must be contiguous. When this is not possible, you can use a virtual link to bridge across an intermediate area. Figure 3-3 shows a virtual link connecting two portions of area 0.

Figure 3-3 OSPF Virtual Link

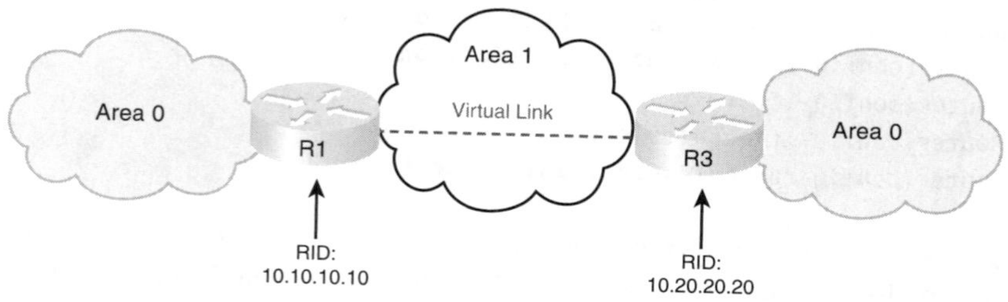

Area 1 is the transit area for the virtual link. Configure each end of a virtual link on the ABRs of the transit area with the command **area** *area-number* **virtual-link** *router-id*. Each end of the link is identified by its RID. The area listed in the command is the transit area, not the area being joined by the link. The configuration for R1 is:

```
R1(config)#router ospf 1
R1(config-router)#area 1 virtual-link 10.20.20.20
```

The configuration for R2 is:

```
R2(config)#router ospf 1
R2(config-router)#area 1 virtual-link 10.10.10.10
```

Verify that the virtual link is up with the **show ip ospf virtual-links** command. Additionally, virtual interfaces are treated as actual interfaces by the OSPF process, and thus, their status can be verified with the **show ip ospf interface** *interface-id* command.

Configuring OSPF Authentication

For security purposes, you can configure OSPF to authenticate every OSPF packet and the source of every OSPF routing update. By default, the router does no authentication. OSPF supports three types of authentication:

- Null authentication for a link that does not use authentication at all
- Simple (plain text) authentication
- MD5 authentication

The following example shows a router configured for simple password authentication in OSPF area 1, using a password of "simple". Note that authentication commands are necessary both under the OSPF process and the interface configuration. All OSPF neighbors reachable through an interface configured for authentication must use the same password. You can, however, use different passwords for different interfaces.

```
Router(config)#int gi0/0
Router(config-if)#ip ospf authentication-key simple
Router(config-if)#ip ospf authentication
Router(config-if)#!
Router(config-if)#router ospf 1
Router(config-router)#area 1 authentication
```

The next example shows the same router configured for OSPF MD5 authentication for area 0, using a password of "secure". Note that the commands are slightly different. The optional keyword **message-digest** is required in two of the commands, and a key number must be specified. Any neighbors reachable through the Gi0/1 interface must also be configured with the same key.

```
Router(config-router)#int gi0/1
Router(config-if)#ip ospf message-digest-key 2 md5 secure
Router(config-if)#ip ospf authentication message-digest
Router(config-if)#!
Router(config-if)#router ospf 1
Router(config-router)#area 0 authentication message-digest
```

CHAPTER 4

IS-IS

Intermediate System-to-Intermediate System (IS-IS) is a link state routing protocol that is part of the OSI family of protocols. Like OSPF, it uses Dijkstra's SPF algorithm to choose routes. IS-IS is a classless interior gateway protocol that uses router resources efficiently and scales to large networks, such as large Internet service providers (ISP).

Table 4-1 lists some IS-IS terms, acronyms, and their meanings.

Table 4-1 IS-IS Acronyms

Term	Acronym	Description
Circuit ID		Identifies a physical interface on the router.
Complete Sequence Number PDU	CSNP	A summary of a router's complete LSDB.
Connectionless Network Protocol	CLNP	OSI protocol used to provide the connectionless services.
Connectionless Network Services	CNLS	OSI data delivery service that provides best-effort delivery.
End System	ES	A host, such as a computer.
Intermediate System	IS	The OSI name for a router.
Intermediate System hello	ISH	Sent by routers to hosts.
IS to IS hello	IIH	Hellos exchanged between routers. Seperate level 1 and level 2 IIHs exist.
Link State Database	LSDB	A database containing all the LSAs the router knows about, and it keeps a separate LSDB for each area it belongs to.
Link State PDU	LSP	A routing update.
Network Entity Title	NET	A router's NSAP. The last byte of a NET is always zero.

continues

Table 4-1 IS-IS Acronyms *continued*

Term	Acronym	Description
Network Service Access Point	NSAP	Address of a CLNS device. Addresses are assigned per device, not per interface as with IP.
NSAP Selector	NSEL	The last byte of a NSAP address. Identifies the process on the device, such as routing.
Protocol Data Unit	PDU	A unit of data.
Partial Route Calculation	PRC	Used to determine end system and IP subnet reachability.
Partial Sequence Number PDU	PSNP	Used to acknowledge receipt of a CSNP and to request more information about a network contained in a CSNP.
Sequence Number Protocol Unit	SNP	An IS-IS packet that is Data sequenced and must be acknowledged. The sequence number helps a router maintain the most recent link state information.
Subnetwork Point Attachment	SNPA	Layer 2 identification for a of router's interface, such as MAC address or DLCI.
Type Length Value	TLV	Fields in the IS-IS updates that contain IP subnet, authentication, and end-system information.

IS-IS Overview

Integrated IS-IS can carry IP network information, but does not use IP as its transport protocol. It uses OSI protocols CLNS and CLNP to deliver its updates. IS-IS sends its messages in PDUs. There are four IS-IS PDU types: Hello, LSP, PSNP, and CSNP.

Types of IS-IS Routers

Figure 4-1 shows an IS-IS network divided into areas. The IS-IS backbone is not a specific area, as in OSPF, but an unbroken chain of routers doing Level 2 routing. R3, R6, and R4 are the backbone in Figure 4-1.

Within an area, routers can be one of three types:

- **Level 1 (L1) router**—R1, R2, and R5 in the figure. Routes to networks only within the local area (intra-area routing). Uses a default route to the nearest Level 2 router for traffic bound outside the area. Keeps one LSDB for the local area. When routing, compares the area of the destination to its area. If they are the same, routes based on system ID. If not, sends traffic to Level 1-2 router.
- **Level 2 (L2) router**—R6 in the figure. Routes to networks in other areas (interarea routing). The routing is based on area ID. Keeps one LSDB for routing to other areas.
- **Level 1-2 (L1-2) router**—R3 and R4 in this figure. Acts as a gateway into and out of an area. Does Level 1 routing within the area and Level 2 routing between areas. Keeps two LSDB: one for the local area and one for interarea routing.

The IS-IS method of selecting routes can result in suboptimal routing between areas. To solve this, RFC 2966 introduces route leaking, which allows some L2 routes to be advertised (or leaked) into L1 areas.

Figure 4-1 IS-IS Network Structure

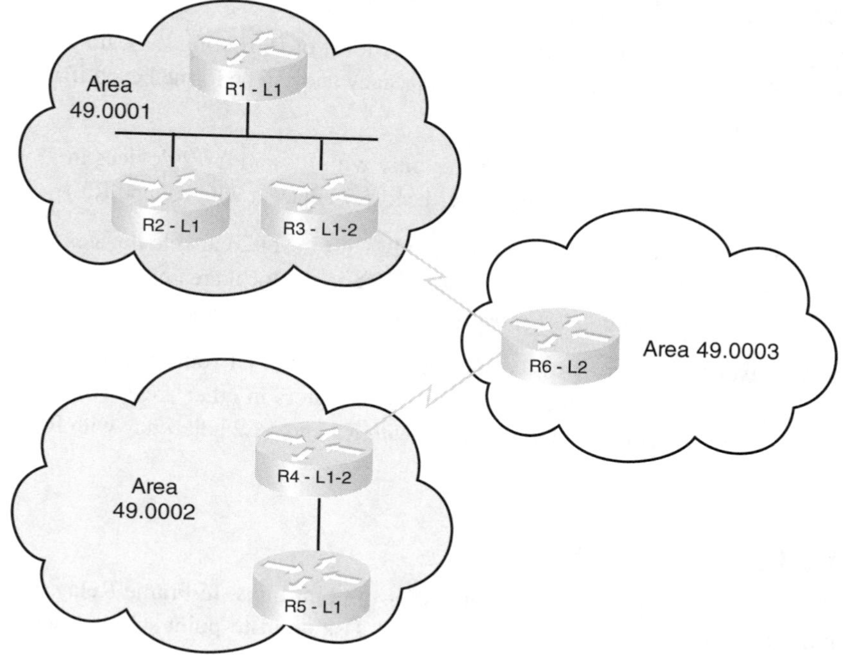

NSAP Address Structure

In the Cisco implementation of integrated IS-IS, NSAP addresses have three parts: the area ID, the system ID, and the NSEL. They are written in hexadecimal and have a maximum size of 20 bytes.

- Area IDs vary from 1 to 13 bytes. Those that begin with 49 designate private area addressing.
- The Cisco system ID must be exactly six bytes. MAC addresses or IP addresses padded with 0s are often used as system IDs.
- The NSEL is exactly one byte in size. A router always has a NSEL of 00.

Figure 4-2 shows the composition of an NSAP address.

Figure 4-2 IS-IS NSAP Address

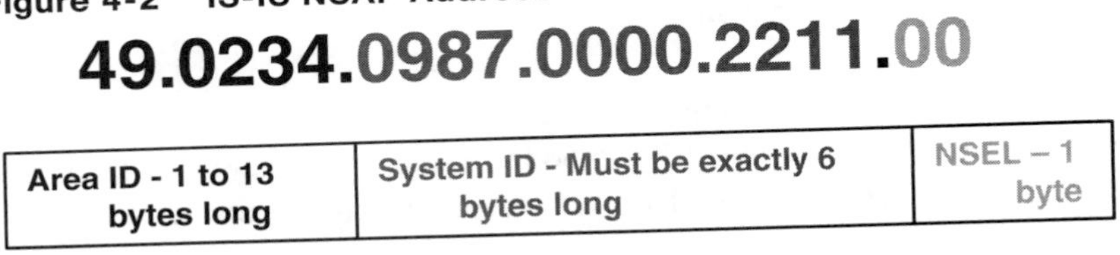

49.0234.0987.0000.2211.00

Area ID - 1 to 13 bytes long	System ID - Must be exactly 6 bytes long	NSEL – 1 byte

Adjacency Formation in IS-IS

IS-IS routers form adjacencies based on the level of IS routing they are doing and their area number. This is a CLNS adjacency and can be formed even if IP addresses don't match.

- Level 1 routers form adjacencies only with L1 and L1-2 devices in their own area. (In Figure 4-1, R1 becomes adjacent with R2 and R3.)
- Level 2 routers form adjacencies only with Level 2-capable devices (either L2 or L1-2 routers). These can be in the local area or in other areas. (In Figure 4-1, R6 becomes adjacent with R3 and R4.)
- Level 1-2 routers form Level 1 adjacencies with L1 routers in their own area, and Level 2 adjacencies with routers in other areas. (In Figure 4-1, R4 has a L1 adjacency with R5 and a L2 adjacency with R6.)

IS-IS Network Types

IS-IS recognizes only broadcast and point-to-point links. In Frame Relay, multipoint interfaces must be fully meshed. Use point-to-point subinterfaces to avoid this.

On a broadcast network, IS-IS routers elect a Designated Intermediate System (DIS). The DIS is elected based on priority, with MAC address as the tie breaker (the lowest number wins for both priority and MAC address). Routers form adjacencies with the DIS and all other routers on the LAN. The DIS creates a pseudonode to represent the network and sends out an advertisement to represent the LAN. All routers advertise only an adjacency to the pseudonode. If the DIS fails, another is elected; no backup DIS exists. The DIS sends Hellos every 3.3 seconds; other routers send them every 10 seconds. The DIS also multicasts a CSNP every 10 seconds.

No DIS exists on a point-to-point link. When an adjacency is first formed over the link, the routers exchange CSNPs. If one of the routers needs more information about a specific network, it sends a PSNP requesting that. After the initial exchange, LSPs are sent to describe link changes, and they are acknowledged with PSNPs. Hellos are sent every 10 seconds.

Configuring IS-IS

The essential tasks to begin IS-IS routing are:

- Enable IS-IS on the router:

  ```
  Router(config)#router isis
  ```

- Configure each router's NET:

  ```
  Router(config-router)#net 49.0010.1111.2222.3333.00
  ```

- Enable IS-IS on the router's interfaces:

  ```
  Router(config)#interface s0/0/0
  Router(config-int)#ip router isis
  ```

You may wish to do some tuning of IS-IS routing. Following are the tasks:

- **Set the IS level.** Cisco routers are L1-2 by default. If the router is completely an internal area router, set the IS level to L1. If the router routes only to other areas and has no internal area interfaces, set the IS level to L2. If the router has both internal and external area interfaces, leave the IS level at L1-2.

  ```
  Router(config-router)is-type {level-1 ¦ level 1-2 ¦ level-2-only}
  ```

- **Set the circuit type on L1-2 routers.** On L1-2 routers, all interfaces send out both L1 and L2 hellos, trying to establish both types of adjacencies. This can waste bandwidth. If only an L1 router is attached to an interface, then change the circuit type for that interface to L1, so that only L1 hellos are sent. If there is only a L2 router attached to an interface, change the circuit type for that interface to L2:

```
Router(config-int)#isis circuit-type {level-1 ¦ level 1-2 ¦
  level-2-only}
```

- **Summarize addresses.** Although IS-IS does CLNS routing, it can summarize the IP addresses that it carries. Summarized routes can be designated as Level 1, Level 2, or Level 1-2 routes. The default is Level 2:

```
Router(config-router)#summary-address prefix mask [level-1 ¦
  level-2 ¦ level-1-2]
```

- **Adjust the metric.** IS-IS uses a metric of 10 for each interface. You can manually assign a metric that more accurately reflects the interface characteristics, such as bandwidth:

```
Router(config-int)#isis metric metric {level-1 ¦ level-2}
```

Verifying and Troubleshooting IS-IS

Table 4-2 shows some IS-IS verification and troubleshooting commands, and describes the information you obtain from these commands.

Table 4-2 IS-IS show Commands

Command	Description
show isis topology	Displays the topology database and least cost paths.
show clns route	Displays the L2 routing table.
show isis route	Displays the L1 routing table. Requires that CLNS routing is enabled.
show clns protocol	Displays the router's IS type, system ID, area ID, interfaces running IS-IS, and any redistribution.
show clns neighbors	Displays the adjacent neighbors and their IS level.
show clns interface	Displays IS-IS details for each interface, such as circuit type, metric, and priority.
show ip protocols	Displays the integrated IS-IS settings.

CHAPTER 5

Optimizing Routing

There are times when you need to go beyond just turning on a routing protocol in your network. You may need to use multiple protocols, control exactly which routes are advertised or redistributed, or which paths are chosen. Most networks use DHCP; your router may need to be a DHCP server, or relay DHCP broadcasts.

Using Multiple Routing Protocols

There are several reasons you may need to run multiple routing protocols in your network. Some include:

- Migrating from one routing protocol to another, where both protocols will run in the network temporarily
- Applications that run under certain routing protocols but not others
- Areas of the network under different administrative control ("layer 8" issues)
- A multi-vendor environment in which some parts of the network require a standards-based protocol

Configuring Route Redistribution

If routinginformation must be exchanged among the different protocols or routing domains, redistribution can be used. Only routes that are in the routing table and learned via the specified protocol are redistributed. Each protocol has some unique characteristics when redistributing, as shown in Table 5-1.

Table 5-1 Route Redistribution Characteristics

Protocol	Redistribution Characteristics
RIP	Metric must be set, except when redistributing static or connected routes, which have a metric of 1.
OSPF	Default metric is 20. Can specify the metric type; the default is E2. Must use subnets keyword or only classful networks are redistributed.
EIGRP	Metric must be set, except when redistributing static or connected routes, which get their metric from the interface. Metric value is "bandwidth, delay, reliability, load, MTU." Redistributed routes have a higher administrative distance than internal ones.
IS-IS	Default metric is 0. Can specify route level; default is L2. Can choose to redistribute only external or internal routes into IS- IS from OSPF and into OSPF from IS-IS.
Static/Connected	To include local networks not running the routing protocol, you must redistribute connected inter faces. You can also redistribute static routes into a dynamic protocol.

You can redistribute only between protocols that use the same protocol stack, such as IP protocols, which cannot advertise IPX routes. To configure redistribution, issue this command under the routing process that is to receive the new routes:

```
Router(config-router)#redistribute {route-source} [metric metric]
  [route-map tag]
```

Seed Metric

Redistribution involves configuring a routing protocol to advertise routes learned by another routing process. Normally, protocols base their metric on an interface value, such as bandwidth, but no interface for a redistributed route exists. Protocols use incompatible metrics, so the redistributed routes must be assigned a new metric compatible with the new protocol.

A route's starting metric is called its *seed metric*. Set the seed metric for all redistributed routes with the **default-metric** [*metric*] command under the routing process. To set the metric for specific routes, either use the **metric** keyword when redistributing or use the **route-map** keyword to link a route map to the redistribution. After the seed metric is specified, it increments normally as the route is advertised through the network (except for certain OSPF routes).

Tools for Controlling/Preventing Routing Updates

Cisco IOS provides several ways to control routing updates. They include:

- Passive interface
- Default and/or static routes
- Distribute list
- Route map
- Change administrative distance

Passive Interface

The **passive-interface** command prevents routing updates from being sent out an interface that runs the routing protocol. RIP and IGRP do not send updates out an interface. It prevents other routing protocols from sending hellos out of an interface; thus, they don't discover neighbors or form an adjacency out that interface. To disable the protocol on one interface, use the command **passive-interface** *interface*. To turn off the protocol on all interfaces, use **passive-interface default**. You can then use **no passive-interface** *interface* for the ones that should run the protocol, as shown:

```
Router(config)#router eigrp 7
Router(config-router)#passive-interface default
Router(config-router)#no passive-interface s0/0/0
```

Distribute Lists

A distribute list allows you to filter routing updates and also routes being redistributed through an access list. Configure an access list that permits the routes to be advertised or redistributed, and then link that access list to the routing process with the **distribute-list** command, given under router configuration mode. This command has two options:

- **distribute-list** *access-list* **in**—Filters updates as they come in an interface. For OSPF, this controls routes placed in the routing table but not the database. For other protocols, this controls the routes the protocol knows about.
- **distribute-list** *access-list* **out**—Filters updates going out of an interface and also updates being redistributed out of another routing protocol into this one.

Route Maps

Route maps are a bit like programs that use a "if/then/else" decision-making capability. They *match* traffic against certain conditions, and then set specified options for that traffic. Each statement has a sequence number, statements are read from the lowest number to highest, and the router stops reading when it gets a match. The sequence number can be used to insert or delete statements. Like an access list, there is an implicit "deny" at the end of each route map; any traffic not matched with a route map statement is denied. Some uses for route maps include:

- Filtering redistributed routes—Use the **route-map** keyword in the redistribute command.
- Policy-based routing—To specify which traffic should be policy routed, based on very granular controls.
- BGP policy—To control routing updates and to manipulate path attributes.

Route Map Syntax

Route maps are created with the global command:

```
Router(config)#route-map {tag} permit ¦ deny [sequence_number]
```

Each statement in a route map begins this same way, with the same route map name but different sequence numbers, and with match and/or set conditions below it. *Permit* means that any traffic matching the match conditions is used. *Deny* means that any traffic matching the match conditions is not used.

Match and Set Conditions

Each route map statement can have from none to multiple **match** and **set** conditions. If no **match** condition exists, the statement matches anything, similar to a "permit any" in an access list. If there is no **set** condition, the matching traffic is either permitted or denied, with no other conditions being set.

Multiple match conditions on the same line use a logical OR. For example, the router interprets **match a b c** as "**match a** or **b** or **c**." Multiple match conditions on different lines use a logical AND. For example, the router interprets the following route map statement as "**match a** and **b** and **c**:"

```
route-map Logical-AND permit 10
 match a
 match b
 match c
```

In route redistribution, some common conditions to **match** include:

- **ip address**—Refers the router to an access list that permits or denies networks.
- **ip next-hop**—Refers the router to an access list that permits or denies next-hop IP addresses.
- **ip route-source**—Refers the router to an access list that permits or denies advertising router IP addresses.
- **metric**—Permits or denies routes with the specified metric from being redistributed.
- **route-type**—Permits or denies redistribution of the route type listed, such as internal or external.
- **tag**—Routes can be labeled (tagged) with a number, and route maps can look for that number.

In route redistribution, some common conditions to **set** are:

- **metric**—Sets the metric for redistributed routes.
- **metric-type**—Sets the type, such as E1 for OSPF.
- **tag**—Tags a route with a number that can be matched on later by other route maps.
- **level**—For IS-IS, sets the IS level for this route.

The following configuration example shows a route map named BGP-LP with three statements that are used to control which routes will be redistributed from OSPF into BGP. The router has already been configured with two access lists, numbered 23 and 103 (not shown.) The first route map statement, with sequence number 10, is a *permit* statement. The **match** condition tells it to use access list 23. Any traffic permitted by access list 23 matches this statement and will be redistributed into BGP. Any traffic explicitly denied by access list 23 will not be redistributed into BGP. The **set** condition tells it to set a BGP local preference for all traffic that matches statement 10. Traffic not matching access list 23 will be checked against the second route map statement.

The second route map statement, sequence number 20, is a *deny* statement that matches access list 103. Any traffic permitted by access list 103 will be denied by this statement, and thus will not be redistributed. Any traffic explicitly denied by access list 103 will be ignored by this statement, and checked against the next route map statement. This route map statement has no **set** conditions. Traffic not matching route map statements 10 or 20 will be checked against statement 30.

The third route map statement, sequence number 30, is a *permit* statement with no **match** or **set** conditions. This statement matches everything and sets nothing, thus permitting all other traffic without changing it. Without this statement, all other traffic would be denied.

Lastly, the route map is applied to the redistribution command, to filter routes redistributed from OSPF into BGP.

```
Router(config)#route-map BGP-LP permit 10
Router(config-route-map)#match ip address 23
Router(config-route-map)#set local-preference 200
Router(config-route-map)#!
Router(config-route-map)#route-map BGP-LP deny 20
Router(config-route-map)#match ip address 103
Router(config-route-map)#!
Router(config-route-map)#route-map BGP-LP permit 30
!
Router(config)#router bgp 65001
Router(config-router)#redistribute ospf 1 route-map BGP-LP
```

Manipulating Administrative Distance

When a router receives routes to the same destination network from more than one routing process, it decides which to put in the routing table by looking at the administrative distance (AD) value assigned to the routing process. The route with the lowest AD is chosen. Table 5-2 shows administrative distance values.

Table 5-2 Administrative Distance

Routing Information Source	Administrative Distance
Connected interface	0
Static route	1
EIGRP summarized route	5
BGP external route	20
EIGRP internal route	90
IGRP	100
OSPF	110
IS-IS	115
RIP	120
EIGRP external route	170
BGP internal route	200
Unknown	255

AD can be changed for all routes of a process or only for specific routes within a process. The command for all IGPs except EIGRP is:

```
Router(config-router)#distance administrative_distance {address
  wildcard-mask} [access-list-number ¦ name]
```

Using the **address/mask** keywords in the command changes the AD of routes learned from the neighbor with that IP address. An entry of **0.0.0.0 255.255.255.255** changes the AD of all routes. Specifying an access list number or name changes the AD only on networks permitted in the ACL.

EIGRP and BGP have different AD values for internal and external routes, so you have to list those separately when using the command with those protocols. BGP also allows you to change the AD for locally generated routes. For these protocols, the commands are:

```
Router(config-router)#distance eigrp internal-distance external-
  distance
Router(config-router)#distance bgp external-distance internal-
  distance local-distance
```

Route redistribution can cause suboptimal routing; one way to correct this is to adjust AD. Figure 5-1 shows a network with two routing domains: RIP and OSPF.

Figure 5-1 Controlling Routing with AD

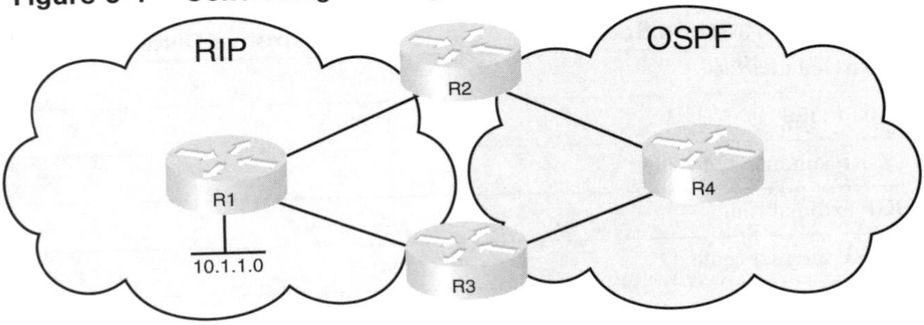

R2 redistributes its RIP routes into OSPF. These routes inherit OSPF's AD when they are advertised to R4. R4 then advertises them to R3 as OSPF routes.

R3 now knows about the 10.1.1.0 network from two routing processes: RIP, with an AD of 120, and OSPF, with an AD of 110. The shortest path is the RIP route through R1. The OSPF path goes through R4 and R2, and then to R1—a much longer path. But, based on AD, R3 puts the OSPF path in its routing table.

To prevent this, increase the AD of the redistributed RIP routes when OSPF advertises them. Note that this doesn't change all OSPF routes, just the ones learned from RIP. The commands given on R2 (the router doing the initial redistribution) are shown in the following:

```
Router(config)#access-list 10 permit 10.1.1.0
!
Router(config)#router ospf 1
Router(config-router)#redistribute rip subnets
Router(config-router)#distance 125 0.0.0.0 255.255.255.255 10
```

The AD is increased to 125 for routes from all neighbors, if they match the network permitted in access list 10. Now R3 hears about the 10.1.1.0 network from RIP with an AD of 120, and from OSPF with an AD of 125. The RIP route is put into the routing table based on its lower AD.

DHCP

DHCP automates the assignment of IP addresses to network hosts. DHCP addresses can be allocated:

- Manually—A specific IP address is assigned to a MAC address.
- Automatic—An IP address is permanently assigned to a host.
- Dynamic—The IP address is assigned for a limited amount of time or until the client releases it.

The process of acquiring an IP address from a DHCP server has four steps:

Step 1. The host broadcasts a DHCPDISCOVER message.

Step 2. The server responds with a DHCPOFFER message containing IP address and optionally other settings.

Step 3. The client broadcasts a DHCPREQUEST message, requesting the offered IP address.

Step 4. The server sends a DHCPACK confirming the address assignment.

Configuring DHCP

Cisco routers can be DHCP clients, servers, or relay agents. To configure an IOS device as a DHCP client, use the **ip address dhcp** command on the interface that needs to obtain the DHCP address. To configure a router as a DHCP server, you must create an IP address pool and assign a network or subnet to that pool. You can optionally add information, such as default gateway, DNS server, lease duration, or options such as Option 150 for Cisco IP phones. Exclude any static IP addresses within the pool, such as the router's address. You may also want to identify an external server to hold the DHCP database of IP address bindings.

Cisco routers have an auto-configuration feature that allows the downloading of some DHCP information from a central server. This saves the trouble of configuring every router with complete DHCP information. To do this, one interface on the router must have a DHCP address. The following example shows a router configured as a DHCP server that imports its domain name, DNS servers, and other information from another DHCP server off interface Gi0/0. The IP address range of 10.6.3.1–10.6.3.5 is excluded from the pool.

```
Router(config)#ip dhcp excluded-address 10.6.3.1 10.6.3.5
!
Router(config)#ip dhcp pool Gator
Router(dhcp-config)#network 10.6.3.0 /24
Router(dhcp-config)#default-router 10.6.3.1
Router(dhcp-config)#import all
!
Router(config)#int gi 0/0
Router(config-if)#ip address dhcp
```

DHCP Relay Agent

Hosts discover their DHCP server by sending broadcasts. If that server is on a different subnet, those broadcasts must be routed to the server as unicasts. You can configure a router to relay DHCP messages with the **ip helper-address** interface command. It is important to understand that this command must be given on the interface that receives the host broadcasts. A Cisco DHCP relay agent functions as follows:

Step 1. A client broadcasts a DHCP request, which is seen by the IOS device (a router, for instance).

Step 2. The router changes the destination address of the packet to the unicast address of the server. It optionally adds option 82 (relay agent option) information.

Step 3. The router sends the unicast packet to the server.

Step 4. The server responds with the IP address and other parameters, such as the default gateway assigned to the client.

Step 5. The router gets the packet from the server, removes any option 82 information, and forwards it to the client.

The **ip helper-address** command enables the relaying of UDP broadcasts only. By default, eight broadcast types are enabled:

- Time, port 37
- TACACS, port 49
- DNS, port 53
- BOOTP/DHCP server, port 67
- BOOTP/DHCP client, port 68
- TFTP, port 69

- NetBIOS name service, port 137
- NetBIOS datagram service, port 138

To disable the forwarding any of these protocols, use the interface command **no ip forward-protocol udp** *port-number*. To add UDP protocols to be relayed, use the interface command **ip forward-protocol udp** *port-number*.

Verify your DHCP configuration with the commands **show ip dhcp database**, **show ip dhcp server statistics**, and **show ip dhcp binding**. Delete address assignments with the **clear ip dhcp binding** {*address* | *} command.

CHAPTER 6

BGP

BGP is an external gateway protocol, meant to be used between different networks. It is the protocol used on the internet. It was built for reliability, scalability and control, not speed. Because of this, it behaves differently from the protocols covered thus far in this book.

BGP Overview

- BGP stands for Border Gateway Protocol.
- BGP uses the concept of autonomous systems. An *autonomous system* is a group of networks under a common administration.
- Autonomous systems run Interior Gateway Protocols (IGP) within the system. They run an Exterior Gateway Protocol (EGP) between them.
- BGP version 4 is the only EGP currently in use.
- BGP neighbors are called peers and must be statically configured.
- BGP uses TCP port 179.
- BGP is a path-vector protocol. Its route to a network consists of a list of autonomous systems on the path to that network.
- BGP's loop prevention mechanism is autonomous system number. When an update about a network leaves an autonomous system, that autonomous system's number is prepended to the list of autonomous systems that have handled that update. When an autonomous system receives an update, it examines the autonomous system list. If it finds its own autonomous system number in that list, the update is discarded.

In Figure 6-1, BGP routers in AS 65100 see network 10.1.1.0 as having an autonomous system path of 65200 65300 65400.

Figure 6-1 BGP AS-Path Advertisement

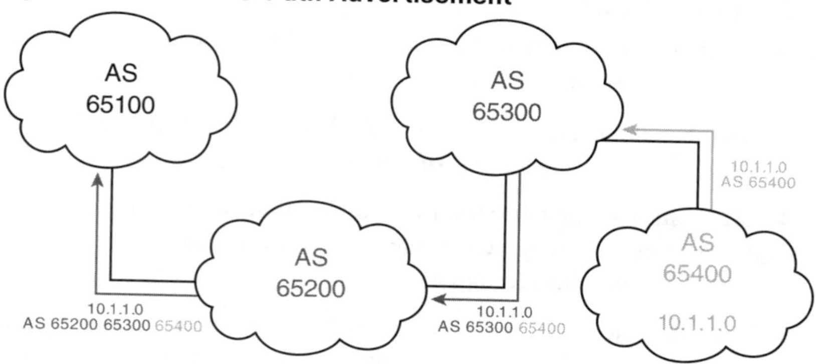

Multihoming

Multihoming means connecting to more than one ISP at the same time. It is done for redundancy and backup in case one ISP fails and for better performance if one ISP provides a better path to often used networks. Three ways exist to receive routes from each ISP:

- Default routes from each provider—This results in low use of bandwidth and router resources. The internal network's IGP metric determines the exit router for all traffic bound outside the autonomous system.
- Default routes plus some more specific routes—This results in medium use of bandwidth and router resources. This allows you to manipulate the exit path for specific routes using BGP, but the IGP metric chooses the exit path for default routes.
- All routes from all providers—This requires the highest use of bandwidth and router resources. It is typically done by large enterprises and ISPs. Path selection for all external routes can be controlled via BGP policy routing tools.

BGP Databases

BGP uses three databases. The first two listed are BGP-specific; the third is shared by all routing processes on the router:

- **Neighbor database**—This is a list of all configured BGP neighbors. To view it, use the **show ip bgp summary** command.
- **BGP database, or RIB (Routing Information Base)**—This is a list of networks known by BGP, along with their paths and attributes. To view it, use the **show ip bgp** command.
- **Routing table**—This is a list of the paths to each network used by the router, and the next hop for each network. To view it, use the **show ip route** command.

BGP Message Types

BGP has four types of messages:

- **Open**—After a neighbor is configured, BGP sends an open message to try to establish peering with that neighbor. Includes information such as autonomous system number, router ID, and hold time.
- **Update**—Message used to transfer routing information between peers.
- **Keepalive**—BGP peers exchange keepalive messages every 60 seconds by default. These keep the peering session active.
- **Notification**—When a problem occurs that causes a router to end the BGP peering session, a notification message is sent to the BGP neighbor and the connection is closed.

Internal and External BGP

Internal BGP (IBGP) is BGP peering relationship between routers in the same autonomous system. External BGP (EBGP) is BGP peering relationship between routers in different autonomous systems. BGP treats updates from internal peers differently than updates from external peers.

In Figure 6-2, routers A and B are EBGP peers. Routers B, C, and D are IBGP peers.

Figure 6-2 Identifying EBGP and IBGP Peers

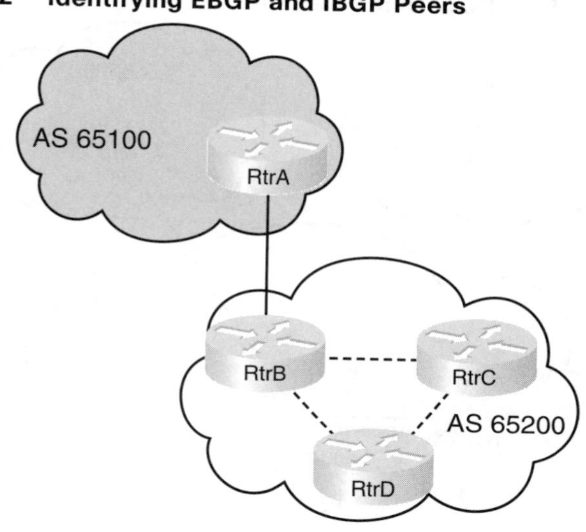

BGP Next-Hop Selection

The next hop for a route received from an EBGP neighbor is the IP address of the neighbor that sent the update.

When a BGP router receives an update from an EBGP neighbor, it must pass that update to its IBGP neighbors without changing the next-hop attribute. The next-hop IP address is the IP address of an edge router belonging to the next-hop autonomous system. Therefore, IBGP routers must have a route to the network connecting their autonomous system to that edge router. For example, in Figure 6-3, RtrA sends an update to RtrB, listing a next hop of 10.2.2.1, its serial interface. When RtrB forwards that update to RtrC, the next-hop IP address will still be 10.2.2.1. RtrC needs to have a route to the 10.2.2.0 network in order to have a valid next hop.

To change this behavior, use the **neighbor** [*ip address*] **next-hop-self** command in BGP configuration mode. In Figure 6-3, this configuration goes on RtrB. After you give this command, RtrB will advertise its IP address to RtrC as the next hop for networks from AS 65100, rather than the address of RtrA. Thus, RtrC does not have to know about the external network between RtrA and RtrB (network 10.2.2.0).

Figure 6-3 BGP Next-Hop Behavior

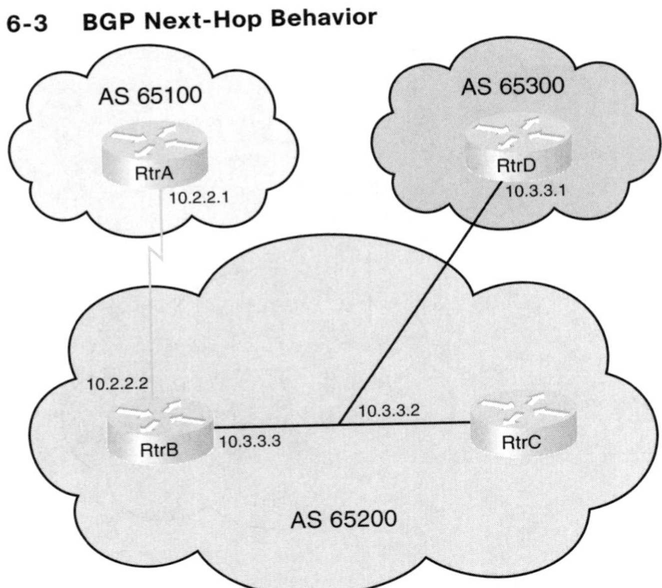

BGP Next Hop on a Multiaccess Network

On a multi-access network, BGP can adjust the next-hop attribute to avoid an extra hop. In Figure 6-3, RtrC and RtrD are EBGP peers, and RtrC is an IBGP peer with RtrB. When C sends an update to D about network 10.2.2.0, it normally gives its interface IP address as the next hop for D to use. But because B, C, and D are all on the same multiaccess network, it is inefficient for D to send traffic to C, and C to then send it on to B. This process unnecessarily adds an extra hop to the path. So, by default, RtrC advertises a next hop of 10.3.3.3 (RtrB's interface) for the 10.2.2.0 network. This behavior can also be adjusted with the **neighbor** [*ip address*] **next-hop-self** command.

BGP Synchronization Rule

The BGP synchronization rule requires that when a BGP router receives information about a network from an IBGP neighbor, it does not use that information until a matching route is learned via an IGP or static route. It also does not advertise that route to an EBGP neighbor unless a matching route is in the routing table. In Figure 6-3, if RtrB advertises a route to RtrC, then RtrC does not submit it to the routing table or advertise it to RtrD unless it also learns the route from some other IGP source.

Recent IOS versions have synchronization disabled by default. It is usually safe to turn off synchronization when all routers in the autonomous system run BGP. To turn it off in earlier IOS versions, use the command **no synchronization** under BGP router configuration mode.

Configuring BGP

Table 6-1 lists the basic BGP configuration commands and their functions.

Table 6-1 Basic BGP Confiuration Commands

Command	Description
router bgp *AS-number*	Starts the BGP routing process on the router.
neighbor *ip-address* **remote-as** *AS-number*	Sets up peering between BGP routers.
neighbor *peer-group-name* **peer-group**	Creates a peer group to which you can then assign neighbors.
neighbor *ip-address* **peer-group** *peer-group-name*	Assigns a neighbor to a peer group.
neighbor *ip-address* **next-hop-self**	Configures a router to advertise its connected interface as the next hop for all routes to this neighbor.
neighbor *ip-address* **update-source** *interface-type number*	Configures a router to use the IP address of a specific interface as the source for its advertisements to this neighbor.
no synchronization	Turns off BGP synchronization.
network *prefix* [**mask** *subnet mask*]	Initiates the advertisement of a network in BGP.

The BGP Network Command

In most IGPs, the network command starts the routing process on an interface. In BGP, the command tells the router to originate an advertisement for that network. The network does not have to be connected to the router; it just has to be in the routing table. In theory, it could even be a network in a different autonomous system (not usually recommended).

When advertising a network, BGP assumes you are using the default classful subnet mask. If you want to advertise a subnet, you must use the optional keyword **mask** and specify the subnet mask to use. Note that this is a subnet mask, not the inverse mask used by OSPF and EIGRP network statements. The routing table must contain an exact match (prefix and subnet mask) to the network listed in the network statement before BGP will advertise the route.

BGP Peering

BGP assumes that external neighbors are directly connected and that they are peering with the IP address of the directly connected interface of their neighbor. If not, you must tell BGP to look more than one hop away for its neighbor, with the **neighbor** *ip-address* **ebgp-multihop** *number-of-hops* command. You might use this command if you are peering with loopback interface IP addresses, for instance. BGP assumes that internal neighbors might not be directly connected, so this command is not needed with IBGP.

BGP Peering States

The command **show ip bgp neighbors** shows a list of peers, and the status of their peering session. This status can include the following states:

- **Idle**—No peering; router is looking for neighbor. Idle (admin) means that the neighbor relationship has been administratively shut down.
- **Connect**—TCP handshake completed.
- **OpenSent, or Active**—An open message was sent to try to establish the peering.
- **OpenConfirm**—Router has received a reply to the open message.
- **Established**—Routers have a BGP peering session. This is the desired state.

You can troubleshoot session establishment with debug commands. Use **debug ip bgp events** or **debug ip bgp ipv4 unicast** (in IOS versions 12.4 and up) to see where the process fails. Some common failure causes include AS number misconfiguration, neighbor IP address misconfiguration, neighbor with no neighbor statement for your router, and neighbor with no route to the source address of your router's BGP messages.

BGP Path Selection

IGPs, such as EIGRP or OSPF, choose routes based on lowest metric. They attempt to find the shortest, fastest way to get traffic to its destination. BGP, however, has a very different way of route selection. It assigns various attributes to each path; these attributes can be administratively manipulated in order to control the path that is selected. It then examines the value of these attributes in an ordered fashion until it is able to narrow all the possible routes down to one path.

BGP Attributes

BGP chooses a route to network based on the attributes of its path. Four categories of attributes exist:

- **Well-known mandatory**—Must be recognized by all BGP routers, present in all BGP updates, and passed on to other BGP routers. For example, AS path, origin, and next hop.
- **Well-known discretionary**—Must be recognized by all BGP routers and passed on to other BGP routers, but need not be present in an update. For example, local preference.
- **Optional transitive**—Might or might not be recognized by a BGP router, but is passed on to other BGP routers. If not recognized, it is marked as partial. For example, aggregator, community.
- **Optional nontransitive**—Might or might not be recognized by a BGP router and is not passed on to other routers. For example, Multi-Exit Discriminator (MED), originator ID.

Table 6-2 lists common BGP attributes, their meanings, and their category.

Table 6-2 BGP Attributes

Attribute	Meaning
AS path	An ordered list of all the autonomous systems through which this update has passed. Well-known, mandatory.
Origin	How BGP learned of this network. i = by **network** command, e = from EGP, ? = redistributed from other source. Well-known, mandatory.
Next hop	The IP address of the next-hop router. Well-known, mandatory.
Local preference	A value telling IBGP peers which path to select for traffic leaving the AS. Well-known, discretionary.

continues

Table 6-2 BGP Attributes *continued*

Attribute	Meaning
Multi-Exit Discriminator (MED)	Suggests to a neighboring autonomous system which of multiple paths to select for traffic bound into your autonomous system. Optional, non-transitive.
Weight	Cisco proprietary, to tell a router which of multiple local paths to select for traffic leaving the AS. Only has local significance.

Influencing BGP Path Selection

BGP was not created to be a fast protocol; it was created to allow as much administrative control over route path selection as possible. Path selection is controlled by manipulating BGP attributes, usually using route maps. You can set a default local preference by using the command **bgp default local-preference** and a default MED for redistributed routes with the **default-metric** command under the BGP routing process. But by using route maps, you can change attributes for certain neighbors only or for certain routes only. The earlier section on route maps contains an example of using a route map to set a local preference of 200 for specific redistributed routes. This is higher than the default local preference of 120, so routers within the AS are more likely to prefer that path than others.

Route maps can also be applied to routes sent to or received from a neighbor. The following example shows a simple route map that sets MED on all routes advertised out to an EBGP neighbor:

```
route-map MED permit 10
set metric 50
!
router bgp 65001
neighbor 10.1.1.1 route-map MED out
```

When attributes are changed, you must tell BGP to apply the changes. Either clear the BGP session (**clear ip bgp** *) or do a soft reset (**clear ip bgp * soft in | out**). Routers using recent IOS versions will do a route refresh when the session in cleared inbound.

BGP Path Selection Criteria

BGP tries to narrow its path selection down to one best path; it does not load balance by default. To do so, it examines the path attributes of any loop-free, synchronized (if synchronization is enabled) routes with a reachable next-hop in the following order:

1. Choose the route with the highest weight.
2. If weight is not set, choose the route with the highest local preference.
3. Choose routes that you advertise.
4. Choose the path with the shortest autonomous system path.
5. Choose the path with the lowest origin code (i is lowest, e is next, ? is last).
6. Choose the route with the lowest MED, if the same autonomous system advertises the possible routes.
7. Choose an eBGP route over an iBGP route.
8. Choose the route through the nearest IGP neighbor.
9. Choose the oldest route.
10. Choose a path through the neighbor with the lowest router ID.
11. Choose a path through the neighbor with the lowest IP address.

To enable BGP to load balance over more than one path, you must enter the command **maximum-paths** *number-of-paths*. BGP can load balance over a maximum of six paths.

BGP Authentication

BGP supports MD5 authentication between neighbors, using a shared password. It is configured under BGP router configuration mode with the command **neighbor** {*ip-address* | *peer-group-name*} **password** *password*. When authentication is configured, BGP authenticates every TCP segment from its peer and checks the source of each routing update. Most ISPs require authentication for their EBGP peers.

Peering will succeed only if both routers are configured for authentication and have the same password. If your router has authentication configured and the neighbor does not, your router will display the error message "%TCP-6-BADAUTH: No MD5 digest from *peer's-IP-address*:11003 to *local-router's-IP-address*:179."

If the neighbor router is configured with a nonmatching password, your router will display the error message "%TCP-6-BADAUTH: Invalid MD5 digest from *peer's-IP-address*:11004 to *local-router's-IP-address*:179."

If a router has a password configured for a neighbor, but the neighbor router does not, a message such as the following will display on the console while the routers attempt to establish a BGP session between them:

```
%TCP-6-BADAUTH: No MD5 digest from [peer's IP address]:11003 to
 [local router's IP address]:179
```

Similarly, if the two routers have different passwords configured, a message such as the following will display on the screen:

```
%TCP-6-BADAUTH: Invalid MD5 digest from [peer's IP address]:11004
 to [local router's IP address]:179
```

CHAPTER 7

IP Multicast

A multicast is a single data stream sent from one source to a group of recipients. Examples might be a stock ticker or live video feed. Figure 7-1 shows an example multicast topology, as contrasted to unicast and broadcast.

Figure 7-1 Multicast Topology

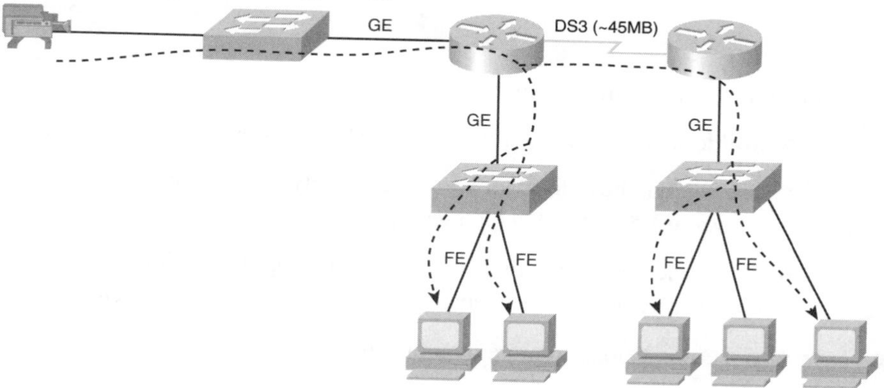

In contrast, a unicast is traffic from one source to one destination (see Figure 7-2).

Figure 7-2 Unicast Topology

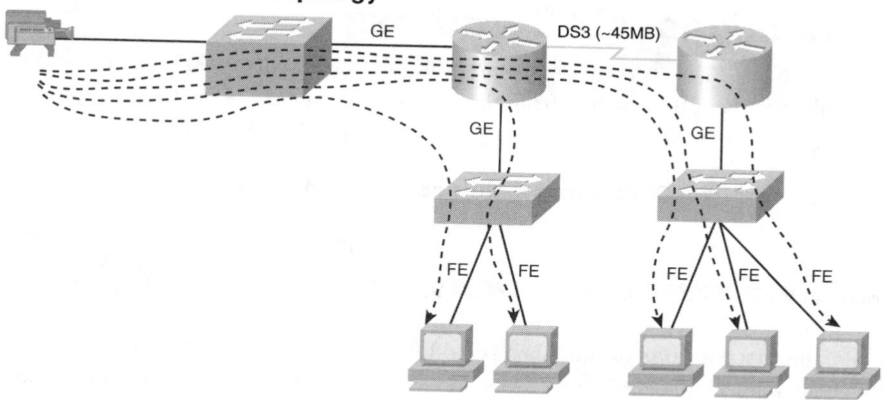

A broadcast is traffic from one source to all destinations (see Figure 7-3). Broadcasts are not routed!

Figure 7-3 Broadcasting

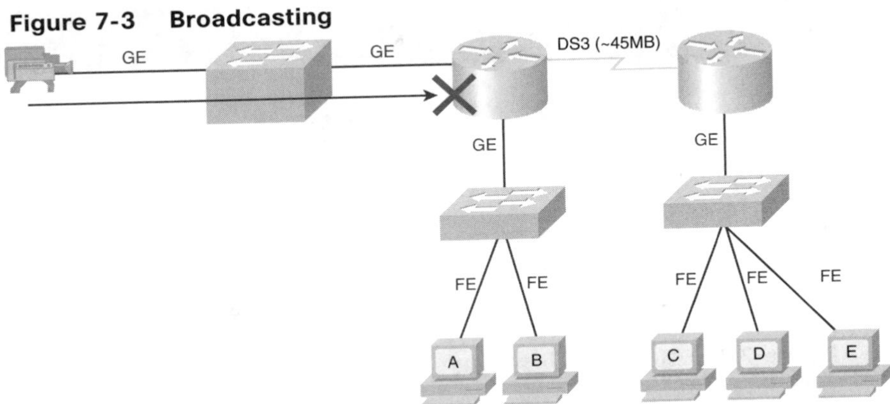

Some features of multicast traffic are:

- Multicast uses UDP, so reliability must be handled by the end host.
- The sending host does not know the identity of the receiving hosts; it knows just a group IP addresses.
- Group membership is dynamic. Hosts join a group, notify their upstream router, and the router begins forwarding data to them.
- Hosts can belong to more than one group.
- Hosts in a group can be located in many different places.

Multicast MAC Address

Multicast MAC addresses all start with the first 25 bits 01005E. The last 23 bits are the left-most bits from the IP address. Figure 7-4 shows how a MAC address of 0100.5E40.0305 maps to a multicast IP address of 227.64.3.5.

Figure 7-4 Computing a Multicast MAC Address

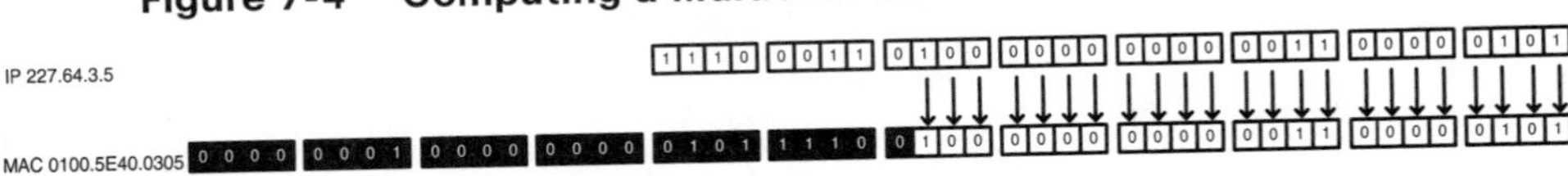

The first four bits of multicast IP addresses are always 1110, and the last 23 bits map to the MAC. That leaves five bits that are dropped. Remember that this is an issue, because every multicast MAC maps to many multicast IPs! Figure 7-5 shows how a MAC address of 0100.5E40.0305 could map to several different multicast IP addresses. Notice that the first two octets can vary in the IP addresses.

Figure 7-5 Overlapping Multicast MAC Addresses

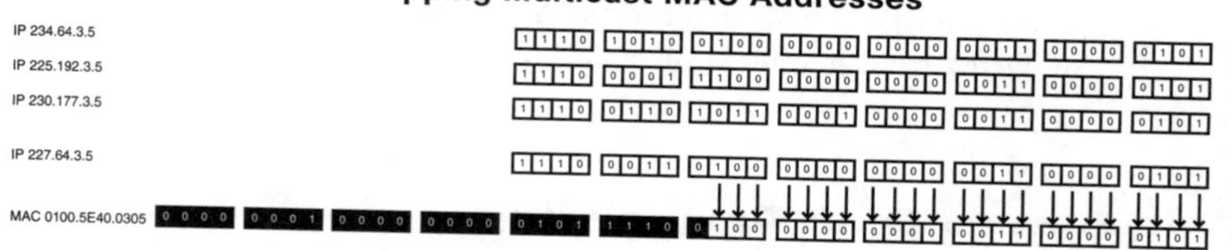

Multicast IP Addresses

Multicasts use the IP address range 224.0.0.0 to 239.255.255.255. The first four bits of the first octet are always binary 1110, and the remaining 28 bits identify the multicast group. Some addresses are reserved:

- 224.0.0.1 is the all-hosts group.
- 224.0.0.2 is the all-routers group.
- The rest of the 224.0.0.0/24 range is reserved for link-local protocols.
- 224.0.1.0 to 238.255.255.255 are for use over the Internet, and they are called globally-scoped addresses.
- Source-specific multicast uses 232.0.0.0/8 addresses.
- 233.0.0.0/8 is used to assign static multicast addresses for use by an organization. The second and third octets of the address are the organization's Autonomous System number. This is called GLOP, which is a combination of global and scope.
- 239.0.0.0/8 is for local use within an organization, and it is called a limited scope or an administratively scoped address.

Multicast Distribution Trees

Multicasts use two different ways to distribute data between a server and hosts:

- A source-based tree is the simplest kind. Its root is the server, and it forms branches throughout the network to all the members of the multicast group. A source tree is identified by (S,G) where S is the IP address of the server and G is the group multicast address. It creates optimal paths between the server and the hosts, but takes more router resources. Every router along the path must maintain path information for every server.

- A shared tree selects a common root called a rendezvous point (RP). The server sends traffic to the RP, which forwards it to hosts belonging to the group. The tree is identified by (*,G) where * means any source and G is the group multicast address. Shared trees use less router resources, but can result in suboptimal paths.

Reverse Path Forwarding

Multicast routers identify upstream ports (pointing to the server or RP) and downstream ports (pointing to other receivers) for each multicast group. The upstream port is found using Reverse Path Forwarding (RPF). RPF involves looking at the routing table to see which interface the router uses to send unicast traffic to that server or RP. That interface is the upstream port, or RPF port, for the multicast group. The RFP check is done every five seconds. It is used in this way:

- If a multicast packet arrives on the RPF port, the router forwards the packet out to the interfaces listed in the outgoing interface list of a multicast routing table.
- If the packet does not arrive on the RPF port, the packet is discarded to prevent loops.

Protocol Independent Multicast (PIM)

PIM is a protocol used between routers to keep track of where to forward traffic for each multicast group. It can use information gathered from any routing protocol. PIM can run in dense mode or sparse mode.

PIM Dense Mode

PIM dense mode uses source-based trees. When running in dense mode, PIM assumes that every router needs to receive multicasts. Any router that doesn't want to receive it must send a prune message upstream to the server. PIM dense mode is most appropriate when:

- Multicast servers and receivers are near each other.
- There are just a few servers and many receivers.
- You have a high volume of multicast traffic.
- The multicast stream is fairly constant.

PIM Sparse Mode

PIM sparse mode uses shared distribution trees. It does not assume that any routers want to receive the multicast, but instead waits to hear an explicit message from them, joining the group. Then it adds branches to the tree to reach the hosts behind those routers. PIM sparse mode uses RPs to connect hosts and servers. After the connection is made, PIM switches over to a source tree. Sparse mode is used when:

- Pockets of users are widely dispersed around the network.
- Multicast traffic is intermittent.

PIM Sparse-Dense Mode

An interface can be configured in sparse-dense mode. Then, if the router knows of an RP for its group, it uses sparse mode. Otherwise, it uses dense mode. In addition, it makes the interface capable of receiving multicasts from both sparse and dense-mode groups.

Configuring Multicast Routing and PIM

Use the following command to enable multicast routing:

```
(config)# ip multicast-routing
```

PIM mode must be configured at each interface with the following command. Configuring PIM on an interface also enables Internet Group Management Protocol (IGMP) on that interface:

```
(config-if)# ip pim {sparse-mode ¦ dense-mode ¦ sparse-dense-mode}
```

When using sparse mode, an RP must be specified. A router knows that it is an RP when it sees its own address in the command:

```
(config)# ip pim rp-address ip-address
```

Auto-RP

Auto-RP automates the discovery of RPs in a sparse or sparse-dense PIM network. RPs advertise themselves to a router designated as an RP mapping agent. The mapping agent then decides on one RP per group and sends that information to the other routers.

To configure a router as an RP, type the following:

```
(config)# ip pim send-rp-announce type number scope ttl
 group-list access-list-number
```

To configure a router as a mapping agent, type the following:

```
(config)# ip pim send-rp-discovery scope ttl
```

PIM Version 2

Cisco routers with recent versions of the IOS use PIM Version 2 by default. Some differences between PIM Version 1 and PIM Version 2 include:

- PIM Version 1 is Cisco proprietary, whereas PIM Version 2 is standards-based.
- Both versions can dynamically map RPs to multicast groups. PIM Version 1 uses an auto-RP mapping agent, and PIM Version 2 uses a bootstrap router (BSR).
- PIM Version 1 uses a Time-to-Live value to bound its announcements, and PIM Version 2 uses a configured domain border.
- In PIM Version 2, sparse and dense mode are group properties, not interface properties.

To configure PIM Version 2, configure at least one router as a BSR, and selected routers as RPs. To configure a BSR, use the following:

```
(config)# ip pim bsr-candidate interface hash-mask-length [priority]
```

To configure a router as a candidate RP, use the following:

```
(config)# ip pim rp-candidate type number ttl group-list access-
 list-number
```

IGMP

When a host wishes to join a multicast group, it sends an Internet Group Management Protocol (IGMP) message to the router. The router periodically checks for group members on each segment. There are three versions of IGMP.

IGMP Version 1

Multicast routers query each segment periodically to see if there are still hosts in multicast groups with a query sent to the all-hosts address of 224.0.0.1. One host on the segment responds. Hosts silently leave a group; the router doesn't know they are gone until it queries and no one responds.

IGMP Version 2

Version 2 adds explicit leave messages that hosts send when they leave a group. Queries are sent to specific multicast group addresses, not the all-hosts address.

IGMP Version 3

Hosts are able to tell the router not only which multicast groups they belong to, but also from which sources they will accept multicasts. It adds two modes for requesting membership in a multicast group:

- Include mode—The receiver lists the group or groups to which it will belong and the servers it will use.
- Exclude mode—The receiver lists the group or groups to which it will belong and the servers it will `not` use.

CGMP

Switches flood multicasts by default. Cisco Group Management Protocol (CGMP) lets a router tell a switch which hosts belong to which multicast group, so the switch can add that information to its port-to-MAC address mapping. Then when a multicast comes in, the switch forwards it only to ports that have hosts belonging to that group. CGMP is Cisco proprietary.

IGMP Snooping

IGMP snooping is another way for the switch to find out which ports have multicast hosts. When it is enabled, the switch opens all multicast packets, looking for IGMP join or leave messages. When it finds one, it records that information and uses it for forwarding multicasts. Because every multicast packet has to be opened, this can cause a performance hit on the switch.

Verifying Multicast Routing

Some commands to verify multicast routing include the following:

- **show ip mroute**—This shows the contents of the multicast routing table. For each group, it lists the mode, the RPF neighbor, the group identifier, and the outgoing interfaces.
- **show ip mroute summary**—Lists each multicast group without as much detail.
- **show ip mroute active**—Shows the active sources and the sending rate of each.
- **show ip mroute count**—Shows traffic statistics for each multicast group.
- **show ip pim interface**—Lists each interface doing multicasting, its PIM mode, and number of neighbors.
- **show ip pim rp**—Lists the RPs the router knows.
- **show ip pim rp-hash**—Shows the RP selected for each multicast group.
- **show ip pim bsr**—Lists the current BSR.

CHAPTER 8

IPv6 Introduction

IPv6 is an extension of IP with several advanced features:

- Larger address space
- Simpler header
- Autoconfiguration
- Extension headers
- Flow labels
- Mobility
- "Baked in" security

Of these, many capabilities have been backported to IPv4. The primary adoption of IPv6 will be driven by the need for more addresses. Given the growth in Internet use and the emergence of large groups of Internet users in developing countries, this is a significant requirement.

IPv6 Routing Prefix

IPv4 addresses are 32 bits long, whereas IPv6 addresses are 128 bits. IPv6 addresses are composed of the following elements (see Figure 8-1):

- The first three bits (/3) of unicast always 001.
- The next 13 bits (/16) are Top-Level Aggregator (TLA) the upstream ISP.
- The next 24 bits (/40) are the next-level aggregator or regional ISP.
- Enterprises are assigned /48 and have 16 bits of subnetting.

Figure 8-1 RFC 2374 IPv6 Address Structure

Format 3b	Top-Level Aggregation 13b	Rsvd8b	Next-Level Aggregation 24b	Site-Level Aggregation 16b	Interface ID 64b

IPv6 Interface ID

The host portion of the address is last 64 bits. It can be assigned manually, using DHCP v6, or using stateless autoconfiguration.

An end-system uses stateless autoconfiguration by waiting for a router to advertise the local prefix. If the end system has a 64-bit MAC, it concatenates the prefix and its MAC to form an IPv6 address. If the end system has a 48-bit MAC, it flips the global/local bit and inserts 0xFFEE into the middle of the MAC. The resulting 64-bit number is called the EUI64. The prefix and EUI64 are concatenated to form the address. Figure 8-2 shows how a host uses its MAC address to create its IPv6 address.

Figure 8-2 EUI64

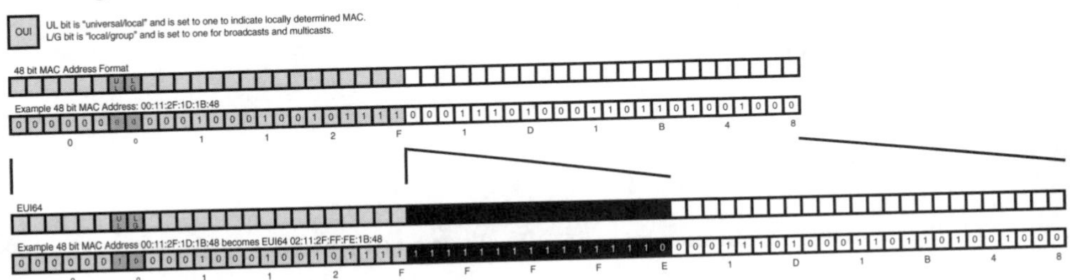

Simplified Presentation of IPv6 Address

There are two ways to shorten the representation of an IPv6 address. Take the example address 4001:0000:0001:0002:0000:0000:0000:ABCD.

- Leading zeros may be omitted. This makes the example 4001:0:1:2:0:0:0:ABCD.
- Sequential zeros may be shown as double colons once per address. This makes the example 4001:0:1:2::ABCD.

IPv6 Header

The IPv6 header, shown in Figure 8-3, is similar o the IPv4 header. The largest changes have to do with the larger addresses, aligning fields to 64-bit boundaries and moving fragmentation to an extension header.

Figure 8-3 IPv6 Header

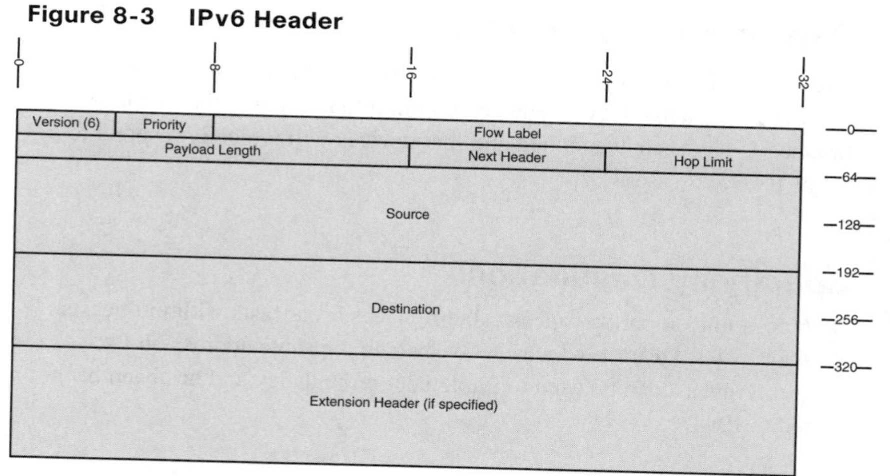

The fields are:

- Version—6.
- Priority—Similar to DSCP in version 4, this eight-bit field is used to describe relative priority.
- Flow—20-bit flow label allows tagging in a manner similar to MPLS.
- Length—The length of the data in the packet.
- Next Header—Indicates how the bits after the IP header should be interpreted. Could indicate TCP or UDP, or it could show an extension header.
- Hop Limit—Similar to TTL.
- Source and Destination—IPv6 addresses.

Zero or more extension headers could follow, including:

- Hop-by-hop options—Options for intermediate devices.
- Destination options—Options for the end node.
- Source routing—Specifies “way stations” that the route must include.
- Fragmentation—Used to divide packets.
- Authentication—Used to attest to source. Replaces the AH header from IPSec.
- Encryption—Replaces the IPSec ESP header.

Advanced Features

"Advanced" features are elements that are not available in IPv4 or have significantly changed. For instance, it's important to know that the idea of broadcasts has been abandoned and that devices will typically respond to a set of IPv6 addresses.

Specifying Destinations

IPv6 does not support broadcasts, but replaces broadcasts with multicasts. IPv6 also uses Anycast, which involves using the same address on two devices. Anycast can be used to implement redundancy and has been back-ported to IPv4.

Specifying Sources

Each IPv6 system must recognize the following addresses:

- Unicast address
- Link local address (FE80/10 | EUI64)
- Loopback (::1)
- All-nodes multicast (FF00::1)
- Site-local multicast (FF02::2)
- Solicited-nodes multicast (FF02::1:FF00/104)

Additionally, some systems will also use the following addresses:

- IPv4 mapped address (0::FFFF | 32-bit, IPv4 address).
- Second unicast address shared with another system (anycast).
- Additional multicast groups.
- Routers must support subnet-router anycast (all zeros EUI64).
- Routers must support local all-routers multicast (FF01::2), link-local (FF02::2), and site-local (FF05:2).
- Routers must support routing protocol multicast groups.

Renumbering

IPv6 supports easy network renumbering. A router sends out a "router advertisement" with a new prefix and a token that instructs end systems to perform stateless autoconfiguration. Hosts then recognize the command and update their addresses.

Anyone who has had to renumber a large range of IPv4 addresses can testify to what a boon this feature will be!

Mobility

IPv6 also includes better support for roaming systems. Using IPv6 Mobility, roamers keep in touch with a "home agent," which is their home router. Traffic sent to the "home address" is forwarded by the agent to the current address. The roamer then sends back a binding update to its corresponding agent so that future traffic is sent directly to the roaming address.

IPv6 Routing

IPv6 is not enabled by default on Cisco routers. To enable IPv6 routing, the command is `Router(config)#`**`ipv6 unicast-routing`**.

After IPv6 is enabled, addresses are assigned to interfaces much like version 4:

```
Router(config-if)#ipv6 address prefix/prefix-length
```

To make this less abstract, a more complete example that shows an IPv6 implementation is shown in Example 8-1.

Example 8-1 Enabling IPv6 Routing and Assigning Addresses

```
RouterA#configure terminal
RouterA(config)#ipv6 unicast-routing
RouterA(config)#interface fastethernet0/0
RouterA(config-if)#description Local LAN
RouterA(config-if)#ipv6 address 4001:0:1:1::2/64
RouterA(config-if)#interface serial 1/0
RouterA(config-if)#description point-to-point line to Internet
RouterA(config-if)#ipv6 address 4001:0:1:5::1/64
```

Static Routing

Static routing with IPv6 works exactly like it does with version 4. Aside from understanding the address format, there are no differences. Static routes are not currently on the BSCI test. The syntax for the IPv6 static route command is shown below, and Example 8-2 is supplied so that the command may be viewed in context as it might be applied.

```
Router(config)# ipv6 route ipv6-prefix/prefix-length {ipv6-address
  ¦ interface-type interface-number [ipv6-address]} [administrative-
  distance] [administrative-multicast-distance ¦ unicast ¦
  multicast] [tag tag]
```

Example 8-2 Configuring Static IPv6 Routes

```
RouterA(config)#ipv6 route 4001:0:1:2::/64 4001:0:1:1::1
RouterA(config)#ipv6 route ::/0 serial1/0
```

RIPng for IPv6

RIPng is the IPv6 of RIP and is defined in RFC 2080. Like RIPv2 for IPv4, RIPng is a distance vector routing protocol that uses a hop count for its metric and has a maximum hop count of 15. RIPng also uses periodic multicast updates—every 30 seconds—to advertise routes. The multicast address is FF02::9.

RIPng is not on the BSCI exam at present, but it is presented here for completeness and to round out your appreciation for IPv6 routing and to prepare the reader for trial implementations of IPv6.

There are two important differences between the old RIP and the next-generation RIP. First, RIPng supports multiple concurrent processes, each identified by a process number (this is similar to OSPFv2). Second, RIPng is initialized in global configuration mode and then enabled on specific interfaces.

Example 8-3 shows the syntax used to apply RIPng to a configuration. Notice that the syntax is very similar to traditional RIP.

Example 8-3 RIPng

```
Router(config)#ipv6 router rip process
Router(config-rtr)#interface type number
Router(config-if)#ipv6 rip process enable
```

Like RIP for IPv4, troubleshoot RIPng by looking at the routing table (**show ipv6 route**), by reviewing the routing protocols (**show ipv6 protocols**), and by watching routing updates propagated between routers (**debug ipv6 rip**).

EIGRP

EIGRP has been expanded to support IPv6, although you'll need to verify that a specific version of IOS is capable of doing this. EIGRP for IPv6 is based on the IPv4 version. EIGRP is still an advanced distance vector routing protocol that uses a complex metric. EIGRP still has a reliable update mechanism and uses DUAL to retain fall-back paths. Like EIGRP in IPv4, it sends multicast hellos every five seconds (but the multicast address is now FF02::A). EIGRP is enabled as described in the following:

```
Router(config)#ipv6 router eigrp as
Router(config-rtr)#router-id ipv4-address¦ipv6-address
Router(config-rtr)#interface type number
Router(config-if)#ipv6 eigrp as
```

Like EIGRP for IPv4, troubleshoot by looking at the routing table (**show ipv6 route**), by reviewing the routing protocols (**show ipv6 protocols**), and by monitoring neighbors (**show ipv6 eigrp neighbors**). Example 8-4 shows the configuration for IPv6 EIGRP. Notice that the routing protocol must be enabled under each interface.

Example 8-4 Configuring EIGRP for IPv6

```
RouterA#configure terminal
RouterA(config)#ipv6 unicast-routing
RouterA(config)#ipv6 router eigrp 1
RouterA(config-rtr)#router-id 10.255.255.1
RouterA(config)#interface fastethernet0/0
RouterA(config-if)#description Local LAN
RouterA(config-if)#ipv6 address 4001:0:1:1::2/64
RouterA(config-if)#ipv6 eigrp 1
RouterA(config-if)#interface serial 1/0
RouterA(config-if)#description point-to-point line to Internet
RouterA(config-if)#ipv6 address 4001:0:1:5::1/64
RouterA(config-if)#ipv6 eigrp 1
```

MP-BGP for IPv6

Multiprotocol BGP (RFC 2858) involves two new extensions to BGP4 that allow BGP to carry reachability information for other protocols, such as IPv6, multicast IPv4, and MPLS. The extensions allow NEXT_HOP to carry

IPv6 addresses and NLRI (network layer reachability information) to an IPv6 prefix.

Example 8-5 shows the BGP commands as they might be applied.

Example 8-5 Configuring BGP IPv6 Routes

```
RouterA#configure terminal
RouterA(config)#ipv6 unicast-routing
RouterA(config)#router bgp 65000
RouterA(config-rtr)#neighbor 4001:0:1:1:5::4 remote-as 65001
RouterA(config-rtr)#address-family ipv6 unicast
RouterA(config-rtr-af)#neighbor 4001:0:1:5::4 activate
RouterA(config-rtr-af)#network 4001:0:1::/48
```

OSPFv3

OSPFv3 is one of the first routing protocols available for IPv6 and. Due to its open-standard heritage, it is widely supported in IPv6. OSPFv3 is the only routing protocol discussed on the BSCI test, so it is covered in more depth here.

OSPFv3, which supports IPv6, is documented in RFC 2740. Like OSPFv2, it is a link-state routing protocol that uses the Dijkstra algorithm to select paths. Routers are organized into areas, with all areas touching area 0.

OSPF speakers meet and greet their neighbors using Hellos, exchange LSAs (link-state advertisements) and DBDs (database descriptors), and run SPF against the accumulated link-state database.

OSPFv3 participants use the same packet types as OSPFv2, form neighbors in the same way, flood and age LSAs identically, and support the same NBMA topologies and rare techniques such as NSSA and on-demand circuits.

OSPFv3 differs from its predecessors principally in its new address format. OSPFv3 advertises using multicast addresses FF02::5 and FF02::6, but uses its link-local address as the source address of its advertisements. Authentication is no longer built in, but relies on the underlying capabilities of IPv6.

OSPFv3 LSAs

OSPFv3 and OSPFv2 use a similar set of LSAs, but version 3 has a few changes from OSPFv2. Types 3 and 4 have been slightly renamed, but still fulfill the same functionality as they did with OSPFv2. Type 8 is new and assists in discovering neighbors. Types 1 and 2 no longer pass routes. Instead they pass router IDs. Prefixes are associated as leaf objects that hang off those nodes and are advertised using Type 9, which is also new.

LSAs are sourced from the link-local address of an interface and destined for a multicast address. FF02::5 is the "all OSPF routers" address and FF02::6 is the "all OSPF DRs" address.

The OSPFv3 LSA types are collected together in Table 8-1. Notice that types one through seven exactly match their OSPFv2 predecessor, while type 8 and type 9 are new to OSPFv3.

Table 8-1 OSPF LSA Types

LSA Type	Name	Description
1	Router-LSA	Advertise RIDs within area
2	Network-LSA	Advertise RIDs within area from DR
3	Inter-Area-Prefix-LSA	Advertise prefixes between areas
4	Inter-Area-Router-LSA	Advertise location of ASBR
5	AS-External-LSA	Advertise redistributed routes
6	Group-Membership	Multicast information
7	Type-7-LSA	Pass external routes through an NSSA
8	Link-LSA	Advertise link-local address to neighbors
9	Intra-Area-Prefix-LSA	Advertise prefixes associated with RID

Configuration

OSPF configuration is similar to RIPng and EIGRP. The routing process is created and routing properties are assigned to it. Interfaces are then associated with the process under interface configuration mode. Assuming that **ipv6 unicast-routing** and interface IP addresses are already in place, the commands to implement OSPFv3 are shown in Example 8-6.

Example 8-6 Configuring OSPF IPv6 Routes

```
Router(config)#ipv6 router ospf process-id
Router(config-rtr)#router-id 32bit-address
Router(config-rtr)#area area range summary-range/prefix-length
Router(config-rtr)#interface type number
Router(config-if)#ipv6 ospf process area area
Router(config-if)#ipv6 ospf process priority priority
Router(config-if)#ipv6 ospf process cost cost
```

Cost may be overridden with the **ipv6 ospf cost** command as shown in Example 8-7.

The **summary-range** command is shown to demonstrate summarization.

Example 8-7 Configuring OSPF IPv6 Routes

```
RouterA#configure terminal
RouterA(config)#ipv6 unicast-routing
RouterA(config)#ipv6 router ospf 1
RouterA(config-rtr)#router-id 10.255.255.1
RouterA(config-rtr)#area 1 range 4001:0:1::/80
RouterA(config-rtr)#interface fastethernet0/0
RouterA(config-if)#description Local LAN
RouterA(config-if)#ipv6 address 4001:0:1:1::2/64
RouterA(config-if)#ipv6 ospf 1 area 1
RouterA(config-if)#ipv6 ospf cost 10
RouterA(config-if)#ipv6 ospf priority 20
RouterA(config-if)#interface serial 1/0
RouterA(config-if)#description multi-point line to Internet
RouterA(config-if)#ipv6 address 4001:0:1:5::1/64
RouterA(config-if)#ipv6 ospf 1 area 1
RouterA(config-if)#ipv6 ospf cost 10
RouterA(config-if)#ipv6 ospf priority 20
```

Troubleshooting

Troubleshoot OSPFv3 just like OSPFv2. Start by looking at **show ipv6 route** to verify routes have been advertised. Assuming the route is in the routing table, test reachability using **ping ipv6**. You can also look at the OSPF setup using **show ipv6 ospf 1 interface**, **show ipv6 ospf**, or **show ipv6 ospf database**.

Integrating IPv4 and IPv6

There are several strategies for migrating from IPv4 to IPv6. Each of these strategies should be considered when organizations decide to make the move to IPv6 because each has positive points to aiding a smooth migration. It should also be said that there does not have to be a global decision on strategy—your organization may choose to run dual-stack in the U.S., go completely to IPv6 in Japan, and use tunneling in Europe. The transition mechanisms include:

- Dual stack—Running IPv6 and IPv4 concurrently.
- IPv6 to IPv4 tunneling (6-to-4)—Routers that straddle the IPv4 and IPv6 worlds to encapsulate the IPv6 traffic inside IPv4 packets.
- Intra-Site Automatic Tunnel Addressing Protocol (ISATAP)—This protocol is similar to 6-to-4, but it treats the IPv4 network as an NBMA network.
- Teredo/Shipworm—Encapsulates IPv6 packets in IPv4/UDP segments.

NAT-PT, ALG, and BIA/BIS

Instead of replacing IPv4, there are several ways to coordinate the functioning of IPv4 and v6 concurrently. NAT-protocol translation is an example of this coexistence strategy. NAT-PT maps IPv6 addresses to IPv4 addresses. If IPv6 is used on the inside of your network, a NAT-PT device will receive IPv6 traffic on its inside interface and replace the IPv6 header with an IPv4 header before sending it to an outside interface. Reply traffic will be able to follow the mapping backward to enable two-way communication.

NAT-PT is able to interpret application traffic and understand when IP information is included in the application data.

It is also possible to connect IPv4 and IPv6 routing domains using application-level gateways (ALG), proxies, or Bump-in-the-API (BIA) and Bump-in-the-Stack (BIS), which are NAT-PT implementations within a host.

PART II

BCMSN

CHAPTER 1

The Evolving Network Model

Cisco has developed specific architecture recommendations for Campus, Data Center, WAN, branches, and telecommuting. These recommendations add specific ideas about how current technologies and capabilities match the network roles within an enterprise.

Each of these designs builds on a traditional hierarchical design and adds features such as security, Quality of Service (QoS), caching, and convergence.

The Hierarchical Design Model

Cisco has used the three level *Hierarchical Design Model* for years. This older model provided a high-level idea of how a reliable network might be conceived, but it was largely conceptual because it did not provide specific guidance. Figure 1-1 is a simple drawing of how the three-layer model might have been built out. A distribution layer-3 switch would be used for each building on campus, tying together the access-switches on the floors. The core switches would link the various buildings together.

Figure 1-1 The Hierarchical Design Model

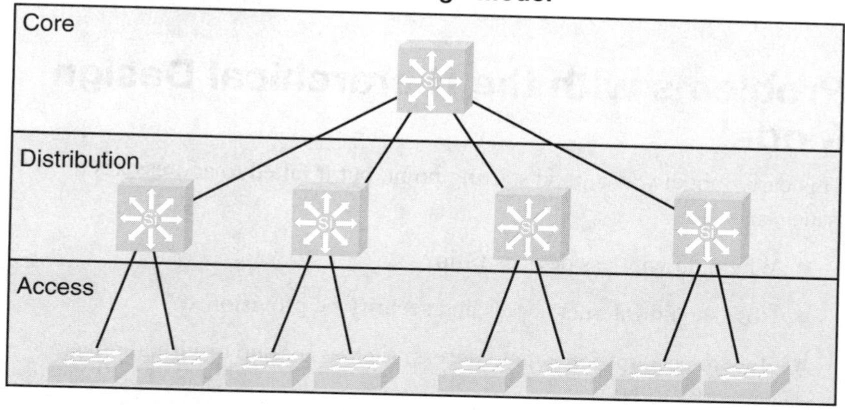

The hierarchical design model divides a network into three layers:

- Access—End stations attach to VLANs.
  - Clients attach to switch ports.
  - VLAN assigned/broadcast domains established.
  - Built using low-cost ports.
- Distribution—Intermediate devices route and apply policies.
  - VLANs terminated, routing between.
  - Policies applied, such as route selection.
  - Access-lists.
  - Quality of Service (QoS).
- Core—The backbone that provides a high-speed path between distribution elements.
  - Distribution devices are interconnected.
  - High speed (there is a lot of traffic).
  - No policies (it is tough enough to keep up).

Later versions of this model include redundant distribution and core devices, and connections that make the model more fault-tolerant. A set of distribution devices and their accompanying access layer switches are called a switch block.

Problems with the Hierarchical Design Model

This early model was a good starting point, but it failed to address key issues, such as:

- Where do wireless devices fit in?
- How should Internet access and security be provisioned?
- How to account for remote-access, such as dial-up or virtual private network (VPN)?
- Where should workgroup and enterprise services be located?

Enterprise Composite Network Model

The newer Cisco model—the Enterprise Composite Model—is significantly more complex and attempts to address the major shortcoming of the Hierarchical Design Model by expanding the older version and making specific recommendations about how and where certain network functions should be implemented. This model is based on the principles described in the Cisco Architecture for Voice, Video, and Integrated Data (AVVID).

The Enterprise Composite Model is broken up into three large sections:

- Enterprise Campus—The portion of the design that is like the old hiearchical model.
- Enterprise Edge—The connections to the public network.
- Service Provider Edge—The different public networks that are attached.

The first section, the Enterprise Campus, looks like the old Hierarchical model with some added details. The Enterprise Campus is shown in Figure 1-2. It features six sections:

- Campus Backbone—The center of the network, like the old "core".
- Building Distribution—Intermediate devices that route from the core to access devices.
- Building Access—Connections for end systems.
- Management—Command, control, and auditing features.
- Edge Distribution—A distribution layer out to the WAN.
- Server Farm—For Enterprise services.

The Enterprise Edge (shown in Figure 1-3) details the connections from the campus to the Wide Area Network and includes:

- E-Commerce—Externally accessible services that have ties to internal data stores.
- Internet Connectivity—Connectivity to outside services.
- Remote Access—Dial and VPN.
- WAN—Internal links.

Figure 1-2 The Enterprise Campus

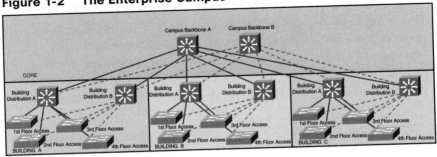

Campus Backbone A
Campus Backbone B
CORE
Building Distribution A
Building Distribution B
1st Floor Access
2nd Floor Access
3rd Floor Access
4th Floor Access
BUILDING A
BUILDING B
BUILDING C

Figure 1-3 The Enterprise Edge

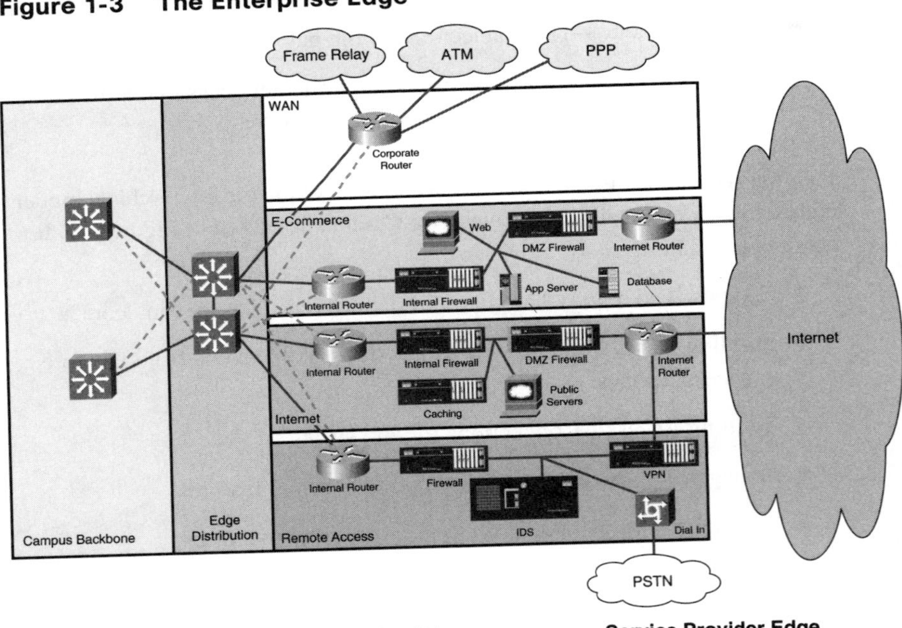

The Service Provider Edge consists of the public networks that facilitate wide-area network connectivity:

- Internet Service Provider (ISP)—Public connectivity
- Public Switched Telephone Network (PSTN)—Dial up
- Frame Relay, ATM, and PPP—Private connectivity

Figure 1-4 puts together the various pieces: Campus, Enterprise Edge, and Service Provider Edge. Security implemented on this model is described in the Cisco SAFE (Security Architecture for Enterprise) blueprint.

Figure 1-4 The Complete Enterprise Composite Model

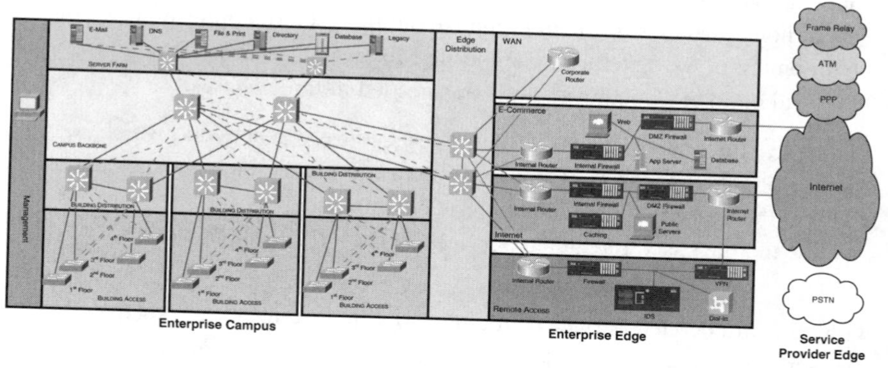

SONA and IIN

Modern converged networks include different traffic types, each with unique requirements for security, QoS, transmission capacity, and delay. These include:

- Voice signaling and bearer
- Core Application traffic, such as Enterprise Resource Programming (ERP) or Customer Relationship Management (CRM)
- Database Transactions
- Multicast multimedia
- Network management
- "Other" traffic, such as web pages, e-mail, and file transfer

Cisco routers are able to implement filtering, compression, prioritization, and policing (dedicating network capacity). Except for filtering, these capabilities are referred to collectively as QoS.

Note

The best way to meet capacity requirements is to have twice as much bandwidth as needed. Financial reality, however, usually requires QoS instead.

CCNP BCMSN

Although QoS is wonderful, it is not the only way to address bandwidth shortage. Cisco espouses an ideal called the Intelligent Information Network (IIN).

IIN describes an evolutionary vision of a network that integrates network and application functionality cooperatively and allows the network to be smart about how it handles traffic to minimize the footprint of applications. IIN is built on top of the Enterprise Composite Model and describes structures overlaid on to the Composite design as needed in three phases.

Phase 1, "Integrated Transport," describes a converged network, which is built along the lines of the Composite model and based on open standards. This is the phase that the industry has been transitioning to for the last few years, and the Cisco Integrated Services Routers (ISR) are an example of this trend.

Phase 2, "Integrated Services," attempts to virtualize resources, such as servers, storage, and network access and move to an "on-demand" model.

By "virtualize" Cisco means that the services are not associated with a particular device or location. Instead, many services can reside in one device to ease management, or many devices can provide one service that is more reliable.

An ISR brings together routing, switching, voice, security, and wireless. It is an example of many services existing on one device. A load balancer, which makes many servers look like one, is a second example.

VRFs are an example of taking one resource and making it look like many. Some versions of IOS are capable of having a router present itself as many virtual router forwarding (VRF) instances, allowing your company to deliver different logical topologies on the same physical infrastructure. Server virtualization is another example. The classic example of taking one resource and making it appear to be many resources is the use of a virtual LAN (VLAN) and a virtual storage area network (VSAN).

Virtualization provides flexibility in configuration and management.

Phase 3, "Integrated Applications," uses application-oriented networking (AON) to make the network application-aware and to allow the network to actively participate in service delivery.

An example of this phase 3 IIN systems approach to service delivery is Network Admission Control (NAC). Before NAC, authentication, VLAN assignment, and anti-virus updates were separately managed. With NAC in place, the network is able to check the policy stance of a client and admit, deny, or remediate based on policies.

IIN allows the network to deconstruct packets, parse fields, and take actions based on the values it finds. An ISR equipped with an AON blade might be configured to route traffic from a business partner. The AON blade can examine traffic, recognize the application, and rebuild XML files in memory. Corrupted XML fields might represent an attack (called *schema poisoning*), so the AON blade could react by blocking that source from further communication. In this example, routing, an awareness of the application data flow, and security are combined to allow the network to contribute to the success of the application.

Services-Oriented Network Architecture (SONA) applies the IIN ideals to Enterprise networks. Figure 1-5 shows how SONA breaks down the IIN functions into three layers:

- Network Infrastructure—Hierarchical converged network and attached end systems.
- Interactive Services—Resources allocated to applications.
- Applications—Includes business policy and logic.

Figure 1-5 IIN and SONA Compared

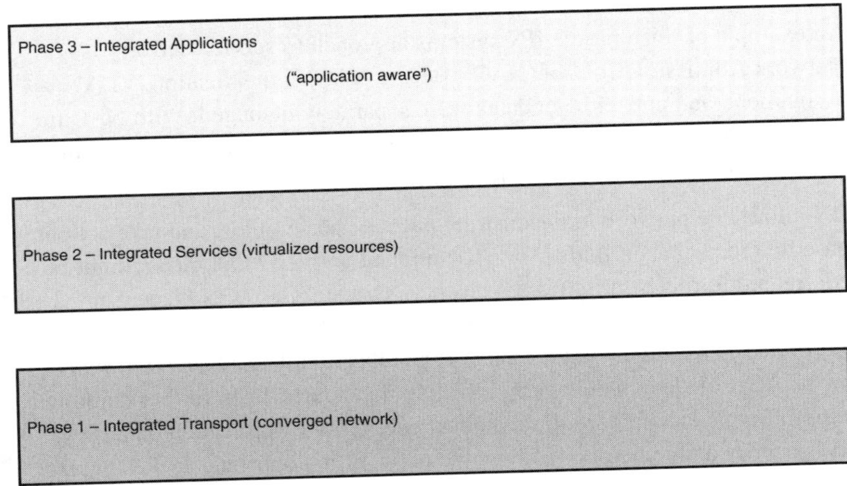
IIN Phases
Phase 3 – Integrated Applications
("application aware")
Phase 2 – Integrated Services (virtualized resources)
Phase 1 – Integrated Transport (converged network)

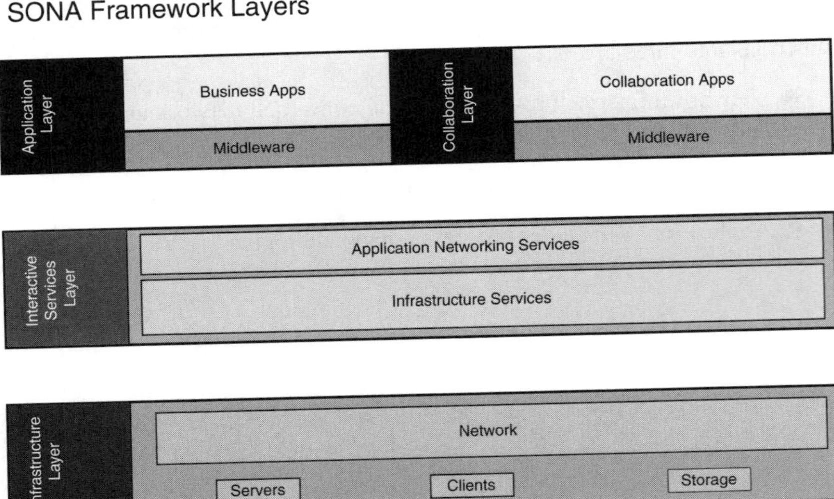
SONA Framework Layers
Application Layer
Business Apps
Middleware
Collaboration Layer
Collaboration Apps
Middleware
Interactive Services Layer
Application Networking Services
Infrastructure Services
Infrastructure Layer
Network
Servers
Clients
Storage

CHAPTER 2

VLAN Implementation

VLANs are used to break large campus networks into smaller pieces. The benefit of this is to minimize the amount of broadcast traffic on a logical segment.

What Is a VLAN?

A virtual LAN (VLAN) is a logical LAN, or a logical subnet. It defines a broadcast domain. A physical subnet is a group of devices that shares the same physical wire. A logical subnet is a group of switch ports assigned to the same VLAN, regardless of their physical location in a switched network.

Two types of VLANs are:

- End-to-end VLAN—VLAN members are assigned by function and can reside on different switches. They are used when hosts are assigned to VLANs based on functions or workgroups, rather than physical location. VLANs should not extend past the Building Distribution submodule. Figure 2-1 shows end-to-end VLANs.
- Local VLAN—Hosts are assigned to VLANs based on their location, such as a floor in a building. A router accomplishes sharing of resources between VLANs. This type is typically found in the Building Access submodule. Figure 2-2 shows an example of local VLANs.

Figure 2-1 End-to-end VLANs

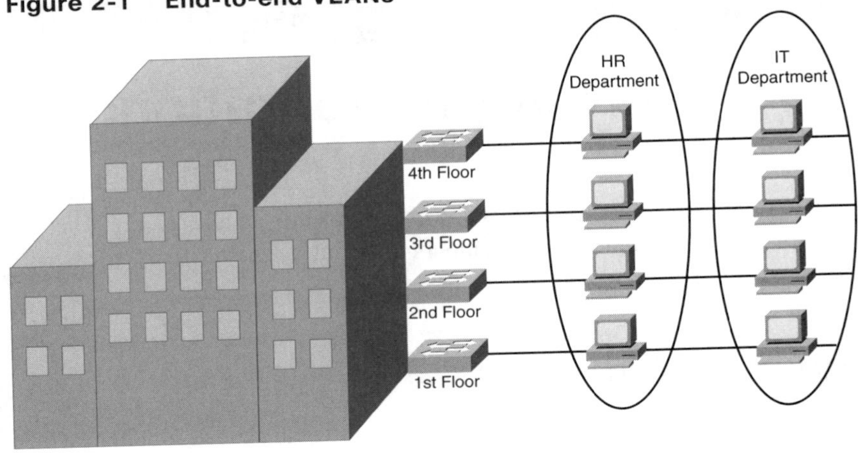

Figure 2-2 Local VLANs

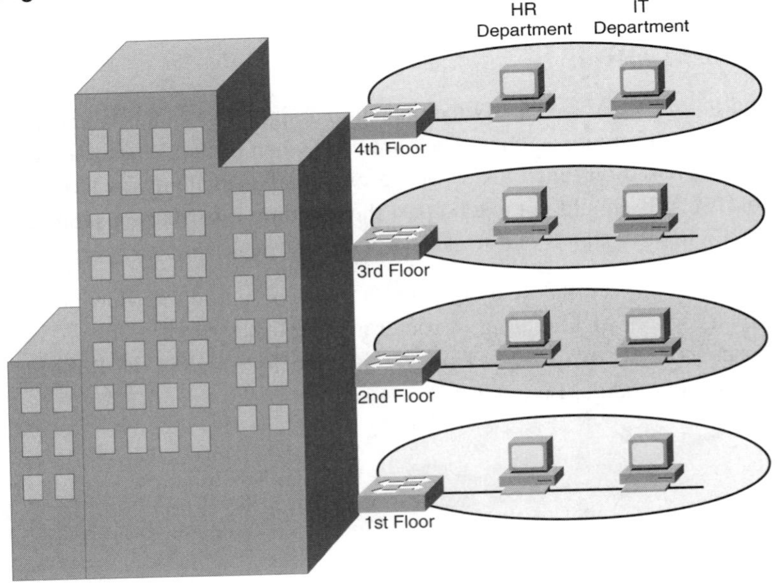

VLAN membership can be assigned either statically by port or dynamically by MAC address using a VLAN Membership Policy Server (VMPS).

Best Practices

VLAN networks need many of the same considerations that normal Ethernet lines demand. For instance, VLANs should have one IP subnet. By supplying consecutive subnets to VLANs, the routing advertisements can be summarized (which has many benefits to convergence).

A stereotypical description of capacity requirements is possible. Access ports are assigned to a single VLAN and should be Fast Ethernet or faster. Ports to the distribution layer should be Gigabit Ethernet or better. Core ports are Gigabit Etherchannel or 10-Gig Ethernet. Remember that uplink ports need to be able to handle all hosts communicating concurrently, and remember that although VLANs logically separate traffic, traffic in different VLANs can still experience contention with other VLANs when both VLANs travel over the same trunk line.

Take into account the entire traffic pattern of applications found in your network. For instance, Voice VLANs pass traffic to a remote Call Manager. Multicast traffic has to communicate back to the routing process and possibly call upon a Rendezvous Point.

Creating a VLAN in Global Config Mode

VLANs must be created before they may be used. VLANs may be created in global configuration mode or in VLAN database mode. Creating VLANs in global configuration is easy—just identify the VLAN number and name it!

```
(config)#vlan 12
(config-vlan)#name MYVLAN
```

Creating a VLAN in Database Mode

Creating a VLAN in VLAN database mode is very similar to global configuration. There are no advantages to either method. Either method creates an entry in a VLAN.DAT file. Remember that copying the configuration, by itself, does not move the VLAN information! To do that you must move the VLAN.DAT file.

```
#vlan database
(vlan)#vlan 12 name MYVLAN
```

Delete a VLAN by using the same command with **no** in front of it. There is no need to include the name when deleting.

Assigning Ports to VLANs

When statically assigning ports to VLANs, first make it an access port, and then assign the port to a VLAN. At the interface configuration prompt:

```
(config-if)#switchport mode access
(config-if)#switchport access vlan 12
```

The commands are similar when using dynamic VLAN assignment. At interface configuration mode:

```
(config-if)#switchport mode access
(config-if)#switchport access vlan dynamic
```

If you use dynamic, you must also enter the IP address of the VMPS server at global configuration mode:

```
(config-if)#vmps server ip address
```

Verifying VLAN Configuration

To see a list of all the VLANs and the ports assigned to them, use the command **show vlan**. To narrow down the information displayed, you can use these keywords after the command: **brief**, **id**, *vlan-number*, or **name** *vlan-name*:

```
ASW# show vlan brief
VLAN Name     Status     Ports
---- -------------------------------- --------- -------------------
----------
1    default     active     Fa0/1, Fa0/2, Fa0/3,
        Fa0/10,Fa0/11,Fa0/12
20   VLAN0020     active     Fa0/5,Fa0/6,Fa0/7
21   VLAN0021     active     Fa0/8,Fa0/9
1002 fddi-default     active
1003 trcrf-default     active
1004 fddinet-default     active
1005 trbrf-default     active
```

Other verification commands include:

- **show running-config interface** *interface-num*—Use the following to verify the VLAN membership of the port:

  ```
  ASW# show run interface fa0/5
  Building configuration...
  Current configuration 64 bytes
  interface FastEthernet 0/5
  switchport access vlan 20
  switchport mode access
  ```

- **show mac address-table interface** *interface-num* **vlan** *vlan-num*—Use the following to view MAC addresses learned through that port for the specified VLAN:

```
ASW# show mac address-table interface fa0/1
          Mac Address Table
------------------------------------------
Vlan    Mac Address       Type          Ports
----    -----------       ----          -----
1       0030.b656.7c3d    DYNAMIC       Fa0/1
Total Mac Addresses for this criterion: 1
```

- **show interfaces** *interface-num* **switchport**—Use the following to see detailed information about the port configuration, such as entries in the Administrative Mode and Access Mode VLAN fields:

```
ASW# show interfaces fa0/1 switchport
Name: Fa0/1
Switchport: Enabled
Administrative Mode: dynamic desirable
Operational Mode: static access
Administrative Trunking Encapsulation: negotiate
Operational Trunking Encapsulation: native
Negotiation of Trunking: On
Access Mode VLAN: 1 (default)
Trunking Native Mode VLAN: 1 (default)
Trunking VLANs Enabled: ALL
Pruning VLANs Enabled: 2-1001
Protected: false
Unknown unicast blocked: false
Unknown multicast blocked: false
Broadcast Suppression Level: 100
Multicast Suppression Level: 100
Unicast Suppression Level: 100
```

Troubleshooting VLAN Issues

The following are three steps in troubleshooting VLAN problems:

- Check the physical connectivity—Make sure the cable, the network adapter, and switch port are good. Check the port's link LED.
- Check the switch configuration—If you see FCS errors or late collisions, suspect a duplex mismatch. Also check configured speed on both ends of the link. Increasing collisions can mean an overloaded link, such as with a broadcast storm.

- Check the VLAN configuration—If two hosts cannot communicate, make sure they are both in the same VLAN. If a host cannot connect to a switch, make sure the host and the switch are in the same VLAN.

VLAN Trunking

A *trunk* is a link that carries traffic for more than one VLAN. Trunks multiplex traffic from multiple VLANs. Trunks connect switches and allow ports on multiple switches to be assigned to the same VLAN.

Two methods of identifying VLANs over trunk links are:

- Inter-Switch Link (ISL)—A Cisco proprietary method that encapsulates the original frame in a header, which contains VLAN information. It is protocol-independent and can identify Cisco Discovery Protocol (CDP) and bridge protocol data unit (BPDU) frames.
- 802.1Q—Standards-based, tags the frames (inserts a field into the original frame immediately after the source MAC address field), and supports Ethernet and Token Ring networks.

When aframe comes into a switch port, the frame is tagged internally within the switch with the VLAN number of the port. When it reaches the outgoing port, the internal tag is removed. If the exit port is a trunk port, then its VLAN is identified in either the ISL encapsulation or the 802.1Q tag. The switch on the other end of the trunk removes the ISL or 802.1Q information, checks the VLAN of the frame, and adds the internal tag. If the exit port is a user port, then the original frame is sent out unchanged, making the use of VLANs transparent to the user.

If a nontrunking port receives an ISL-encapsulated frame, the frame is dropped. If the ISL header and footer cause the MTU size to be exceeded, it might be counted as an error.

If a nontrunking port receives an 802.1Q frame, the source and destination MAC addresses are read, the tag field is ignored, and the frame is switched normally at Layer 2 .

Configuring a Trunk Link

Ports can become trunk ports either by static configuration or dynamic negotiation using Dynamic Trunking Protocol (DTP). A switch port can be in one of five DTP modes:

- Access—The port is a user port in a single VLAN.
- Trunk—The port negotiates trunking with the port on the other end of the link.
- Non-negotiate—The port is a trunk and does not do DTP negotiation with the other side of the link.
- Dynamic Desirable—Actively negotiates trunking with the other side of the link. It becomes a trunk if the port on the other switch is set to **trunk**, **dynamic desirable**, or **dynamic auto** mode.
- Dynamic Auto—Passively waits to be contacted by the other switch. It becomes a trunk if the other end is set to **trunk** or **dynamic desirable** mode.

Configure a port for trunking at the interface configuration mode:

```
(config-if)#switchport mode {dynamic {auto ¦ desirable} ¦ trunk}
```

If dynamic mode is used, DTP negotiates the trunking state and encapsulation. If trunk mode is used, you must specify encapsulation:

```
(config-if)#switchport trunk  encapsulation {isl ¦ dot1q ¦ negotiate}
```

Native VLAN with 802.1Q

If you are using 802.1Q, specify a native VLAN for the trunk link with the command:

```
(config-if)#switchport trunk native vlan vlan-num
```

Frames from the native VLAN are sent over the trunk link untagged. Native VLAN is the VLAN the port would be in if it were not a trunk, and it must match on both sides of the trunk link. VLAN 1 is the default native VLAN for all ports.

VLAN Mapping

ISL trunking recognizes only VLANs numbered 1–1001, but 802.1Q can use VLANs 0–4094. If you are using both ISL and 802.1Q in your network and have VLANs numbered above 1001, you have to map the 802.1Q VLANS to ISL numbers. Some rules about mapping VLANs include:

- You can configure only eight mappings.
- Mappings are local to the switch; the same mappings must be configured on all switches in the network.
- You can map only to Ethernet ISL VLANs.
- The 802.1Q VLANs with the same number as mapped ISL VLANs are blocked. (For example, you map 802.1Q VLAN 1500 to ISL VLAN 150, then 802.1Q VLAN 150 is blocked on that switch.)
- You should not map the 802.1Q native VLAN.

VLANs Allowed on the Trunk

By default, a trunk carries traffic for all VLANs. You can change that behavior for a particular trunk link by giving the following command at the interface config mode:

```
switchport trunk allowed vlan vlans
```

Make sure that both sides of a trunk link allow the same VLANs.

Verifying a Trunk Link

Two commands you can use to verify your trunk configuration are:

```
#show running-config
#show interfaces [interface-num] switchport | trunk
```

Using the **trunk** keyword with the **show interfaces** command gives information about the trunk link:

```
# show interfaces fastethernet 0/1 trunk
Port        Mode          Encapsulation  Status        Native vlan
Fa0/1     desirable      n-802.1q         trunking       1
Port       Vlans allowed on trunk
Fa0/1      1-150
<further output omitted>
```

802.1Q Tunnels

Tunneling is a way to send 802.1Q-tagged frames across a foreign network (such as a Service Provider's network) and still preserve the original 802.1Q tag (see Figure 2-3). The SP configures their end of the trunk link as a tunnel port and assigns a VLAN to carry your traffic within their network. The SP switch then adds a second 802.1Q tag to each frame that came in the tunnel port. Other switches in the SP network see only this second tag, and do not read the original tag. When the frame exits the SP network, the extra tag is removed, leaving the original 802.1Q tag to be read by the receiving switch in your network.

Figure 2-3 802.1q

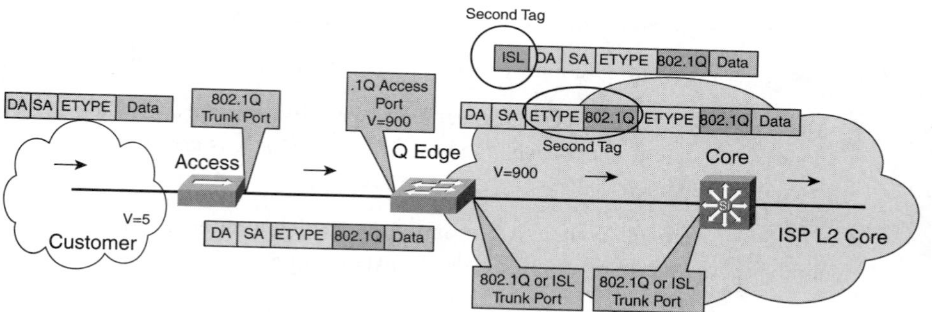

Layer 2 Protocol Tunneling (GBPT)

If a Service Provider separates sections of your network, you can use Layer 2 protocol tunneling to tunnel CDP, Spanning Tree Protocol (STP), and VLAN Trunking Protocol (VTP) frames across the SP's cloud. This is called Generic Bridge PDU Tunneling (GBPT). Frames from the above control protocols are encapsulated as they enter the SP's network on a tunnel port, and de-encapsulated when they exit that network.

Troubleshooting Trunking

Troubleshooting trunking links happens mostly at the physical and datalink layers. Start with the most basic assumptions and work your way "up" the OSI model. It is important to show that physical layer connectivity is present, before moving on to, for instance before trying to troubleshoot IP problems.

- Are both sides of the link in the correct trunking mode?
- Is the same trunk encapsulation on both sides?
- If 802.1Q, is the same native VLAN on both sides?
- Are the same VLANs permitted on both sides?

VLAN Trunking Protocol (VTP)

VTP is a protocol that runs over trunk links and synchronizes the VLAN databases of all switches in the VTP domain. A VTP domain is an administrative group—all switches within that group must have the same VTP domain name configured or they do not synchronize databases.

VTP works by using Configuration Revision numbers and VTP advertisements:

- All switches send out VTP advertisements every five minutes, or when there is a change to the VLAN database (when a VLAN is created, deleted, or renamed).
- VTP advertisements contain a Configuration Revision number. This number is increased by one for every VLAN change.
- When a switch receives a VTP advertisement, it compares the Configuration Revision number against the one in its VLAN database.
- If the new number is higher, the switch overwrites its database with the new VLAN information, and forwards the information to its neighbor switches.
- If the number is the same, the switch ignores the advertisement.
- If the new number is lower, the switch replies with the more up-to-date information contained in its own database .

VTP Switch Roles

A switch can be a VTP:

- Server—The default VTP role. Servers can create, delete, and rename VLANs. They originate both periodic and triggered VTP advertisements and synchronize their databases with other switches in the domain.

- Client—Clients cannot make VLAN changes. They originate periodic VTP advertisements and synchronize their databases with other switches in the domain.
- Transparent—It can create, delete, and rename VLANs, but its VLANs are only local. It does not originate advertisements or synchronize its database with any other switches. It forwards VTP advertisements out its trunk links, however.

VTP Pruning

By default, switches flood broadcasts, multicasts, and unknown unicasts across trunk links. Suppose a host in VLAN 10 on Switch B sends a broadcast. Hosts in VLAN 10 on Switch C need to see that broadcast, but Switch A has no ports in VLAN 10, so it doesn't need to receive the broadcast traffic.

Enabling VTP pruning causes the switch to keep track of VLAN port assignments in its downstream switches. The switch then sends flooded traffic only on trunks toward switches that have ports assigned to the VLAN originating the traffic. It prunes flooded traffic from all other trunks. VTP pruning increases the available bandwidth by preventing unnecessary traffic on trunk links.

There are two versions of VTP: Version 1 and Version 2. To use Version 2, all switches in the domain must be capable of using it. Configure one server for Version 2, and the information is propagated through VTP. Version 2 has the following added features:

- It supports Token Ring VLANs.
- Transparent switches pass along messages from both versions of VTP.
- Consistency checks are performed only when changes are configured through the CLI or SNMP.

Configuring VTP

VTP configuration is done at the global config mode. To configure the switch's VTP mode:

```
(config)#vtp {server | client |transparent}
```

To configure the VTP domain name :

```
(config)#vtp domain name
```

To configure a VTP password (all switches in the domain must use the same password):

```
(config)#vtp password password
```

To configure the switch to use VTP Version 2:

```
(config)#vtp version 2
```

To enable pruning:

```
vtp pruning
```

To specify which VLANs are to be pruned:

```
(config-if)#switchport trunk pruning vlan {add ¦ except ¦ none ¦
 remove} vlan-list [,vlan[,vlan[,,,]]
```


Verifying and Monitoring VTP

To get basic information about the VTP configuration, use **show vtp status**. The example shows the default settings:

```
# show vtp status
VTP Version    : 1
Configuration Revision    : 0
Maximum VLANs supported locally    : 1005
Number of existing VLANs    : 5
VTP Operating Mode    : Server
VTP Domain Name    :
(config)#
VTP Pruning Mode    : Disabled
VTP V2 Mode    : Disabled
VTP Traps Generation    : Disabled
MD5 digest    :
```

Troubleshooting VTP

The following are some common things to check when troubleshooting problems with VTP:

- Make sure you are trunking between the switches. VTP is sent only over trunk links.
- Make sure the domain name matches on both switches (name is case sensitive).
- If the switch is not updating its database, make sure it is not in transparent mode.
- If using passwords, make sure they all match. To remove a password, use **no vtp password**.

Adding a New Switch to a VTP Domain

Adding a new switch in client mode does not prevent it from propagating its incorrect VLAN information. A server synchronizes to a client if the client has the higher configuration revision number. You must reset the revision number back to 0 on the new switch. The easiest way to do this is to change the domain name. Then change it back to the correct one, and attach the switch to the network.

CHAPTER 3

Spanning Tree

Ethernet network design balances two separate imperatives. First, Ethernet has no capacity for detecting circular paths. If such paths exist, traffic loops around and accumulates until new traffic is shut out (this is called a broadcast storm). Second, having secondary paths is good preparation for inevitable link failure.

Spanning Tree is a protocol that prevents loop formation by detecting redundant links and disabling them until needed. Designers can therefore build redundant links and the protocol will allow one to pass traffic and keep the other in reserve. When the active link fails, the secondary link is enabled quickly.

Understanding the Spanning Tree Protocol

Switches either forward or filter Layer 2 frames. The way they make the forwarding/filtering decision can lead to loops in a network with redundant links. Spanning Tree is a protocol that detects potential loops and breaks them.

A Layer 2 switch is functionally the same thing as a transparent bridge. Transparent bridges:

- Learn MAC (Media Access Control) addresses by looking at the source address of incoming frames. They build a table mapping MAC address to port number.
- Forward broadcasts and multicasts out all ports except the on which they came. (This is called flooding.)
- Forward unknown unicasts out all ports except the one on which they came. An unknown unicast is a message bound for a unicast MAC address that is not in the switch's table of addresses and ports.
- Do not make any changes to the frames as they forward them.

Spanning Tree Protocol (STP) works by selecting a root bridge, then selecting one loop-free path from the root bridge to every other switch. (STP uses the term bridge because it was written before there were switches.) Consider the following switched network (see Figure 3-1).

Figure 3-1 Example Switched Topology

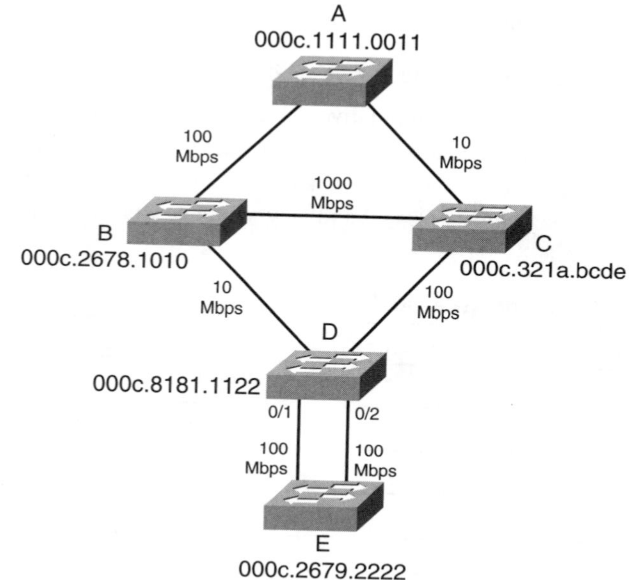

Spanning Tree must select:

- One root bridge
- One root port per nonroot bridge
- One designated port per network segment

Spanning Tree Election Criteria

Spanning Tree builds paths out from a central point along the fastest available links. It selects path according to the following criteria:

1. Lowest root bridge ID (BID)
2. Lowest path cost to the root
3. Lowest sender bridge ID
4. Lowest sender port ID (PID)

When reading the path selection criteria, remember the following:

- Bridge ID—Bridge priority: Bridge MAC address.
- Bridge priority—2-btye value, 0–65,535 (0–0xFFFF).
- Default priority is 32,768 (0x8000).
- Port ID—Port priority: port number.
- Port priority—A 6-bit value, 0–63, default is 32.
- Path cost—This is the cumulative value of the cost of each link between the bridge and the root. Cost values were updated in 2000 and you should see only new cost values, but both are given in the following table (see Table 3-1). Old and new switches work together.

Table 3-1 Spanning Tree Costs

Link Speed	Old Cost	New Cost
10 Mbps	100	100
100 Mbps	10	19
1 Gbps	1	4
10 Gbps	1	2

The STP Election

Spanning Tree builds paths out from a starting point, the "root" of the tree. The first step in selecting paths is to identify this root device. Then, each device selects its best path back to the root, according to the criteria laid out in the previous sections (lowest root BID, lowest cost, lowest advertising BID, lowest port).

Root Bridge Election

Looking at Figure 3-1, first select the root bridge. Assume each switch uses the default priority.

- Switch A BID = 80-00-00-0c-11-11-00-11
- Switch B BID = 80-00-00-0c-26-78-10-10
- Switch C BID = 80-00-00-0c-32-1a-bc-de
- Switch D BID = 80-00-00-0c-81-81-11-22
- Switch E BID = 80-00-00-0c-26-79-22-22

Switch A has the lowest BID, so it is the root. Each nonroot switch must now select a root port.

Root Port Election

The root port is. the port that leads back to the root. Continuing with Figure 3-1, once A is acknowledged as the root, the remaining bridges sort out their lowest cost path back to the A.

- **Switch B**—Uses the link to A with a cost of 19 (link speed of 100 Mbps).
- **Switch C**—The connected link has a cost of 100 (Ethernet), the link through B has a path cost of 38 (two 100 Mbps links), and so B is chosen.
- **Switch D**—The link through B has a path cost of 119, the path cost through C to A is 119, the path through C then B is 57, so C is chosen.
- **Switch E**—The lowest path cost is the same for both ports (76 through D to C to B to A). Next check sender BID—sender for both ports is D, so that it does not break the tie. Next check sender Port ID. Assuming default port priority, the PID for 0/1 is lower than the PID for 0/2, so the port on the left is the root port.

Designated Port Election

Designated ports are ports that lead away from the root. Obviously, all ports on the root bridge are designated ports (A-B and A-C in Figure 3-2).

- Segment B-D—B has the lowest path cost to root (19 vs 119), so it is designated for this segment.
- Segment C-D—C has the lowest path cost to the root (100 vs 119), so it is designated for this segment.
- Segment B-C—B has the lowest path cost to the root (19 vs 100), so it is designated for this segment.
- Both segments D-E—D has the lowest cost to the root (57 vs 76), so it is designated for both segments.

Now the looped topology has been turned into a tree with A at the root. Notice that there are no more redundant links.

Figure 3-2 The Active Topology After Spanning Tree Is Complete

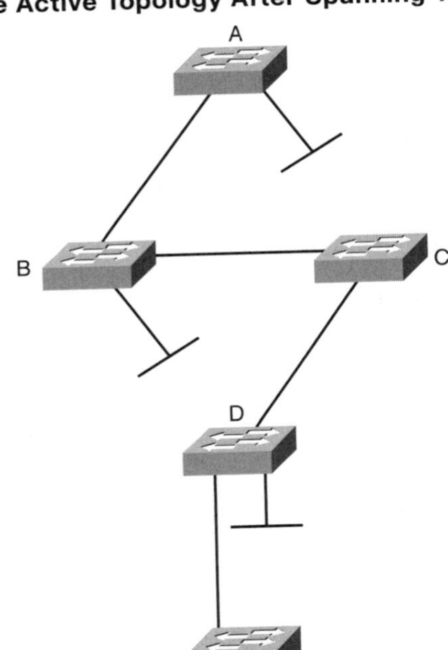

Bridge Protocol Data Units (BPDU)

Switches exchange BPDUs. There are two types of BPDUs: Configuration and Topology Change (TCN).

Configuration BPDUs are sent every two seconds from the root toward the downstream switches. They:

- Are used during an election.
- Maintain connectivity between switches.
- Send timer information from the root.

TCN BPDUs are sent toward the root when:

- There is a link failure.
- A port starts forwarding, and there is already a designated port.
- The switch receives a TCN from a neighbor.

When a switch receives a TCN BPDU, it acknowledges that with a configuration BPDU that has the TCN Acknowledgment bit set.

When the root bridge receives a TCN, it starts sending configuration BPDUs with the TCN bit set for a period of time equal to max age plus forward delay. Switches that receive this change their MAC table aging time to the Forward Delay time, causing MAC addresses to age faster. The topology change also causes an election of the root bridge, root ports, and designated ports.

BPDU Fields

Some of the fields in the BPDU include:

- Root bridge ID—The BID of the current root.
- Sender's root path cost—The cost to the root.
- Sender's bridge ID—Sender's priority concatenated to MAC.
- Sender's port ID—The port number, transmitted as final tie-breaker.
- Hello time—Two seconds by default.
- Forward Delay—15 seconds by default.
- Max Age—20 seconds by default.

Spanning Tree Port States

When a port is first activated, it transitions through the following stages shown in Table 3-2.

Table 3-2 Spanning Tree Port States

Port State	Timer	Actions
Blocking	Max Age (20 sec)	Discards frames, does not learn MAC addresses, receives BPDUs.
Listening	Forward Delay (15 sec)	Discards frames, does not learn MAC addresses, receives BPDUs to determine its role in the network.
Learning	Forward Delay (15 sec)	Discards frames, does learn MAC addresses, receives and transmits BPDUs.
Forwarding		Accepts frames, learns MAC addresses, receives and transmits BPDUs.

Designing for Spanning Tree

To optimize data flow in the network, design and configure switches for the following STP roles:

- Primary and secondary root bridges (set priority values)
- Designated and root ports (set port priorities/path cost)
- Enable STP enhancements, such as Root Guard

Spanning Tree and PVST

With PVST (Per Vlan STP), there is a different instance of STP for each VLAN. To derive the VLAN BID, the switch picks a different MAC address from its base pool for each VLAN. Each VLAN has its own root bridge, root port, and so on. You can configure these so that data flow is optimized, and traffic load is balanced among the switches.

Spanning Tree is enabled by default on every VLAN.

Configuring Spanning Tree

To change the STP priority value, use the following:

```
Switch (config)#spanning-tree vlan vlan_no priority value
```

To configure a switch as root without manually changing priority values, use the following:

```
Switch(config)# spanning-tree vlan vlan_no root {primary ¦
 secondary}
```

To change the STP port cost for an access port, use the following:

```
Switch(config-if)# spanning-tree cost value
```

To change the STP port cost for a VLAN on a trunk port, use the following:

```
Switch(config-if)# spanning-tree vlan vlan_no cost value
```

To display STP information for a VLAN, use the following:

```
Switch# show spanning-tree vlan vlan_no
```

To display the STP information for an interface, use the following:

```
Switch# show spanning-tree interface interface_no [detail]
```

To verify STP timers, use the following:

```
Switch#show spanning-tree bridge brief
```

Spanning Tree Enhancements

Cisco has some proprietary enhancements to Spanning Tree that help speed up network convergence. They include:

- PortFast
- UplinkFast
- BackboneFast

Portfast

Portfast is for access (user) ports only. It causes the port to bypass the STP listening and learning states and transition directly to forwarding. Connecting a switch to a Portfast port can cause loops to develop.

```
(config-if)#spanning-tree portfast
```

UplinkFast

UplinkFast is for speeding convergence when a direct link to an upstream switch fails. The switch identifies backup ports for the root port (these are called an uplink group). If the root port fails, then one of the ports in the uplink group is unblocked and transitions immediately to forwarding—it bypasses the listening and learning stages. It should be used in wiring closet switches with at least one blocked port.

The command to enable uplinkfast is shown below. Please note that uplinkfast is enabled globally, so the command affects all ports and all VLANs.

```
(config)# spanning-tree uplinkfast
```

BackboneFast

BackboneFast is used for speeding convergence when a link fails that is not directly connected to the switch. It helps the switch detect indirect failures. If a switch running BackboneFast receives an inferior BPDU from its designated bridge, it knows a link on the path to the root has failed. (An inferior BPDU is one that lists the same switch for root bridge and designated bridge.)

The switch then tries to find an alternate path to the root by sending a Root Link Query (RLQ) frame out all alternate ports. The root then responds with an RLQ response, and the port receiving this response can transition to forwarding. Alternate ports are determined in this way:

- If the inferior BPDU was received on a blocked port, then the root port and any other blocked ports are considered alternates.
- If the inferior BPDU was received on the root port, then all blocked ports are considered alternates.
- If the inferior BPDU was received on the root port and there are no blocked ports, the switch assumes it has lost connectivity with the root and advertises itself as root.

Configure this command on all switches in the network:

```
(config)#spanning-tree backbonefast
```

Rapid Spanning Tree (RSTP)

Rapid Spanning Tree (RSTP) 802.1w is a standards-based, non-proprietary way of speeding STP convergence. Switch ports exchange an explicit handshake when they transition to forwarding. RSTP describes different port states than regular STP, as shown in the Table 3-3.

Table 3-3 Comparing 802.1d and 802.1w Port States

STP Port State	Equivalent RSTP Port State
Disabled	Discarding
Blocking	Discarding
Listening	Discarding
Learning	Learning
Forwarding	Forwarding

RSTP Port Roles

RSTP also defines different Spanning Tree roles for ports:

- Root port—The best path to the root (same as STP).
- Designated port—Same role as with STP.
- Alternate port—A backup to the root port.

- Backup port—A backup to the designated port.
- Disabled port—One not used in the Spanning Tree.
- Edge port—One connected only to an end user.

BPDU Differences in RSTP

In regular STP, BPDUs are originated by the root and relayed by each switch. In RSTP, each switch originates BPDUs, whether or not it receives a BPDU on its root port. All eight bits of the BPDU type field are used by RSTP. The TC and TC Ack bits are still used. The other six bits specify the port's role and its RSTP state, and are used in the port handshake. The RSTP BPDU is set to Type 2, Version 2. PVST is done by Rapid PVST+ on Catalyst switches.

RSTP Fast Convergence

The Rapid Spanning tree process understands and incorporates topology changes much quicker than the previous version.

- RSTP uses a mechanism similar to BackboneFast—When an inferior BPDU is received, the switch accepts it. If the switch has another path the root, it uses that and informs its downstream switch of the alternate path.
- Edge ports work the same as Portfast ports—They automatically transition directly to forwarding.
- Link type—If you connect two switches through a point-to-point link and the local port becomes a designated port, it exchanges a handshake with the other port to quickly transition to forwarding. Full-duplex links are assumed to be point-to-point, half-duplex links are assumed to be shared.
- Backup and alternate ports—Ports that can transition to forwarding when no BPDUs are received from a neighbor switch (similar to UplinkFast).

If an RSTP switch detects a topology change, it sets a TC timer to twice the hello time and sets the TC bit on all BPDUs sent out to its designated and root ports until the timer expires. It also clears the MAC addresses learned on these ports.

If an RSTP switch receives a TC BPDU, it clears the MAC addresses on that port and sets the TC bit on all BPDUs sent out its designated and root ports until the TC timer expires.

Multiple Spanning Tree (MST)

With Multiple Spanning Tree (MST), you can group VLANs and run one instance of Spanning Tree for a group of VLANs. This cuts down on the number of root bridges, root ports, designated ports, and BPDUs in your network. Switches in the same MST Region share the same configuration and VLAN mappings. Configure MST with these commands:

```
(config)# spanning-tree mode mst
(config)# spanning-tree mst configuration
(config-mst)# name region_name
(config-mst)# revision number
(config-mst)# instance number vlan vlan_range
(config-mst)# end
```


To be compatible with 802.1Q trunking, which has one common Spanning Tree (CST) for all VLANs, MST runs one instance of an Internal Spanning Tree (IST). The IST appears as one bridge to a CST area and is MST instance number 0. The original MST Spanning Trees (called M-Trees) are active only in the region—they combine at the edge of the CST area to form one.

EtherChannels

EtherChannel is a way of combining several physical links between switches into one logical connection. Normally, Spanning Tree blocks redundant links; EtherChannel gets around that and allows load balancing across those links. Load is balancing on the basis of such things as source or destination MAC address or IP address. The Etherchannel load-balancing method is configured at global configuration mode.

```
(config)#port-channel load-balance type
```

A logical interface—the Port Channel interface—is created. Configuration can be applied to both the logical and physical interfaces.

Some guidelines for EtherChannels are as follows:

- Interfaces in the channel do not have to be physically next to each other or on the same module.

- All ports must be the same speed and duplex.
- All ports in the bundle should be enabled.
- None of the bundle ports can be a SPAN port.
- Assign an IP address to the logical Port Channel interface, not the physical ones.
- Put all bundle ports in the same VLAN, or make them all trunks. If they are trunks, they must all carry the same VLANs and use the same trunking mode.
- Configuration you apply to the Port Channel interface affects the entire EtherChannel. Configuration you apply to a physical interface only affects that interface.

Configuring an EtherChannel

Basically, for a Layer 3 EtherChannel, you should configure the logical interface and then put the physical interfaces into the channel group:

```
(config)#interface port-channel number
(config-if)#no switchport
(config-if)#ip address address mask
```

Then, at each port that is part of the EtherChannel, use the following:

```
(config)#interface {number | range interface - interface}
(config-if)#channel-group number mode {auto | desirable | on}
```

Putting the IP address on the Port Channel interface creates a Layer 3 EtherChannel. Simply putting interfaces into a channel group creates a Layer 2 EtherChannel, and the logical interface is automatically created.

The Cisco proprietary Port Aggregation Protocol (PAgP) dynamically negotiates the formation of a channel. There are three PAgP modes:

- On—The port channels without using PAgP negotiation. The port on the other side must also be set to On.
- Auto—Responds to PAgP messages but does not initiate them. Port channels if the port on the other end is set to Desirable. This is the default mode.
- Desirable—Port actively negotiates channeling status with the interface on the other end of the link. Port channels if the other side is Auto or Desirable.

There is also a non-proprietary protocol called Link Aggregation Control Protocol (LACP), IEEE 802.3ad, which does the same thing. LACP has two modes:

- Active—Port actively negotiates channeling with the port on the other end of the link. A channel forms if the other side is Passive or Active.
- Passive—Responds to LACP messages but does not initiate them. A channel forms if the other end is set to Active.

If you want to use LACP, specify it under the interface and put the interface in either active or passive mode:

```
(config-if)#channel-protocol lacp
```


Verifying an EtherChannel

Some typical commands for verifying include:

- **#show running-config interface** *number*
- **#show interfaces** *number* **etherchannel**
- **#show etherchannel** *number* **port-channel**
- **#show etherchannel summary**

Additional Spanning Tree Features

Some additional features available to help you tune Spanning Tree include:

- BPDU Guard
- BPDU Filtering
- Root Guard
- UDLD
- Loop Guard

BPDU Guard

BPDU Guard is used to prevent loops if another switch is attached to a Portfast port. When BPDU Guard is enabled on an interface, it is put into an error-disabled state (basically, shut down) if a BPDU is received on the interface. It can be enabled at either global config mode—in which case it affects all Portfast interfaces, or at interface mode. Portfast does not have to be enabled for it to be configured at a specific interface. The following configuration example shows BPDU guard being enabled.

```
(config)#spanning-tree portfast bpduguard default
(config-if)#spanning-tree bpduguard enable
```

BPDU Filtering

BPDU filtering is another way of preventing loops in the network. It also can be enabled either globally or at the interface, and functions differently at each. In global config, if a Portfast interface receives any BPDUs, it is taken out of Portfast status. At interface config mode, it prevents the port from sending or receiving BPDUs. The commands are:

- (config)# **spanning-tree portfast bpdufilter default**
- (config-if)# **spanning-tree bpdufilter enable**

Root Guard

Root Guard is meant to prevent the wrong switch from becoming the Spanning Tree root. It is enabled on ports other than the root port and on switches other than the root. If a Root Guard port receives a BPDU that might cause it to become a root port, then the port is put into "root-inconsistent" state and does not pass traffic through it. If the port stops receiving these BPDUs, it automatically re-enables itself.

```
(config-if)# spanning-tree guard root
```

Unidirectional Link Detection (UDLD)

A switch notices when a physical connection is broken by the absence of Layer 1 electrical keepalives (Ethernet calls this a link beat). However, sometimes a cable is intact enough to maintain keepalives, but not to pass data in both directions. This is a Unidirectional Link. Unidirectional Link Detection (UDLD) detects a unidirectional link by sending periodic hellos out to the interface. It also uses probes, which must be acknowledged by the device on the other end of the link. UDLD operates at Layer 2. The port is shut down if a unidirectional link is found.

To enable UDLD on all fiber-optic interfaces, use the following command:

```
(config)# udld enable
```

Although this command is given at global config mode, it applies only to fiber ports.

To enable UDLD on non-fiber ports, give the same command at interface config mode.

To disable UDLD on a specific fiber port, use the following command:

```
(config-if)# udld disable
```

To disable UDLD on a specific non-fiber port, use the following command:

```
(config-if)#no udld enable
```

To re-enable all interfaces shut by UDLD, use the following:

```
#udld reset
```

To verify UDLD status, use the following:

```
#show udld interface
```


Loop Guard

Loop Guard prevents loops that might develop if a port that should be blocking inadvertently transitions to the forwarding state. This can happen if the port stops receiving BPDUs (perhaps because of a unidirectional link or a software/configuration problem in its neighbor switch). When one of the ports in a physically redundant topology stops receiving BPDUs, the STP conceives the topology as loop-free. Eventually, the blocking port becomes designated and moves to forwarding state, thus creating a loop. With Loop Guard enabled, an additional check is made.

If no BPDUs are received on a blocked port for a specific length of time. Loop Guard puts that port into "loop inconsistent" blocking state, rather than transitioning to forwarding state. Loop Guard should be enabled on all switch ports that have a chance of becoming root or designated ports. It is most effective when enabled in the entire switched network in conjunction with UDLD.

To enable Loop Guard for all point-to-point links on the switch, use the following command:

```
(config)# spanning-tree loopguard default
```

To enable Loop Guard on a specific interface, use the following:

```
(config-if)# spanning-tree guard loop
```

Loop Guard automatically re-enables the port if it starts receiving BPDUs again.

Troubleshooting STP

Some common things to look for when troubleshooting Spanning Tree Protocol include:

- Duplex mismatch—When one side of a link is half-duplex and the other is full-duplex. This causes late collisions and FCS errors.
- Unidirectional link failure—The link is up but data flows only in one direction. It can cause loops.
- Frame corruption—Physical errors on the line cause BPDUs to be lost, and the port incorrectly begins forwarding. This is caused by duplex mismatch, bad cable, or cable too long.
- Resource errors—STP is implemented in software, so a switch with an overloaded CPU or memory might neglect some STP duties.
- Port Fast configuration errors—Connecting a switch to two ports that have Port Fast enabled. This can cause a loop.
- STP tuning errors—Max age or forward delay set too short can cause a loop. A network diameter that is set too low causes BPDUs to be discarded and affects STP convergence.

Identifying a Bridging Loop

Suspect a loop if you see the following:

- You capture traffic on a link, and see the same frames multiple times.
- All users in a bridging domain have connectivity problems at the same time.
- There is abnormally high port utilization.

To remedy a loop quickly, shut redundant ports and then enable them one at a time. Some switches allow debugging of STP (not 3550/2950) to help in diagnosing problems.

What to Use Where

Confused by all the acronyms and STP features? Figure 3-3 shows the STP features you might use in your network and where you might use them.

Figure 3-3 Example Switched Topology

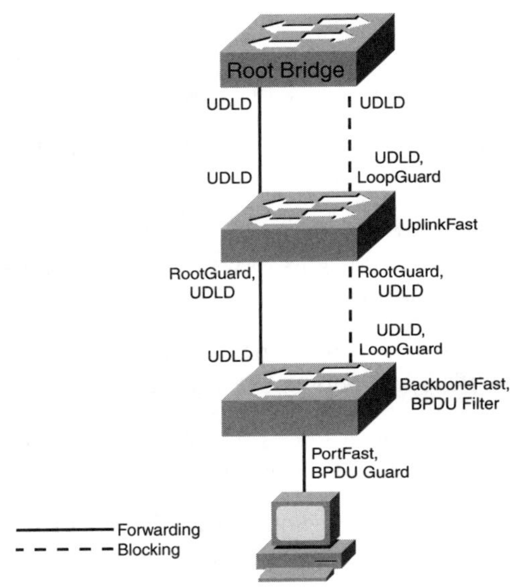

CHAPTER 4

InterVLAN Routing

VLANs divide the network into smaller broadcast domains, but also prohibit communication between domains To enable communication between those groups—without also passing broadcasts—routing is used.

InterVLAN Routing Using Multilayer Switches

Port roles:

- Virtual LAN (VLAN) Port—Acts as layer 2 switching port with a VLAN.
- Static VLAN—Use the **switchport** command to identify VLAN.
- Dynamic VLAN—Use VLAN Membership Policy Server (VMPS).
- Trunk port—Passes multiple VLANs and differentiates by tagging.

Use the **switchport** command to set parameters:

- ISL(Interswitch Link) or 802.1Q
- Switched Virtual Interface (SVI)—Virtual routed port in a VLAN
  - — Use to route or fallback bridge between VLANs
  - — Default SVI for VLAN 1 automatically created
  - — Associate with VLAN using **interface** *vlan-num*
- Routed port—Acts as layer 3 routed port
  - — Place in layer 3 mode with **no switchport**
  - — Not associated with VLAN
  - — Turn on routing using **ip routing**
  - — Assign address and enable routing protocols as needed

InterVLAN Routing

Multilayer switches do the following:

- Enable IP routing using **ip routing**
- Create SVI using **interface** *vlan-num*
- Assign an IP address to each interface

A router on a stick attaches the router to the switch using a trunk line (ISL or 802.1Q). Following are features of these:

- Easy to implement
- Use existing equipment
- Much more latency than Multi-layer switching (MLS) solution
- Configure by creating subinterface with **interface fastethernet 1/0.7**
- Associate the VLAN to the interface with command **encapsulation isl 7** or **encapsulation dot1q 7**
- ISL—No address on main interface
- 802.1Q—Address on main interface for native (untagged) VLAN

Multilayer Switching

This next section walks through the switching process and focuses on order of operations. The order things happen is extremely important for two reasons. First, order of events is good test material. Second, understanding the processing order allows you to evaluate how the various filtering and forwarding mechanisms interact (examples include error checking, access-lists, VLAN access-lists, routing, and QoS).

Understanding the Switching Process

Steps involved in layer 2 forwarding are as follows:

- Input
    1. Receive frame.
    2. Verify frame integrity.

3. Apply inbound VLAN ACL (Virtual Local Area Network Access List).
4. Look up destination MAC (Media Address Code).

- Output
    1. Apply outbound VLAN ACL.
    2. Apply outbound QoS ACL.
    3. Select output port.
    4. Queue on port.
    5. Rewrite.
    6. Forward.

Steps involved in layer 3 forwarding are as follows:

- Input
    1. Receive frame.
    2. Verify frame integrity.
    3. Apply inbound VLAN ACL.
    4. Look up destination MAC.

- Routing
    1. Input ACL.
    2. Switch if entry cached.
    3. Identify exit interface and next-hop address using routing table.
    4. Output ACL.

- Output
    1. Apply outbound VLAN ACL.
    2. Apply outbound QoS ACL.
    3. Select output port.
    4. Queue on port.
    5. Rewrite source and destination MAC, IP checksum and frame check sequence, and decrement TTL (Time to Live field in the IP header).
    6. Forward.

Understanding the Switching Table

Content Addressable Memory (CAM) is used for MAC tables for layer two switching.

- Used for Catalyst 4500 layer 2 forwarding tables
- Used for Catalyst 6500 layer 2 and Netflow forwarding tables
- Contains binary values (0 or 1)
- Match must be exact

In comparison, MLS uses Ternary Content Addressable Memory (TCAM).

- Used for Catalyst 3500/3700, 4500, and 6500 layer 3 switching
- Ternary (3) values (0, 1, or wildcard)
- Entries are in VMR form
  - — Value—Pattern to be matched.
  - — Mask—Masking bits associated with pattern.
  - — Result—Consequences of a match (permit/deny or more complex information).

Understanding Switch Forwarding Architectures

In a Centralized Forwarding model, the CPU controls forwarding decisions:

- Decision made by single table
- Used by 4500 and 6500

With Distributed Forwarding, the forwarding decisions are spread throughout the interface ASICs:

- Decision made at port or module
- Used by 3500/3700 and 6500 with distributed forwarding card
- NetFlow switching
- Decision made cooperatively by Route Processor and MLS
- First packet switched in software, result cached
- Subsequent packets switched in hardware

Cisco Express Forwarding (CEF) uses a different kind of memory to facilitate forwarding:

- Uses TCAM
- Topology-based switching (via Forwarding Information Base [FIB])
- Can be centralized or distributed

Multilayer Switching

Multilayer Switching (MLS) is a switch feature that allows the switch to route traffic between VLANs and routed interfaces in a highly optimized and efficient manner. Cisco Express Forwarding (CEF) is an example technology used to facilitate MLS (see Figure 4-1). Cisco Express Forwarding (CEF) does the following:

Figure 4-1 Cisco Express Forwarding

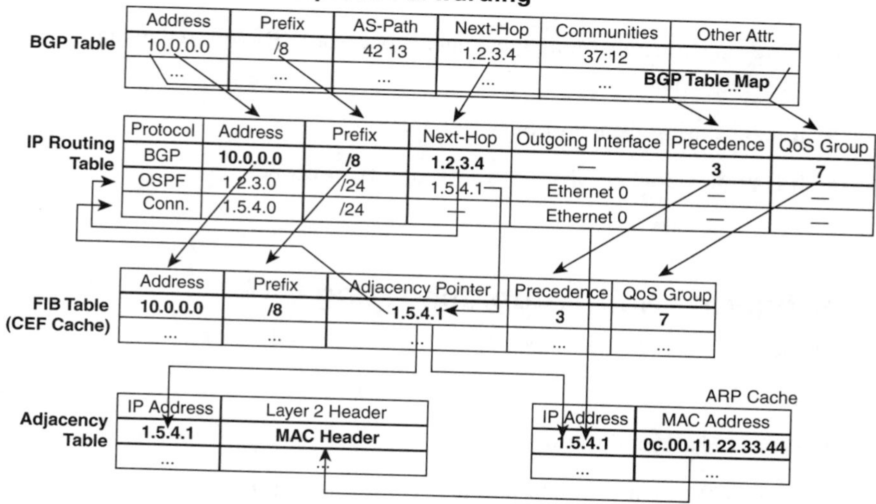

- Separates control plane hardware from data plane hardware.
- Controls plane runs in software and builds FIB and adjacency table.
- The data plane uses hardware to forward most IP unicast traffic.
- Handles traffic that must be forwarded in software (much slower) and includes:
  - — Packets originating from device.
  - — Packets with IP header options.

— Tunneled traffic.

— 802.3 (IPX) frames.

— Load sharing traffic.

— FIB is an optimized routing table, stored in TCAM.

— Builds adjacencies from ARP data.

— Eliminates recursive loops.

ARP Throttling

ARP throttling is a tool to limit ARPs into a VLAN. ARPs, you may recall, are sent as broadcast. Once an ARP is sent for a given IP, the switch prevents repetitive ARPs for a short period of time:

- First packet to destination forwarded to Route Processor.
- Subsequent traffic dropped until MAC is resolved.
- It prevents overwhelming the Route Processor (RP) with redundant ARP requests.
- It helps during Denial of Service attacks.
- It is removed when MAC is resolved in two seconds.

Configuring and Troubleshooting CEF

By default, CEF is on and supports per destination load sharing.

To disable CEF:

- 4500—Use (config)#**no ip cef**.
- 3500/3700—On each interface, use (config)#**no ip route-cache cef**.
- 6550 with policy feature card, distributed FC, and multilayer switch FC—Cannot be disabled.

View CEF information with the following:

```
#show interface fastethernet 2/2 | begin L3
```

View switching statistics with the following:

```
#show interface fastethernet 2/2 | include switched
```

View FIB with the following:

```
#show ip cef
```

View detailed CEF FIB entry with the following:

```
#show ip cef fastethernet 2/2 10.0.0.1 detail
```

Troubleshoot CEF drops with the following:

```
#debug ip cef drops
```

Troubleshoot packets not forwarded by CEF with the following:

```
#debug ip cef receive
```

Troubleshoot CEF events with the following:

```
#debug ip cef events
```

CHAPTER 5

Layer 3 Redundancy

Specifying a default gateway leads to a single point of failure. Proxy Address Resolution Protocol (ARP) is one method for hosts to dynamically discover gateways, but it has issues in a highly-available environment. With Proxy ARP:

- Hosts ARP for all destinations, even remote.
- Router responds with its MAC.
- Problem: Slow failover because ARP entries take minutes to timeout.

Instead of making the host responsible for choosing a new gateway, Layer 3 redundancy protocols allow two or more routers to support a shared MAC address. If the primary router is lost, the backup router assumes control of traffic forwarded to that MAC. This section refers to routers, but includes those Layer 3 switches that can also implement Layer 3 redundancy.

Hot Standby Router Protocol (HSRP)

HSRP is a Cisco proprietary protocol.

With HSRP, two or more devices support a virtual router with a fictitious MAC address and unique IP address. Hosts use this IP address as their default gateway, and the MAC address for the Layer 2 header. The virtual router's MAC address is 0000.0c07.AC*xx*, where *xx* is the HSRP group. Multiple groups (virtual routers) are allowed.

The *Active* router forwards traffic. The *Standby* is backup. The standby monitors periodic hellos (multicast to 224.0.0.2, UDP port 1985) to detect a failure of the active router. On failure, the standby device starts answering messages sent to the IP and MAC addresses of the virtual router.

The active router is chosen because it has the highest HSRP priority (default priority is 100). In case of a tie, the router with the highest configured IP address wins the election. A new router with a higher priority does not cause an election unless it is configured to *preempt*—that is, take over from a lower priority router. Configuring a router to preempt also insures that the highest priority router regains its active status if it goes down but then comes back online again.

Interface tracking reduces the active router's priority if a specified circuit is down. This allows the standby router to take over even though the active router is still up.

HSRP States

HSRP devices move between these states:

- Initial—HSRP is not running.
- Learn—The router does not know the virtual IP address and is waiting to hear from the active router.
- Listen—The router knows the IP and MAC of the virtual router, but it is not the active or standby router.
- Speak—Router sends periodic HSRP hellos and participates in the election of the active router.
- Standby—Router monitors hellos from active router and assumes responsibility if active router fails.
- Active—Router forwards packets on behalf of the virtual router.

Configuring HSRP

To begin configuring HSRP, use the **standby** *group-number* **ip** *virtual-IP-address* command in interface configuration mode. Routers in the same HSRP group must belong to the same subnet/virtual LAN (VLAN.) Give this command under the interface connecting to that subnet or VLAN. For instance, use the following to configure the router as a member of HSRP group 39 with virtual router IP address 10.0.0.1:

```
Router(config-if)#standby 39 ip 10.0.0.1
```

Tune HSRP with four options: Priority, Preempt, Timers, and Interface Tracking.

Manually select the active router by configuring its priority higher than the default of 100:

```
Router(config-if)#standby 39 priority 150
```

Along with configuring priority, configure **preempt** to allow a router to take over if the active router has lower priority, as shown in the following commands. This helps lead to a predictable data path through the network. The second command shown delays preemption until the router or switch has fully booted, and the routing protocol has converged. Time how long it takes to boot and add 50 percent to get the delay value in seconds:

```
Router(config-if)#standby 39 preempt
Router(config-if)#standby 39 preempt delay minimum 90
```

Speed convergence by changing the hello and hold timers. The following sets the hello interval to 2 seconds and the hold time to 7 seconds. They can be set between 1–255 seconds (the default hello is 3 seconds and hold time is 10 seconds):

```
Router(config-if)#standby 39 timers 2 7
```

Tracking an interface can trigger an election if the active router is still up, but a critical interface (such as the one to the Internet) is down. In the following, if serial 1/0/0 is down, the router's HSRP priority is decremented by 100:

```
Router(config-if)#standby 39 track s1/0/00 100
```

Note

The standby router must be configured with the preempt command for it to take control.

Multiple HSRP standby groups can be configured, and the same router can be active for some groups and standby for others by adjusting priorities. You can have a maximum of 255 groups. When using Layer 3 switches, configure the same switch as the primary HSRP router and the Spanning Tree root.

To view the HSRP status, use the **show standby interface** *interface* command, or **show standby brief**. To monitor HSRP activity, use the **debug standby** command.

Virtual Router Redundancy Protocol (VRRP)

Virtual Router Redundancy Protocol (VRRP) is similar to HSRP, but it is an open standard (RFC 2338). Two or more devices act as a virtual router. With VRRP, however, the IP address used can be either a virtual one or the actual IP address of the primary router.

The VRRP *Master* router forwards traffic. The master is chosen because 1) it owns the real address, or 2) it has the highest priority (default is 100). If a real address is being supported, the owner of real address *must* be master. A *Backup* router takes over if the master fails, and there can be multiple backup routers. They monitor periodic hellos multicast by the master to 224.0.0.18, using UDP port 112, to detect a failure of the master router.

Multiple VRRP groups are allowed, just as with HSRP.

Routers in the same VRRP group must belong to the same subnet/VLAN. To enable VRRP, give this command **vrrp** *group-number* **ip** *virtual-IP-address* under the interface connecting to that subnet or VLAN:

```
Router(config-if)#vrrp 39 ip 10.0.0.1
```

Control the master and backup elections by configuring priority values from 1–255. If a master VRRP router is shutdown, it advertises a priority of 0. This triggers the backup routers to hold an election without waiting for the master's hellos to time out.

```
Router(config-if)#vrrp 39 priority 175
```

VRRP uses the following timers:

- Advertisement, or hello, interval in seconds. Default is 1 second.
- Master down interval. Equals (3 x advertisement interval) plus skew time. Similar to a hold or dead timer.
- Skew time. (256–priority) / 256. This is meant to ensure that the highest priority backup router becomes master, since higher priority routers have shorter master down intervals.

To change the timers on the master, use the following command because it is the router that advertises the hellos:

```
Router(config-if)#vrrp 39 timers advertise 5
```

To change the timers on the backup routers, use the following command because they hear the hellos from the master:

```
Router(config-if)#vrrp 39 timers learn
```

GLBP

One issue with both HSRP and VRRP is that only the primary router is in use, the others must wait for the primary to fail before they are used. These two protocols use groups to get around that limitation. However, Gateway

Load Balancing Protocol (GLBP) allows the simultaneous use of up to four gateways, thus maximizing bandwidth. With GLBP, there is still one virtual IP address. However, each participating router has a virtual MAC address, and different routers' virtual MAC addresses are sent in answer to ARPs sent to the virtual IP address. GLBP can also use groups up to a maximum of 1024 per physical interface.

The load sharing is done in one of three ways:

- Weighted load balancing—Traffic is balanced proportional to a configured weight.
- Host-dependent load balancing—A given host always uses the same router.
- Round-robin load balancing—Each router MAC is used to respond to ARP requests in turn.

GLBP routers elect an Active Virtual Gateway (AVG). It is the only router to respond to ARPs. It uses this capacity to balance the load among the GLBP routers. The highest priority router is the AVG; the highest configured IP address is used in case of a tie.

The actual router used by a host is its Active Virtual Forwarder (AVF). GLBP group members multicast hellos every 3 seconds to IP address 224.0.0.102, UDP port 3222. If one router goes down, another router answers for its MAC address.

Configure GLBP with the interface command **glbp** *group-number* **ip** *virtual-IP-address,* as shown:

```
Router(config-if)#glbp 39 ip 10.0.0.1
```

To ensure deterministic elections, each router can be configured with a priority. The default priority is 100:

```
Router(config-if)#glbp 39 priority 150
```

Hello and hold (or dead) timers can be configured for each interface with the command **glbp** *group-number* **timers** [**msec**] *hello-time* [**msec**] *hold-time*. Values are in seconds unless the **msec** keyword is used.

GLBP can also track interfaces; if an interface goes down, another router answers for the first router's MAC address.

CHAPTER 6

Using Wireless LANs

Wireless LAN Overview

Devices on a wireless LAN (WLAN) transmit and receive data using radio or infrared signals, sent through an access point (AP). WLANs function similarly to Ethernet LANs with the access point providing connectivity to the rest of the network as would a hub or switch. WLANs use an Institute of Electrical and Electronics Engineers (IEEE) standard that defines the physical and data link specifications, including the use of Media Access Control (MAC) addresses. The same protocols (such as IP) and applications (such as IPSec) can run over both wired and wireless LANs.

WLANs are local to a building or a campus, use customer-owned equipment, and are not usually required to have radio frequency (RF) licenses.

Service Set Identifiers (SSID) correspond to a VLAN and can be used to segment users. SSIDs can be broadcast by the access point, or statically configured on the client, but the client must have the same SSID as the AP to register with it. SSIDs are case sensitive. Clients associate with access points as follows:

Step 1. The client sends a probe request.

Step 2. The AP sends a probe response.

Step 3. The client initiates an association to an AP. Authentication and any other security information is sent to the AP.

Step 4. The AP accepts the association.

Step 5. The AP adds the client's MAC address to its association table.

Characteristics of Wireless LANs

The following lists some characteristics of wireless LANs, and the data transmitted over wireless networks.

- WLANs use Carrier Sense Multi-Access/Collision Avoidance (CSMA/CA). Wireless data is half-duplex. CSMA/CA uses Request to Send (RTS) and Clear to Send (CTS) messages to avoid collisions.
- WLANs use a different frame type than Ethernet.
- Radio waves have unique potential issues. They are susceptible to interference, multipath distortion, and noise. Their coverage area can be blocked by building features, such as elevators. The signal might reach outside the building and lead to privacy issues.
- WLAN hosts have no physical network connection. They are often mobile and often battery-powered. The wireless network design must accommodate this.
- WLANs must adhere to each country's RF standards.

Clients can roam between APs that are configured with the same SSIDs/VLANs. Layer 2 roaming is done between APs on the same subnet; Layer 3 roaming is done between APs on different subnets.

WLAN Topologies

Use of the Cisco Aironet line of wireless products falls into three categories:

- Client access, which allows mobile users to access the wired LAN resources
- Wireless connections between buildings
- Wireless mesh

Wireless connections can be made in *ad-hoc* mode or *infrastructure* mode. *Ad-hoc* mode (or Independent Basic Service Set [IBSS]) is simply a group of computers talking wirelessly to each other with no access point (AP). It is limited in range and functionality. *Infrastructure* mode's BSS uses one AP to connect clients. The range of the AP's signal, called its microcell, must encompass all clients. The Extended Service Set (ESS) uses multiple APs with overlapping microcells to cover all clients. Microcells should overlap by 10–15 percent for data, and 15–20 percent for voice traffic. Each AP should use a different channel.

Wireless repeaters extend an AP's range. They use the same channel as their AP, they must be configured with the AP's SSID, and they should have 50 percent signal overlap.

Workgroup bridges connect to devices without a wireless network interface card (NIC) to allow them access to the wireless network.

Wireless mesh networks can span large distances because only the edge APs connect to the wired network. The intermediate APs connect wirelessly to multiple other APs and act as repeaters for them. Each AP has multiple paths through the wireless network. The Adaptive Wireless Path (AWP) protocol runs between APs to determine the best path to the wired network. APs choose backup paths if the best path fails.

WLAN Standards

WLANs use three unlicensed frequency bands: 900 MHz, 2.4 GHz, and 5 GHz. These bands are all in the Industrial, Scientific, and Medical (ISM) frequency range. Higher frequency bands allow greater bandwidth, but have smaller transmission ranges. Within all bands, the data rate decreases as the client moves away from the AP.

802.11b Standard

802.11b is a widely adopted standard that operates in the 2.4 GHz range and uses Direct Sequence Spread Spectrum (DSSS). It has four data rates: 1, 2, 5.5, and 11 Mbps. 802.11b provides from 11–14 channels, depending on country standards, but only three channels have nonoverlapping frequencies: 1, 6, and 11. Cisco recommends a maximum of 25 users per cell; expect an actual peak throughput of about 6.8 Mbps.

Note

Japan provides a 14 channel, which does not overlap with channel 11 and gives a fourth available nonoverlapping channel.

802.11a Standard

802.11a operates in the 5 GHz range and uses Orthogonal Frequency-Division Multiplexing (OFDM). It has eight data rates: 6, 9, 12, 18, 24, 36, 48, and 54 Mbps. 802.11a provides from 12–23 nonoverlapping channels, depending on country regulations. Portions of the 5 GHz range are allocated to radar, so 802.11a uses Dynamic Frequency Selection (DFS) to check for radar signals and choose a different channel if it detects them. It also uses Transmit Power Control (TMC) to adjust client power, so that they use only enough to stay in contact with the AP. DFS and TMC are part of the 802.11h specification. Cisco recommends a maximum of 15 users per cell; expect an actual peak throughput of about 32 Mbps.

802.11g Standard

802.11g operates in the same 2.4 GHz range as 802.11b and uses the same three nonoverlapping channels: 1, 6, and 11. It can provide higher data rates; however. 802.11g uses DSSS to provide 1, 2, 5.5, and 11 Mbps throughput, which makes it backward compatible with 802.11b. It uses OFDM to provide 6, 9, 12, 18, 24, 36, 48, and 54 Mbps throughput, as does 802.11a.

802.11b/g access points can register both 802.11b and 802.11g clients. Because 802.11b clients do not understand OFDM messages, when 802.11b clients register, the AP implements an RTS/CTS protection mechanism against collisions. When a client wants to talk, it sends an RTS message. The AP must answer with a CTS message before the client is allowed to transmit. This creates overhead for the AP and causes a drop in overall throughput for all clients. Cisco recommends a maximum of 20 users per cell; expect an actual peak throughput of about 32 Mbps.

Wireless Security

Wireless security methods, listed from weakest to strongest, include:

- Wired Equivalent Privacy (WEP)—It uses static keys, weak authentication, and is not scalable.
- 802.1x Extensible Authentication Protocol (EAP)—Uses RADIUS for authentication, dynamic keys, and stronger encryption. Cisco supports it via Lightweight EAP (LEAP) and Protected EAP (PEAP).
- Wi-Fi Protected Access (WPA)—This is a Wi-Fi Alliance standard. Uses Temporal Key Integrity Protocol (TKIP) for encryption, dynamic keys, and 802.1x user authentication. Cisco supports it via Lightweight EAP (LEAP), Protected EAP (PEAP), and Extensible Authentication Protocol-Flexible Authentication via Secure Tunneling (EAP-FAST).
- WPA2—The Wi-Fi Alliance's implementation of the 802.11i standard, which specifies the use of Advanced Encryption Standard (AES) for data encryption and uses 802.1x authentication methods. Can also use TKIP encryption.

WPA/WPA2 Authentication

When a host wanting WLAN access needs to be authenticated in a network using WPA or WPA2, the following steps occur:

Step 1. An 802.1x/EAP supplicant on the host contacts the AP (or WLAN controller, if it is a lightweight AP) using 802.1x.

Step 2. The AP or WLAN controller uses RADIUS to contact the AAA server, and attempts to authentication the user.

Step 3. If the authentication succeeds, all traffic from the client to the AP is encrypted.

Cisco Wireless Network Components

This section is mainly concerned with Cisco products and is quite marketing oriented. Cisco supported two types of wireless solutions: one using autonomous access points, and one using lightweight (or "dumb") access points in combination with WLAN controllers. The wired network infrastructure is the same for both types: switches and routers.

Cisco Unified Wireless Network

The Cisco Unified Wireless Network concept has five components that work together to create a complete network, from client devices to network infrastructure, to network applications. Cisco has equipment appropriate to each component. Table 6-1 lists components and equipment.

Table 6-1 Cisco Unified Wireless Network Components

Component	Description and Devices
Client Devices	Cisco Aironet client, and Cisco compatible third-party vendor clients.
Mobility Platform	Aironet APs and bridges, using LWAPP.
Network Unification	Leverages existing wired network. 2000- and 4400-series WLAN controllers and switch and router modules.
World-Class Network Management	Visualize and secure the WLAN. WCS for location tracking, RF management, wireless IPS, and WLC management.
Unified Advanced Services	Applications such as wireless IP phones, location appliances, and RF firewalls.

You should review the following link for more information on Cisco wireless controllers and access points before you take the exam: http://www.cisco.com/en/US/products/hw/wireless/products_category_buyers_guide.htmlWireless Clients.

Cisco has a wireless NIC that can be installed on Windows 2000 and Windows XP systems. It comes with some utilities: Aironet Desktop Utility (ADU), Aironet Client Monitor (ACM), and Aironet Client Administration Utility (ACAU). Cisco recommends using the ADU and ACM utilities to control your wireless card, rather than the built-in Windows controls to get the increased functionality Cisco provides. The Cisco ACAU allows loading and configuration of the Cisco client software over the network, using encrypted files. There is also an Aironet Site Survey Utility to scan for APs and get information about them.

Cisco wireless IP phones have the same features as Cisco wired IP phones and can use LEAP for authentication.

The Cisco Compatible Extensions Program tests other vendors' devices for compatibility with Cisco wireless products. Using products certified by this program ensures full functionality of Cisco enhancements and proprietary extensions. A list of these products can be found at www.cisco.com/go/cisco-compatible/wireless.

Autonomous APs

Autonomous APs run Cisco IOS, are programmed individually, and act independently. They can be centrally managed with the CiscoWorks Wireless LAN Solution Engine (WLSE) and can use Cisco Secure Access Control Server (ACS) for RADIUS and TACAS+ authentication. Redundancy consists of multiple APs.

Lightweight Access Points

Lightweight APs divide the 802.11 processing between the AP and a Cisco Wireless LAN Controller (WLC). This is sometimes called "split MAC," because they split the functions of the MAC layer—Layer 2. Their management components also include the Wireless Control System (WCS) and a location-tracking appliance. Redundancy consists of multiple WLCs. The AP handles real-time processes, and the WLC handles processes such as:

- Authentication
- Client association/mobility management

- Security management
- QoS policies
- VLAN tagging
- Forwarding of user traffic

The Lightweight Access Point Protocol (LWAP) supports the split MAC function in traffic between a lightweight AP and its controller. LWAP uses AES-encrypted control messages and encapsulates, but does not encrypt, data traffic. LWAP operates at Layer 2, and also at Layer 3 over UDP. (However, Layer 2 operation has been deprecated by Cisco.) The controller can be either in the same broadcast domain and IP subnet or in a different broadcast domain and IP subnets for Layer 3 operation. The AP follows this process to discover its controller:

Step 1. The AP requests a DHCP address. The DHCP response includes the management IP address of one or more WLCs.

Step 2. The AP sends an LWAPP Discovery Request message to each WLC.

Step 3. The WLCs respond with an LWAPP Discovery Response that includes the number of APs currently associated to it.

Step 4. The AP sends a Join Request to the WLC with the fewest APs associated to it.

Step 5. The WLC responds with a Join Response message, the AP and the controller mutually authenticate each other and derive encryption keys to be used with future control messages. The WLC then configures the AP with settings, such as SSIDs, channels, security settings, and 802.11 parameters.

The Cisco Aironet 2000 series WLC can handle up to six APs; thus, it is sized for small- to medium-sized operations.

The Cisco Aironet 4400 series WLC supports medium to large facilities with the 4402 handling up to 50 APs, and the 4404 handling up to 100 APs.

Wireless LAN Antennas

Several concepts are important in understanding wireless antennas:

- Gain—The energy an antenna adds to the RF signal.
- Directionality—How the radio coverage is distributed.

- Polarization—The physical orientation the RF element. Cisco Aironet antennas use vertical polarization.
- Multipath Distortion—Receiving both direct and reflected signals arriving from different directions.
- Effective Isotropic Radiated Power (EIRP)—The AP radio's effective transmission power. Includes gain from the antenna and loss from the antenna's cable.

Gain

Cisco measures gain in dBi, which stands for *decibel isotropic* and is a measure of decibels relative to an isotropic source in free space. A *decibel* is the ratio between two signal levels. An *isotropic* antenna is a theoretical one in which the signal spreads out evenly in all directions from one point. Thus, dBi is the ratio of an antenna's signal to that of an isotropic antenna.

Directionality

Omnidirectional antennas have signals that theoretically extend in all directions, both vertically and horizontally. When gain in increased, the signal expands horizontally, but decreases vertically. One omnidirectional example is the dipole "Rubber Duck" antenna.

Directional antennas aim their signal in a specific direction. Signals can spread fairly wide in one direction or can be narrowly focused. Some examples include the Diversity Patch Wall Mount Antenna, Yagi, and dish antennas.

Multipath Distortion

Because radio waves are transmitted in many directions, not all go in a straight line to every client's antenna. Some bounce off walls or other objects and arrive at the client in varying intervals. Thus, the client receives several copies of the same RF signal, which can cause degraded data quality. This is *multipath distortion*, or *multipath interference*. Diversity systems try to minimize this by using two antennas; you might try moving antennas or changing the frequency if this is a problem in your facility. OFDM uses multiple frequencies operating together to increase performance in multipath situations.

EIRP

EIRP is the actual power of the signal that comes from the antenna, measured in Decibel Milliwatts (dBm). (0 dBm equals 1 milliwatt of power.) EIRP is calculated by taking the transmitter power, subtracting the amount of signal lost traversing the cable between the transmitter and antenna, and adding the antenna's gain. This can be expressed:

EIRP = (power – cable loss) + antenna gain.

Different countries have different rules about the amount of EIRP allowed. For instance, the maximum in the United States is 36 dBm. To minimize signal loss, use the shortest low-loss cable possible. Wider cables conserve more signal but are also more expensive.

Power over Ethernet (PoE) Switches

Access points can receive their power over Ethernet cables from Power over Ethernet (PoE) switches, routers with PoE switch modules, or midspan power injectors, thus alleviating the need for electrical outlets near them. APs require up to 15W of power, so plan your power budget accordingly. Two power standards are the Cisco Prestandard PoE and the IEEE's 802.3af standard. Both have a method for sensing that a powered device is connected to the port. 802.3af specifies a method for determining the amount of power needed by the device. Cisco devices, when connected to Cisco switches, can additionally use CDP to send that information. Power can be supplied over the data pairs—1, 2, 3, and 6—or over the unused pairs of 4, 5, 7, and 8.

Cisco PoE switches are configured by default to automatically detect and provide power. To disable this function, or to re-enable it, use the interface command **power inline** {**never** | **auto**}. To view interfaces and the power allotted to each, use **show power inline** [*interface*].

Configuring Wireless LAN Devices

Autonomous APs must be configured individually, while the WLC provides configuration to lightweight APs. WLAN clients must also be configured; this process varies depending on the client software used.

Configuring Autonomous Access Points

Autonomous APs can be configured in one of three ways:

- IOS Command Line—Either via Telnet or the console port.
- Web browser—This is the Cisco preferred way.
- CiscoWorks WLSE—For centralized configuration control.

The AP must already have an IP address to use any of these except the console port. It attempts to obtain one via DHCP by default. This link has directions and screen shots for both the command line and web browser configuration: http://www.cisco.com/en/US/products/ps6087/products_installation_and_configuration_guides_list.html.

Aironet 1100, 1200, and 1300 series APs perform various functions:

- Wireless AP
- Root bridge
- Nonroot bridge
- Repeater
- Scanner
- Workgroup bridge

Configuring a WLAN Controller

Cisco lightweight APs receive their configuration from the Wireless LAN Controller, which must be configured first. Initial configuration of the lightweight WLC can be done via command line using the console port or via web browser using the service port. Subsequent configuration can be done via:

- IOS Command Line—Either by Telnet, SSH, or the console port.
- Web browser—Using the WLC's IP address and Internet Explorer.
- Cisco Wireless Control System—For centralized configuration control.

You need to configure the WLC with information such as VLANs, SSIDs, and security policies. It downloads a configuration to its associated APs, and you can also configure, monitor, or reset individual APs through the web browser of the WLC. Review the material at this link for screen shots and WLC configuration information: http://www.cisco.com/en/US/products/ps6366/products_configuration_guide_book09186a00806b0077.html.

WLCs use several different types of physical and logical interfaces that are described in Table 6-2.

Table 6-2 Wireless LAN Controller Interfaces

Interface Type	Description
Service Port	Used for out of band management and initial setup. Must be a unique subnet. Not present on the 2006 WLC.
Management Interface with it. One per WLC.	Used by the APs to find their WLC and associate
AP-Manager Interface	Used for LWAPP traffic between controller and APs. Can have multiple AP-Manager interfaces.
Virtual Interface	IP address used for mobility group when implementing layer 3 roaming.
User Interface	Used to carry data traffic from users. One per VLAN.

CHAPTER 7

VoIP in a Campus Network

Many companies are integrating Voice over IP (VoIP) into their networks. Figure 7-1 shows some components of a VoIP system, which can include the following:

- IP phones—Provide voice and applications to the user.
- Voice gateways—Translates between PSTN and IP calls and provides backup to the Cisco CallManager (IP PBX, or Call Agent).
- Gatekeepers—An optional component that can do call admission control, allocate bandwidth for calls, and resolve phone numbers into IP addresses.
- Cisco CallManager—Serves as an IP PBX. Registers phones, controls calls.
- Video conferencing unit—Allows voice and video in the same phone call.
- Multipoint control unit—Allows multiple participants to join an audio and/or video conference call.
- Application server—Provides services such as Unity voice mail.

Figure 7-1 Some Components of a VoIP System

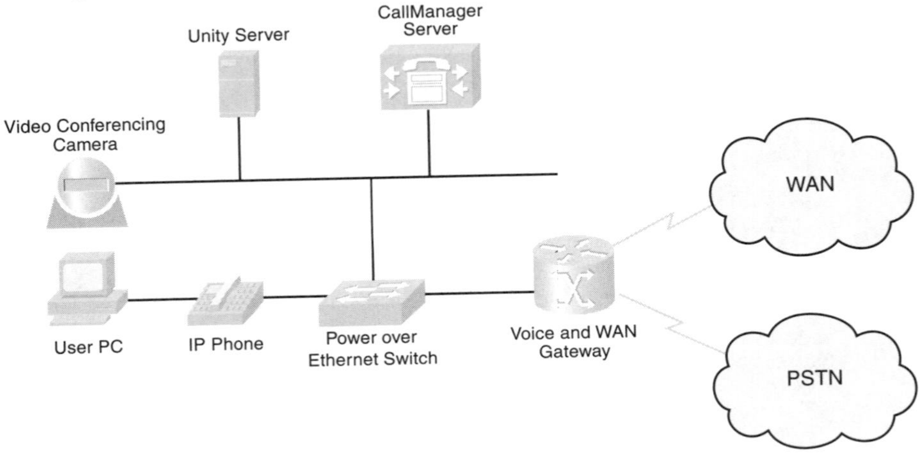

Voice and data have different network requirements. Although TCP data adjusts to dropped packets, packet loss is one of the biggest enemies of voice transmissions and is often caused by jitter and congestion. Jitter (variable delay) causes buffer over- and under-runs. Congestion at the interface can be caused by traffic from a fast port being switched to exit out a slower port, which causes the transmit buffer to be overrun.

VoIP traffic consists of two types: voice bearer and call control signaling. Voice bearer traffic is carried over the UDP-based Real Time Protocol (RTP). Call control uses one of several different protocols to communicate between the phone and CallManager and between the CallManager and the voice gateways.

Preparing the Network for VoIP

When adding voice or video to an existing network, you should examine several things in advance to provide the high level of availability users expect in their phone system:

- What features are needed?—Power for IP phones, voice VLANs on the switches, network redundancy for high availability, security for voice calls, and Quality of Service (QoS) settings.
- The physical plant—Cabling at least CAT-5.
- Electrical power for the IP phones—Use either inline power from Catalyst switch or power patch panel. Need uninterruptible power supply (UPS) with auto-restart, monitoring, and 4-hour response contract. May need generator backup. Maintain correct operating temperatures.
- Bandwidth—Commit no more than 75 percent of bandwidth. Consider all types of traffic—voice, video, and data. Have more than enough bandwidth if possible. Include both voice and call-control traffic in your planning.
- Network management—Need to monitor and proactively manage the network so that it does not go down.

Network and Bandwidth Considerations

The network requirements for VoIP include:

- Maximum delay of 150–200 ms (one-way)

- No more than 1 percent packet loss
- Maximum average jitter of 30 ms
- Bandwidth of 21–106 kbps per call, plus about 150 bps per phone for control traffic

A formula to use when calculating bandwidth needed for voice calls is as follows:

(Packet payload + all headers) * Packet rate per second

Auxiliary (or Voice) VLANs

Cisco switches can be configured to dynamically place IP telephones into a VLAN separate from the data VLANs. They can do this even when the phone and PC are physically connected to the same switch port. This is called an auxiliary VLAN or a voice VLAN. Voice VLANs allow phones to be dynamically placed in a separate IP subnet from hosts, to have QoS (using 802.1Q/p headers) and security policies applied, and makes troubleshooting easier.

QoS for VoIP

QoS gives special treatment to certain traffic at the expense of others. Using QoS in the network has several advantages:

- Prioritizes access to resources, so that critical traffic can be served.
- Allows good management of network resources.
- Allows service to be tailored to network needs.
- Allows mission-critical applications to share the network with other data.

People sometimes think that there is no need for QoS strategies in a LAN. However, switch ports can experience congestion because of port speed mismatches, many people trying to access the switch backbone, and many people trying to send traffic to the same switch port (such as a server port).

QoS Actions

Three QoS strategies are commonly implemented on interfaces where traffic enters the switch:

- Classification—Distinguishing one type of traffic from another. After traffic is classified, other actions can be performed on it. Some classification methods include access lists, ingress interface, and NBAR.
- Marking—At layer 2, placing 802.1p class of service (CoS) value within the 802.1Q tag. At layer 3, setting IP Precedence or Differentiated Services Code Point (DSCP) values on the classified traffic.
- Policing—Determining whether or not a specific type of traffic is within preset bandwidth levels. If so, it is usually allowed and might be marked. If not, the traffic is typically marked or dropped. CAR and class-based policing are examples of policing techniques.

Other QoS techniques are typically used on outbound interfaces:

- Traffic shaping and conditioning—Attempts to send traffic out in a steady stream at a specified rate. Buffers traffic that goes above that rate and sends it when there is less traffic on the line.
- Queuing—After traffic is classified and marked, one way it can be given special treatment is to be put into different queues on the interface to be sent out at different rates and times. Some examples include priority queuing, weighted fair queuing, and custom queuing. The default queuing method for a switch port is FIFO.
- Dropping—Normally interface queues accept packets until they are full and then drop everything after that. You can implement prioritized dropping, so that less important packets are dropped before more important ones—such as with Weighted Random Early Detection (WRED).

DSCP Values

Differentiated services provide levels of service based on the value of certain bits in the IP or ISL header or the 802.1Q tag. Each hop along the way must be configured to treat the marked traffic the way you want—this is called per-hop behavior (PHB).

In the Layer 3 IP header, you use the 8-bit ToS field. You can set either IP Precedence using the top 3 bits or Differentiated Services Code Points (DSCP) using the top 6 bits of the field. The bottom 2 bits are set aside for congestion notification. The default DSCP value is zero, which corresponds to best-effort delivery.

The six DSCP bits can be broken down into two sections: The first 3 bits define the DiffServ Assured Forwarding (AF) class, and the next 2 bits define the drop probability within that class. The sixth bit is 0 and unused. AF classes 1–4 are defined, and within each class, 1 is low drop probability, 2 is medium, and 3 is high (meaning that traffic is more likely to get dropped if there is congestion). These are shown in Table 7-1. Each hop still needs to be configured for how to treat each AF class.

Table 7-1 DSCP Assured Forwarding Values

	Low Drop	Medium Drop	High Drop
Class 1	AF11	AF12	AF13
Class 2	AF21	AF22	AF23
Class 3	AF31	AF32	AF33
Class 4	AF41	AF42	AF43

Voice bearer traffic uses an Expedited Forwarding value of DSCP 46 to give it higher priority within the network.

Trust Boundaries

When IP traffic comes in already marked, the switch has some options about how to handle it. It can:

- Trust the DSCP value in the incoming packet, if present.
- Trust the IP Precedence value in the incoming packet, if present.
- Trust the CoS value in the incoming frame, if present.
- Classify the traffic based on an IP access control list or a MAC address access control list.

Mark traffic for QoS as close to the source as possible. If the source is an IP telephone, it can mark its own traffic. If not, the building access module switch can do the marking. If those are not under your control, you might need to mark at the distribution layer. Classifying and marking slows traffic flow, so do not do it at the core. All devices along the path should then be configured to trust the marking and provide a level of service based on it. The place where trusted marking is done is called the *trust boundary*.

Configuring VoIP Support on a Switch

Manual Configuration

To associate a voice VLAN with a switch port, use the following:

```
Switch(config-if)#switchport voice vlan vlan-ID
```

To configure an IOS switch to trust the markings on traffic entering an interface, use the following:

```
Switch(config-if)#mls qos trust {dscp | cos}
```

To configure the switch to trust the traffic markings only if a Cisco phone is connected, use the following:

```
Switch(config-if)#mls qos trust device cisco-phone
```

To set a COS value for frames coming from a PC attached to the phone, use the following:

```
Switch(config-if)#switchport priority extend cos cos-value
```

To verify the interface parameters, use the following:

```
Switch(config-if)#show interfaces interface switchport
```

To verify the QoS parameters on an interface, use the following:

```
Switch(config-if)#show mls qos interface interface
```

Using AutoQoS

When AutoQoS is enabled, the switch configures its interfaces based on a best-practices template. AutoQoS has the following benefits:

- Automatic discovery and classification of network applications.
- Creates QoS policies for those applications.
- Configures the switch to support Cisco IP phones as well as network applications. Manual configuration can be done afterward, also.
- Sets up SNMP traps for network reporting.
- Configures consistently across your network when used on all routers and switches.

CDP must be enabled for AutoQoS to function properly with Cisco IP phones.

AutoQoS commands for switches running the Catalyst OS are listed in Table 7-2.

Table 7-2 AutoQoS Commands for Catalyst OS

Command	Description
set qos autoqos	Globally enables AutoQoS on the switch.
set port qos *mod/port* **autoqos trust** [**cos**|**dscp**]	Configures the port to trust either the COS or DSCP markings of all traffic coming in the port.
set port qos *mod/port* **autoqos voip** [**ciscosoftphone** | **ciscoipphone**] [**trust**]	Configures the port to trust traffic markings only if a Cisco phone or a computer with a Cisco softphone is connected to the port. Requires that CDP be enabled.

AutoQoS commands for switches running Native IOS are shown in Table 7-3.

Table 7-3 AutoQoS Commands for IOS

Command	Description
(config-if)#**auto qos voip trust**	Configures the port to trust the COS on all traffic entering the port.
(config-if)#**auto qos voip cisco-phone**	Configures the port to trust traffic markings only if a Cisco phone is connected to the port. Requires that CDP be enabled.
#**show auto qos** [**interface** *interface*]	Shows the AutoQoS configuration. Does not show any manual QoS configuration—use **show run** to see that.

CHAPTER 8

Campus Network Security

Attention has traditionally been paid to network perimeter security, such as firewall, and to mitigating Layer 3 attacks. However, networks must be protected against Layer 2 attacks, also. These are launched from devices inside the network by either a rogue device or a legitimate device that has been compromised. Rogue devices might be placed maliciously or might just be connected to an access switch by an employee wanting more switch port or wireless access. They include:

- Wireless routers or hubs
- Access switches
- Hubs

A switch might become the Spanning Tree root bridge, and disrupt user traffic. Use **root guard** and **bpdu guard** commands to prevent this. (Spanning tree security is discussed later in this chapter.)

There are four typical types of attacks against a switched network:

- MAC-based attacks, such as MAC address flooding
- VLAN-based attacks, such as VLAN hopping and attacks against devices on the same VLAN
- Spoofing attacks, such as DHCP spoofing, MAC spoofing, Address Resolution Protocol (ARP) spoofing, and Spanning Tree attacks
- Attacks against the switch, such as Cisco Discovery Protocol (CDP) manipulation, Telnet attacks, and Secure Shell (SSH) attacks

MAC Address Flooding

In a MAC address flooding attack, the attacker fills the switch's Content Addressable Memory (CAM) table with invalid MAC addresses. After the table is full, all traffic with an address not in the table is flooded out all interfaces. This has two bad effects—more traffic on the LAN and more work for the switch. Additionally, the intruder's traffic is also flooded, so they have access to more ports than they would normally have. After the attack stops, CAM entries age out and life returns to normal. However, meanwhile the attacker might have captured a significant amount of data.

Port security and port-based authentication can help mitigate MAC address attacks.

Port Security

Port security limits the number of MAC addresses allowed per port and can also limit which MAC addresses are allowed. Allowed MAC addressed can be manually configured or the switch can sticky learn them. Table 8-1 lists port security commands; these are given at the interface.

Table 8-1 Port Security Commands

Command	Description
switchport port-security	Enables port security on that interface.
switchport port-security maximum *value*	Specifies the max MAC addresses allowed on this port. Default is 1.
switchport port-security violation {**shutdown** | **restrict** | **protect**}	Configures the action to be taken when the maximum number is reached and a MAC address not associated with the port attempts to use the port, or when a station whose MAC address is associated with a different port attempt to access this port. Default is **shutdown**.
switchport port-security mac-address *mac-address*	Statically associates a specific MAC address with a port.
switchport port-security mac-address sticky	Enables the switch port to dynamically learn secure MAC addresses. MAC addresses learned through that port, up to the maximum number, if a maximum is configured, are treated as secure MAC addresses.
show port security [**interface** *interface* | **address**]	Verifies port security actions.

Port-Based Authentication

802.1x authentication requires a computer (called a client) to be authenticated before it is allowed access to the LAN. This can be combined with port security to allow only authenticated clients with specified MAC addresses to access a port. When a computer connects to a switch port configured for 802.1x authentication, the following steps occur:

Step 1. The port is in the *unauthorized* state, allowing only 802.1x EAP over LAN (EAPOL) traffic.

Step 2. The client connects to the port. The switch either requests authentication or the client sends an EAPOL frame to begin authentication.

Step 3. The switch relays authentication information between the client and a RADIUS server that acts in proxy for the client.

Step 4. If authentication succeeds, the port transitions to the *authorized* state, and normal LAN traffic is allowed through it.

Table 8-2 shows commands to configure 802.1x authentication on a switch.

Table 8-2 Configuring 802.1x Port Authentication

Command	Description
(config)#**aaa new-model**	Enables AAA on the switch.
(config)#**aaa authentication dot1x default group radius**	Creates a AAA method list that says to use 802.1x authentication by default, using a RADIUS server (configured separately).
(config)#**dot1x system-auth-control**	Globally enabled 802.1x authentication on the switch.
(config-if)#**dot1x port-control auto**	Enables 802.1x authentication on an interface of the switch.
show dot1x	Verifies 802.1x authentication.

VLAN-Based Attacks

VLAN-based attacks include VLAN hopping, in which a station is able to access a VLAN other than its own. This can be done with switch spoofing or with 802.1Q double-tagging.

Switch Spoofing

Switch spoofing involves a station configured to negotiate a trunk link between itself and the switch. By default, switches dynamically negotiate trunking status using Dynamic Trunking Protocol (DTP). If a computer is able to use DTP to establish a trunk link to the switch, it will receive all traffic bound for VLANs allowed on that trunk. By default, all VLANs are allowed on a trunk.

You can mitigate this by turning off DTP on all ports that should not become trunks, such as most access ports, using the interface command **switchport nonegotiate**. If the port should be an access port, configure it as such with the interface command **switchport mode access**. Additionally, shut down all unused ports and assign them to an unused VLAN. The commands to do this are:

```
Switch(config)#interface interface
Switch(config-if)#switchport mode access
Switch(config-if)#switchport access vlan vlan
Switch(config-if)#shutdown
```


802.1Q Double-Tagging

A double-tagging attack is possible with 802.1Q trunking because it does not tag frames from the native VLAN. In this attack, the attacking computer sets up a trunk port between itself and the switch, then generates frames with two 802.1Q tags. The first tag matches the native VLAN of the trunk port, and the second matches the VLAN of a host it wants to attack, as shown in Figure 8-1.

Figure 8-1 VLAN Hopping by 802.1Q Double-Tagging

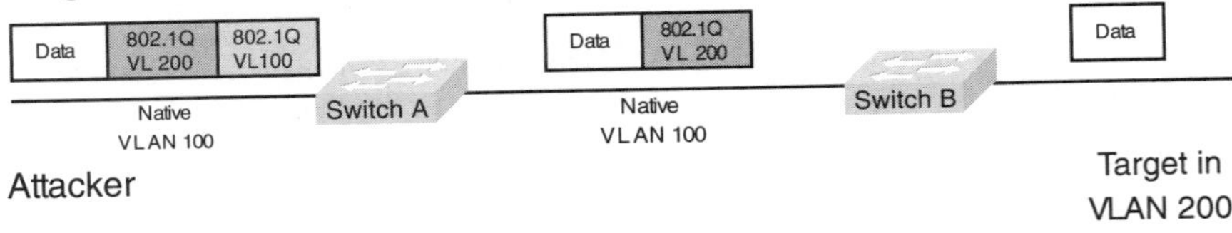

Switch A removes the first tag for VLAN 100, because it matches the native VLAN for that link. It forwards the frame out all links with the same native VLAN, including its link to Switch B. Switch B sees the frame come in with an 802.1Q tag for VLAN 200, so it forwards it out the VLAN 200 link to the victim computer.

To mitigate this type of attack, use the same strategies used for switch spoofing. You can also use VLAN access control lists, called *VACLs*, or implement Private VLANs.

VACLs

Cisco switches support of various kinds of ACLs:

- Traditional Router ACL (RACL)
- QoS ACL
- VACL

VLAN access control lists (VACLs) are similar to route-maps in that they are composed of statements that contain match and set conditions. In a VACL, the "set" conditions are called "actions." Actions include **forward**, **drop**, and **redirect**. Like route-maps, VACL statements are numbered for ordering. After configuration, VACLs are applied to traffic to specified VLANs.

The following is a sample VACL that instructs the switch to drop traffic matching ACL 101 (not shown), and forward all other traffic:

```
Switch(config)#vlan access-map Drop101 5
Switch(config-access-map)#match ip address 101
Switch(config-access-map)#action drop
Switch(config-access-map)#vlan access-map Drop101 10
Switch(config-access-map)#action forward!
Switch(config)#vlan filter Drop101 vlan_list 10
```

To view VACL settings, use the commands **show vlan access-map** *vacl_name* or **show vlan filter access-map** *vacl_name*.

Private VLANs

Private VLANs (PVLANs) allow service providers to isolate customers into separate multi-access domains. Using a VLAN for each customer is not scalable, because a switch's maximum VLANs would limit the number of customers an ISP can have. Each VLAN requires a separate IP subnet, which could also be a limiting factor.

PVLANs divide a VLAN into secondary VLANs, letting you isolate a set of ports from other ports within the same VLAN. There are two types of secondary VLANs:

- Community VLANs—Ports can communicate with other ports in the same community VLAN.
- Isolated VLANs—Ports cannot communicate with each other.

Ports within a private VLAN can be one of three types:

- Community—Communicates with other community ports and with promiscuous ports.
- Isolated—Communicates only with promiscuous ports.
- Promiscuous—Communicates with all ports.

Table 8-3 shows the commands to configure a primary private VLAN, secondary PVLANs, and their associated ports.

Table 8-3 Configuring Private VLANs

Command	Description
vlan *vlan-id*	Enters VLAN configuration mode.
private-vlan {**community** | **isolated** | **primary**}	Configures the VLAN as a private VLAN and specifies the type. Repeat this command to configure all primary and secondary VLANs.
vlan *primary-vlan-id*	Enters configuration mode for the primary VLAN.
private-vlan association *secondary_vlan_list*	Associates secondary VLANs with the primary one. Separate the secondary VLAN numbers with a comma, no spaces.
switchport mode private-vlan (for {**host** | **promiscuous**}	Configures a port as either a host port community or isolated) or a promiscious port.
switchport private-vlan host-association *primary_vlan_ID secondary_vlan_ID*	Associates a host port with its primary and secondary PVLANs.
private-vlan mapping *primary_vlan_ID secondary_vlan_list*	Associates a promiscuous port with its primary and secondary PVLANs.
show interfaces *interface* **switchport**	Verifies the VLAN configuration.
show interfaces private-vlan mapping	Verify the private VLAN configuration.

Spoof Attacks

Spoof attacks include DHCP spoofing, MAC address spoofing, and ARP spoofing.

DHCP Spoofing

A DHCP spoofing attacker listens for DHCP requests and answers them, giving its IP address as the client default gateway. The attacker then becomes a "man-in-the-middle" as all off-net traffic flows through it.

DHCP snooping can prevent DHCP spoofing attacks. When DHCP snooping is enabled, only ports that uplink to an authorized DHCP server are trusted, and allowed to send all types of DHCP messages. All other ports on the switch are untrusted and can send only DHCP requests. If a DHCP response is seen on an untrusted port, the port is shut down. The switch can also be configured to send information, such as port ID, using DHCP option 82.

Note

DHCP snooping configuration is user impacting, because the switch drops all DHCP requests until the ports are configured. You should do this during off hours or during a maintenance window.

Configure DHCP snooping with the following commands, either globally or for a particular VLAN. Configure only individual ports that uplink to DHCP servers as trusted ports.

```
Switch(config)#ip dhcp snooping
Switch(config)#ip dhcp snooping information option
Switch(config)#ip dhcp snooping vlan number number
Switch(config-if)#ip dhcp snooping trust
Switch#show ip dhcp snooping
```

To extend the protection further, IP Source Guard tracks the IP addresses of the host connected to each port and prevents traffic sourced from another IP address from entering that port. The tracking can be done based on just an IP address or on both IP and MAC addresses.

Enable IP Source Guard for both IP and MAC addresses on host access interfaces with the command **ip verify source vlan dhcpsnooping port-security**.

ARP Spoofing

In an ARP spoofing attack, the attacker sends out gratuitous (unsolicited) ARP messages giving the IP address of the local default gateway, with its own MAC address as the layer 2 address. Local devices overwrite their existing correct ARP information with the incorrect one, and, thus, they forward off-net traffic to the attacker (it becomes a "man-in-the-middle"). If the attacker then forwards it on to the legitimate router, this type of attack might go undetected by the users.

Dynamic ARP Inspection (DAI) can work with DHCP spoofing to stop ARP spoofing. DAI defines trusted and untrusted interfaces. It intercepts ARP messages on untrusted ports, and checks them against the IP address/MAC address bindings in the DHCP snooping database. They must match for the switch to forward the traffic. Access ports should be configured as untrusted, and ports that connect to other switches or to a router should be trusted.

Enable DAI on a VLAN, or multiple VLANs, and configure trusted interfaces. You can optionally configure a rate limit, or configure which addresses DAI matches against (the default is IP and MAC address). The basic commands are:

```
Switch(config)#ip arp inspection vlan vlan_id
Switch(config-if)#ip arp inspection trust
```


Securing Spanning Tree

Spanning Tree tuning can help prevent a rogue device from becoming root bridge or otherwise disrupting your user traffic. There are several tools at your disposal—Figure 8-2 shows where each could be used in a switched network.

Figure 8-2 Securing Spanning Tree

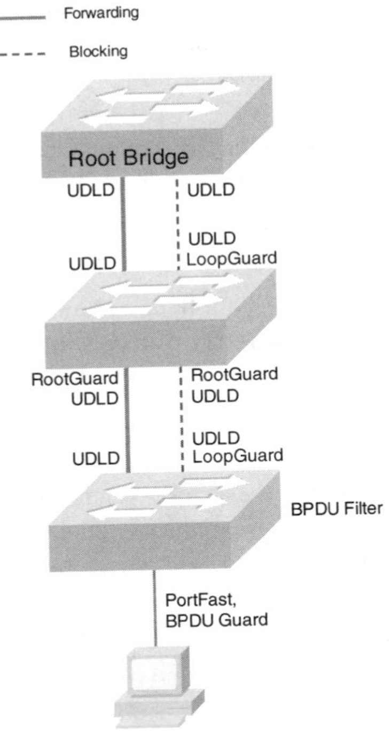

BPDU Guard

BPDU Guard prevents loops if another switch is attached to a Portfast port. When BPDU Guard is enabled on an interface, it is put into an error-disabled state (basically, it is shut down) if a BPDU is received on the interface. It can be enabled at either global configuration mode—in which case it affects all Portfast interfaces—or at interface mode. Portfast does not have to be enabled for it to be configured at a specific interface.

```
Switch(config)#spanning-tree portfast bpduguard default
Switch(config-if)#spanning-tree bpduguard enable
```

BPDU Filtering

BPDU filtering is another way of preventing loops in the network. It also can be enabled either globally or at the interface, and it functions differently at each. In global configuration, if a Portfast interface receives any BPDUs, it is taken out of Portfast status. At interface configuration mode, it prevents the port from sending or receiving BPDUs. The commands are:

```
Switch(config)#spanning-tree portfast bpdufilter default
Switch(config-if)#spanning-tree bpdufilter enable
```


Root Guard

Root Guard is meant to prevent the wrong switch from becoming the spanning-tree root. It is enabled on ports other than the root port and on switches other than the root. If a Root Guard port receives a BPDU that causes it to become a root port, the port is put into a "root-inconsistent" state and does not pass traffic through it. If the port stops receiving these BPDUs, it automatically re-enables itself.

```
Switch(config-if)#spanning-tree guard root
Switch#show spanning-tree inconsistentports
```

Prevent Spanning Tree Loops

A switch notices when a physical connection is broken by the absence of Layer 1 electrical keepalives (Ethernet calls this a link beat). However, sometimes a cable is intact enough to maintain keepalives, but not to pass data in both directions. This is a unidirectional link.

Unidirectional Link Detection (UDLD)

UDLD detects a unidirectional link by sending periodic hellos out the interface. It also uses probes, which must be acknowledged by the device on the other end of the link. UDLD operates at Layer 2. The port is shut down if a unidirectional link is found.

To enable UDLD on all fiber-optic interfaces, use this command:

```
Switch(config)#udld enable
```

Although this command is given at global configuration mode, it applies only to fiber ports. To enable UDLD on nonfiber ports, give the same command at interface config mode.

To disable UDLD on a specific fiber port, use this command:

```
Switch(config-if)#udld disable
```

To disable UDLD on a specific nonfiber port, use this command:

```
Switch(config-if)#no udld enable
```

To re-enable all interfaces shut by UDLD, use the following:

```
Switch#udld reset
```

To verify UDLD status, use the following:

```
Switch#show udld interface
```

Loop Guard

Loop Guard prevents loops that might develop if a port that should be blocking inadvertently transitions to the forwarding state. This can happen if the port stops receiving BPDUs (perhaps because of a unidirectional link or a software/configuration problem in its neighbor switch). When one of the ports in a physically redundant topology stops receiving BPDUs, the STP conceives the topology as loop-free. Eventually, the blocking port becomes designated and moves to a forwarding state, thus creating a loop. With Loop Guard enabled, an additional check is made.

If no BPDUs are received on a blocked port for a specific length of time, Loop Guard puts that port into loop inconsistent blocking state, rather than transitioning to a forwarding state. Loop Guard should be enabled on all switch ports that have a chance of becoming root or designated ports. It is most effective when enabled in the entire switched network, in conjunction with UDLD.

To enable Loop Guard for all point-to-point links on the switch, use the following command:

```
Switch(config)#spanning-tree loopguard default
```

To enable Loop Guard on a specific interface, use:

```
Switch(config-if)#spanning-tree guard loop
```

Loop Guard automatically re-enables the port if it starts receiving BPDUs once again.

Securing Your Switch

Here are some basic security suggestions for network devices:

- Use passwords that are not susceptible to a dictionary attack. Add numbers or substitute numbers and symbols for letters.
- Limit Telnet access using access lists.
- Use SSH instead of Telnet.
- Physically secure access to the device.
- Use banners that warn against unauthorized access.
- Remove unused services, such as finger, the TCP and UDP small servers, service config, and HTTP server.
- Set up and monitor Syslog.
- Disable automatic trunking on all nontrunk ports.
- Disable CDP on ports where it is not needed.

PART III

ISCW

CHAPTER 1

Network Conceptual Models

Conceptual models allow network designers to move from looking at the network as a collection of devices to viewing it as a way to provide services to users, no matter where the users and the services are located. Cisco currently defines three models as the building blocks of a world-class enterprise network: the Intelligent Information Network, the Service-Oriented Network Architecture, and the Cisco Enterprise Architecture.

Intelligent Information Network

The Intelligent Information Network (IIN) seeks to create a holistic network that integrates with and enables your business processes. It allows centralized control and interoperation of distributed systems. This control and interoperability can provide increased network security and efficiency.

The IIN consists of three components:

- **Integrated transport**—Data, voice, and video all transported over a secure IP network.
- **Integrated services**—Shared/virtualized resources, such as storage and servers.
- **Integrated applications**—The network is application aware, enhancing the efficiency of applications. This component includes Application-Oriented Networking (AON), which offloads shared, common functions, such as logging and security, to the network.

Service-Oriented Network Architecture

An intelligent network is delivered using the Service-Oriented Network Architecture (SONA) framework. SONA sees a converged network as the connecting thread for all the portions of the network and the services provided. The network is application aware; that is, it contains the intelligence needed to tie all the various types of traffic together to deliver required services. SONA defines three layers:

- **Network Infrastructure**—IT resources such as servers, users, WANs, and office locations all connected and accessible to each other
- **Integrated Services**—Services such as voice, network management, mobility, security, and storage that are delivered using the network infrastructure
- **Application**—Business applications that function using the integrated services

In an enterprise, the campus and branch offices, teleworker access, and WAN access all fall under the Network Infrastructure layer of the SONA. This categorization allows workers in all types of locations to access the services and applications of the other layers. The Cisco Enterprise Architecture defines how each of these components should be designed and structured.

Cisco Enterprise Architecture

The Cisco Enterprise Architecture model divides the network into building blocks and gives best practices for the architecture of each one. The traditional three-layer model (Core, Distribution, and Access) is still around and can be integrated into the design of components of the Enterprise Architecture model.

Enterprise Architecture building blocks include the following:

- **Campus**—The enterprise core, or headquarters. The campus building block contains routing, switching, security, Voice over IP (VoIP), wireless, and so on.
- **Data center**—Server and application resources. Redundant data centers provide business continuity and allow load balancing.
- **Branch office**—Remote locations that contain services similar to the campus but are administered centrally rather than at each location.
- **Teleworker**—Either a small office, home office, or a mobile user. Extends data (and possibly voice) services to these users over a virtual private network (VPN) using broadband WAN access.
- **WAN**—Connects all the different blocks together. Converges voice, video, and data over an IP WAN that provides security, quality of service (QoS), and ubiquitous access.

WAN options between the campus and branch offices include traditional Layer 2 connections such as Frame Relay, ATM, and leased lines. Multiprotocol Label Switching (MPLS) can provide any-to-any connectivity between the sites and is highly scalable. IPsec VPNs across the Internet can also be used.

This short cut is concerned mainly with how the campus, branch, and small office, home office (SOHO)/teleworker portions of the network use the WAN to communicate with each other to provide network services to their users.

CHAPTER 2

Providing SOHO/Teleworker Connectivity

The traditional teleworker solution consists of a virtual private network (VPN) client on the user's computer connecting over the Internet to a VPN concentrator, firewall, or Cisco Adaptive Security Appliance (ASA) at the corporate site. This requires only a dialup or broadband Internet connection and a dialup or broadband modem. However, this approach has several shortcomings:

- Dialup does not provide the necessary bandwidth to take advantage of all the corporate services, such as Voice over IP (VoIP).
- There is no centralized control of the teleworker equipment, so security, virus protection, and so forth are left to the teleworker to implement.
- There is no control over quality of service (QoS) for advanced services.
- It is hard for corporate IT staff to support.

The Cisco Business-Ready Teleworker Solution addresses these issues with the traditional teleworker approach. It seeks to secure corporate data by using IPsec VPNs, allow corporate control of the connection components, and provide a scalable architecture as part of disaster planning. It consists of an always-on broadband connection, a corporate-owned and -managed router configured for VPN and QoS, IP phone, and (optionally) video equipment.

Two typical broadband connection types are digital subscriber line (DSL) and cable.

Broadband Cable

CATV, or Community Antenna Television, was originally developed to provide improved TV signals by sharing antennas and satellite dishes. It used coaxial cable to transport the TV signals to each subscriber. Current systems typically use a combination of fiber and coaxial. When both fiber and coaxial cables are used, the system is referred to as a *hybrid fiber-coaxial* (HFC) *network.*

Broadband cable uses frequency-division multiplexing (FDM) to deliver data over a radio frequency (RF) network. Cable provides relatively inexpensive high-speed Internet access that supports analog and digital video, voice, and data. Its downsides include possible bandwidth and security issues because it is a shared medium. The provider can increase bandwidth by using smaller service areas and more channels. Security can be addressed by the user within the cable modem or with an onsite router.

Cable Components

Five basic components comprise a cable TV/data system:

- **Antenna site**—Receives TV signals from antennas or satellite dishes.
- **Headend site**—Converts TV signals for distribution to end users and converts data for transport to and from end users. Similar to a telephone central office.
- **Transportation network**—Links the antenna site to the headend or the headend to the distribution network. Can use microwave, coaxial cable, or fiber cable.
- **Distribution network**—Carries signals between the end user and the transportation network. Consists of trunks and feeder cables. Backbone trunks are either fiber or coaxial cable. Feeder cables are usually coaxial and connect the distribution network to the subscriber drops.
- **Subscriber drops**—Connects the customer premises equipment (CPE) such as TV, set-top box, or cable modem to the distribution network. Uses coaxial cable.

Figure 2-1 shows more detail about how these components work together to deliver combined cable TV and data to an end user. Each acronym and component is further explained following the figure.

Figure 2-1 Components of a Cable System

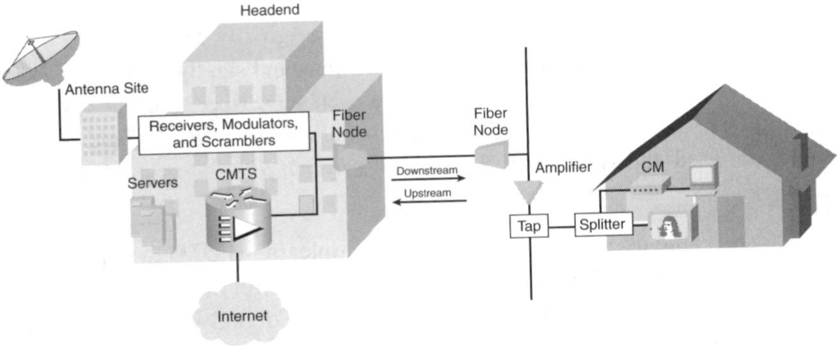

In Figure 2-1, video signals are received at the antenna site and sent to the local headend site. Feeds from other headend sites might be used, too. Each TV channel has receivers, modulators, and scramblers. The signals are transferred via RF to a fiber transmitter. Data signals from the Internet or various servers (such as e-mail or content servers) are modulated by the Cable Modem Termination System (CMTS) router and sent as RF signals to the fiber transmitter. They are then translated to optical signals and sent downstream, toward the end users. A fiber node in the distribution network translates them back to RF signals and sends them over the coaxial cable. Signals are boosted at intervals by an amplifier. A tap divides the signal for sending to a particular subscriber's residence. At the residence, a splitter divides the signals into data and video. Video is sent to the TV or set-top box, and data is sent to a cable modem (CM). The cable modem demodulates the signal back to digital.

Cable Standards

Worldwide, three standards control cable TV systems:

- **National Television Standards Committee (NTSC)**—Analog television standard used in North America. Specifies a 6-MHz channel width.
- **Phase-Alternating Line (PAL)**—Color television standard used in most of the rest world. Specifies 6-, 7-, or 8-MHz channel widths.
- **Systéme Electronic Couleur avec Mèmoire (SECAM)**—Standard used in France and some Eastern European countries. Specifies an 8-MHz channel.

The standard for sending data over cable systems is Data-Over-Cable Service Interface Specifications (DOCSIS). This standard, developed by Cablelabs, defines physical and data link layer requirements for cable modems. Cablelabs also certifies cable modems and CMTS systems to work with the standard. At the physical layer, DOCSIS specifies channel widths and modulation methods. At the data link layer it specifies access methods, some QoS capabilities, and some security features.

Cable RF waves use different frequencies for upstream and downstream signaling. Downstream signals are allowed 810 MHz of bandwidth, in the 50- to 860-MHz range. This is then further subdivided into channels of 6-, 7-, or 8-MHz depending on the standard used. Upstream signals have only 37 MHz of bandwidth, in the 5- to 42-MHz range.

Provisioning the Cable Modem

Cable modems communicate with their CMTS across whatever physical networks connect them. The service provider must have the necessary auxiliary services, such as DHCP, TFTP, and Time of Day (TOD), available at its headend. When a cable modem boots, it registers with the CMTS and acquires its configuration using the following steps:

Step 1. The cable modem scans for a downstream channel to use for communication with the CMTS. Once it finds a channel, the CM locks it in.

Step 2. CMTS tells the CM the parameters to use for upstream messages.

Step 3. Communication is established at Layers 1 and 2 (physical and data link layers).

Step 4. The cable modem broadcasts for a DHCP server. It obtains an IP address, the address of the TFTP and TOD servers, and the name of the TFTP file to download.

Step 5. The cable modem downloads the DOCSIS configuration file from the TFTP server.

Step 6. The cable modem forwards the configuration file to the CMTS and attempts to register with it. If the configuration is valid, the modem is registered. The two devices negotiate QoS and security settings.

Step 7. The user device—either a PC or a router—requests an IP address, DNS server, and default gateway information from the cable provider.

Digital Subscriber Line

Voice does not use all the available bandwidth on a phone line—it uses frequencies only up to about 3 kHz. DSL was created to use the space between 3 kHz and 1 MHz to send data traffic over a telephone local loop. Thus, both voice and data can be sent simultaneously over the same connection (some variants of DSL use the entire spectrum, however, so no voice can be sent). DSL is a physical layer medium that extends between the subscriber's DSL modem and the provider's DSL access multiplexer (DSLAM.)

Types of DSL

Asymmetrical DSL has higher downstream (from the provider's central office [CO] to the subscriber) bandwidth than upstream (from the subscriber to the CO.) Symmetrical DSL has the same bandwidth both downstream and upstream. You will sometimes see these referred to as "asynchronous" and "synchronous" DSL.

The various types of DSL include the following:

- **ADSL**—Asymmetric DSL supports both voice and data. Downstream bandwidth goes up to 8 Mbps; upstream goes up to 1 Mbps. Two other versions, ADSL2 and ADSL2+, provide 24 Mbps downstream and 1.5 Mbps upstream. The maximum distance from the CO is 18,000 feet, or 5.46 km.
- **RADSL**—Rate-adaptive DSL changes the rate based on the local loop.
- **VDSL**—Very-high-rate DSL can be either symmetric or asymmetric and can carry voice along with data. Maximum symmetric bandwidth is 26 Mbps; maximum asymmetric is 52 Mbps downstream and 13 Mbps upstream. The maximum distance from the CO is 4,500 feet, or 1.37 km.
- **IDSL**—ISDN DSL carries only digital data (other forms of DSL send analog signals). It uses both ISDN B channels and the D channel, for a symmetric bandwidth of 144 kbps. The maximum distance for IDSL is 18,000 feet, or 5.46 km.

- **SDSL**—Symmetric DSL carries only data, with a maximum for both downstream and upstream of 768 kbps. The distance limitation is 22,000 feet, or 6.7 km. It is a proprietary technology that uses only one twisted pair of wires.
- **HDSL**—High-data-rate DSL uses two twisted pairs of wires to achieve a maximum symmetrical bandwidth of 2.048 Mbps. Its maximum distance from the CO is 12,000 feet, or 3.7 km. HDSL carries only data, no voice.
- **G.SHDSL**—Symmetric high-speed DSL has a symmetrical data rate of 2.3 Mbps and the longest maximum distance: 28,000 feet, or 8.52 km. It also carries only data, no voice.

ADSL

ADSL is a popular residential service because it can carry both voice and data over one twisted pair of wires. This capability is accomplished by using either a splitter or a filter. A splitter takes the incoming analog signals and splits off the frequencies under 4 MHz to a voice line. It sends all other traffic to the DSL line. Splitters are more typically used at the CO than the subscriber premises because they require a technician to install them. A filter, or microfilter, requires no installation. It simply connects to the phone line on one end and the telephone on the other. It passively filters out any signals in the DSL range so that only voice reaches the telephone.

Figure 2-2 shows how ADSL components work together in a typical residential implementation. The telephone company's CO forwards both plain old telephone service (POTS) and DSL data traffic over the same line to the subscriber. The line enters at the network interface device (NIDS) and branches toward the telephone and the PC. A low-pass filter blocks everything but voice frequencies from reaching the phone. A DSL modem (or router with a DSL interface) forwards data to the PC. When the CO receives traffic from the subscriber, a splitter sends voice frequencies to the PSTN switch and DSL frequencies to the DSLAM. The DSLAM sends data traffic to a router for forwarding to the Internet.

Figure 2-2 Components of an ADSL System

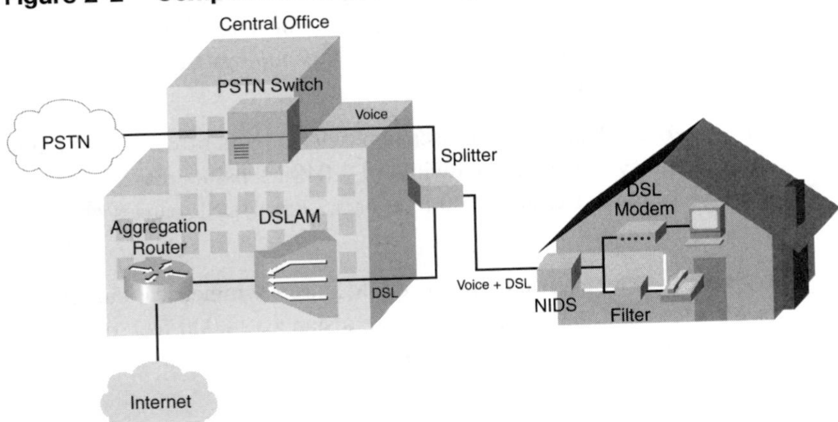

Carrierless Amplitude and Phase Line Coding

Carrierless Amplitude and Phase (CAP) is a DSL line-coding method that divides the bandwidth into three channels: one for voice, one for downstream data, and one for upstream data. Each type of traffic is carried within one frequency band, and so CAP is termed a *single-carrier modulation technique*. The bands are fairly wide. Voice uses 0 to 4 kHz, upstream traffic uses 25 to 160 kHz, and downstream uses 240 kHz to 1.5 MHz. CAP is simple to understand and implement but does not scale as well as Discrete Multi-Tone (DMT) modulation.

Discrete Multi-Tone Line Coding

Discrete Multi-Tone (DMT) is the most widely used method of ADSL line coding. It divides the DSL frequency band into 256 channels of 4 kHz each. Some channels are duplex and used for both downstream and upstream traffic. Others are used only for downstream. Channel quality is constantly monitored, and the channels used can be changed when conditions warrant. DMT is more complex than CAP but is also more flexible and scalable and can achieve higher speeds.

A version of DMT, G.Lite ADSL, uses half the number of channels as DMT.

Layer 2 over DSL

Recall that DSL is a Layer 1 (physical layer) technology. There are three methods of carrying data at Layer 2 over DSL:

- **Bridging**—Based on RFCs 1483 and 2684. Ethernet traffic is just bridged from the subscriber PCs, through the DSL modem and the DSLAM, to a provider router. Bridging is not as secure or scalable as other methods.
- **PPP over Ethernet (PPPoE)**—The most common Layer 2 method of carrying data over DSL. PPP traffic is encapsulated in Ethernet frames.
- **PPP over ATM (PPPoA)**—PPP packets are routed over ATM between the subscriber equipment and the provider.

PPPoE

When PPPoE is used, a PPP session is established, similar to when using dialup. Either Password Authentication Protocol (PAP) or Challenge Handshake Authentication Protocol (CHAP) authentication can be used. The provider's aggregation router and the subscriber's CPE establish a session between them. There are three ways to do this:

- The PPP client on a subscriber router with a DSL interface terminates both the DSL and the PPP sessions. The router can allow multiple users over the DSL with just one PPP login, by acting as a DHCP server and doing Network Address Translation (NAT) or Port Address Translation (PAT) for the subscriber users. The router obtains its outside IP address via PPP's IP Control Protocol (IPCP.)
- A DSL modem terminates the DSL session, and the PPP client on a CPE router terminates the PPP session. The router can act as a DHCP server and do NAT/PAT, to allow multiple internal users. It obtains its outside address via IPCP.
- A DSL modem terminates the DSL session, and a PPP client on the subscriber PC terminates the PPP session. Traffic is bridged from the PC to the aggregation router. This allows only a single DSL user. If multiple users are at the same residence, they must each have their own PPP login, and they each obtain an IP address via IPCP.

PPP was created to be used over a point-to-point connection, and Ethernet is inherently multipoint, so PPPoE uses a PPP server discovery process. After a server has been discovered, a virtual point-to-point link can be established, and the PPP session process can continue. The PPP server discovery stage has four steps:

Step 1. The PPP client sends a PPPoE Active Discovery Initiation (PADI) broadcast.

Step 2. Any PPP servers (aggregation routers) reply with a PPPoE Active Discovery Offer (PADO), sent as a unicast to the client's MAC address.

Step 3. The client replies to the server with a PPPoE Active Discovery Request (PADR).

Step 4. The server confirms the association with a PPPoE Active Discovery Session-confirmation (PADS) message.

When these steps have been completed, the normal PPP session negotiations proceed, and a session is established.

PPPoA

PPPoA requires a CPE router; traffic is routed from the subscriber PCs to the aggregation router—it cannot be bridged as with PPPoE. The PPP session is established between the CPE router and the aggregation router. Multiple users are supported if the CPE router is configured to do DHCP and NAT. Traffic between the CPE router and the aggregation router is encapsulated as ATM at Layer 2, rather than Ethernet. Therefore, the CPE router must have an ATM interface.

Configuring DSL CPE

When a CPE router is used as the PPP client, it must be configured. The configuration will differ depending on whether you are using PPPoE or PPPoA. PPPoE can be used with an Ethernet or an ATM interface on the router connecting to the DSL network. An Ethernet interface is used if the router connects to a DSL modem; an ATM interface is used if the router connects directly to the DSL network. A dialer interface must also be created and configured with PPP parameters.

Configuring PPPoE CPE

The following tasks must be completed to configure a CPE router with for PPPoE:

1. Configure the internal and external interfaces.
2. Configure a dialer interface.
3. Configure NAT/PAT.

4. Configure the router to act as a DHCP server.
5. Configure a default route.

First, configure the internal Ethernet interface with an IP address. It will be the default gateway for the users. Also, configure it as the inside interface for NAT.

Do not put an IP address on the external Ethernet interface. Enable PPPoE on it, and assign it to a PPPoE client dialer pool. The final configuration on the two Ethernet interfaces should be similar to that shown in Example 2-1.

Example 2-1 Configuring Ethernet Interfaces for PPPoE

```
interface FastEthernet0/0
 description DSL interface
 no ip address
 pppoe enable
 pppoe-client dial-pool-number 1
!
interface FastEthernet0/1
 description Internal interface
 ip address 172.16.1.1 255.255.255.0
 ip nat inside
```

If the external interface is ATM, the configuration changes slightly. You must configure the ATM permanent virtual circuit (PVC) information and assign the interface to a PPPoE client dialer pool. Leave the DSL operating mode at its default to auto-detect the correct modulation, as shown in Example 2-2.

Example 2-2 Configuring an ATM Interface for PPPoE

```
interface ATM1/0
 description DSL interface
 no ip address
 dsl operating-mode auto
 pvc 1/100
  pppoe-client dial-pool-number 1
```

Second, configure a dialer interface and assign it to the same dialer pool as the Ethernet interface. Give it a PPP encapsulation and configure the PPP parameters on it. Make it the NAT outside interface. Limit the maximum transmission unit (MTU) size to 1492 bytes, to allow for the PPP and Ethernet headers. Because DSL is an always-on connection, a dialer list is

CCNP ISCW

not required. Your configuration should look similar to Example 2-3. Verify PPP operation with the **show ppp session** command. You can also debug PPP with the commands **debug ppp authentication** and **debug ppp negotiation**.

Example 2-3 Configuring a Dialer Interface for PPPoE

```
interface Dialer1
 ip address negotiated
 ip mtu 1492
 ip nat outside
 encapsulation ppp
 dialer pool 1
 ppp authentication chap
 ppp chap password dslpass
```

Next, configure the router to do NAT or PAT. NAT translates one internal address to one external one. PAT can translate multiple internal addresses to one external one. Most residential and SOHO subscribers use PAT. To configure it, identify the traffic that must be translated using an access list. Then tell the router to translate those IP addresses to the IP address of the dialer interface, and to "overload" that external IP address. The **overload** command causes the router to use PAT. Be sure to designate the inside and outside interfaces (see Example 2-1 for those commands.) PAT configuration is done in global command mode, and shown in Example 2-4.

Verify your NAT/PAT operation with the **show ip nat translations** command.

Example 2-4 Configuring NAT/PAT

```
access-list 100 permit ip 172.16.1.0 0.0.0.255 any
!
ip nat inside source list 100 interface Dialer1 overload
```

The next task is to configure the router to serve IP addresses to internal hosts. To set up basic DHCP, create a pool of addresses for assigning to clients, specify the clients' default gateway, and import the DNS information obtained from the DSL provider via PPP. Example 2-5 shows what this might look like. On the router, verify IP address assignment using the command **show ip dhcp binding**. On a Windows-based user computer, verify the IP address using the DOS command **ipconfig /all**.

Example 2-5 Configuring a Router as a DHCP Server

```
ip dhcp pool Users
  import all
   network 172.16.1.0 255.255.255.0
   default-router 172.16.1.1
```

Finally, configure a static default route. It should point to the dialer interface rather than an IP address, as shown in Example 2-6.

Example 2-6 Configuring a Static Default Route

```
ip route 0.0.0.0 0.0.0.0 Dialer1
```

Configuring PPPoA CPE

Cisco routers support three types of PPPoA connections:

- Cisco proprietary PPPoA
- The Internet Engineering Task Force (IETF)'s Multiplex (MUX)-encapsulated PPPoA
- The IETF's Logical Link Control (LLC)-encapsulated PPPoA

Configuring PPPoA involves almost the same tasks as configuring PPPoE. You still must set up the internal Ethernet interface, a dialer interface, PAT, DHCP, and a static default route. The main difference is in the configuration of the external interface. Because it is ATM, you need to configure virtual path identifier (VPI) and virtual circuit identifier (VCI) information to match that of the provider. The type of ATM encapsulation must be specified, and the PPPoA enabled, and linked to the virtual dialer interface. A dialer pool is associated with PVC, as shown in Example 2-7.

Example 2-7 Configuring the PPPoA ATM Interface

```
interface ATM1/0
 description DSL interface
 no ip address
 dsl operating-mode auto
 pvc 1/100
  encapsulation aal5mux ppp dialer
  dialer pool-member 1
```

Troubleshooting ADSL

When troubleshooting ADSL problems, start with checking Layer 1 physical connectivity. If that checks out okay, progress to checking Layer 2 connectivity. Finally, check Layer 3.

Troubleshooting ADSL at Layer 1

Try the following procedures when troubleshooting DSL physical layer problems:

1. Check for the carrier detect light on the router's ATM interface. If it is off, use the **show interfaces atm** *interface_number* command to check the interface status. If the interface status is down, try swapping out the RJ-11 cable connecting to the wall jack. The middle pins are used with ADSL signaling. If that doesn't work, contact the provider to make sure that the DSL service has been started.
2. If the interface status shown in the **show interfaces atm** command is "administratively down," enable the interface with the command **no shutdown**.
3. If there is a carrier detect light, check communication with the DSLAM. The subscriber DSL modem should *train* to the DSLAM. This allows them to negotiate settings such as speed. To verify this, use the **show dsl interface atm** *interface_number* command and look for the Modem Status field. It should say "Showtime." There should also be a nonzero value in the Speed field.
4. Check the DSL modulation type. Verify with the provider that your router's chipset is supported and find out what operating mode it should be in to support the correct modulation. Set this on the router with the command **dsl operating-mode** {**auto** | **ansi-dmt** | **itu-dmt** | **splitterless**}. If the modulation type is unknown, use the **auto** option.

Troubleshooting ADSL at Layer 2

If the interface status shows that it is up, and the line protocol is up, move to troubleshooting Layer 2 issues. Try the following to look for PVC or PPP problems:

1. Use the command **ping-atm-interface-atm** *interface_number vpi vci* **seg-loopback** to check that your PVC is configured on the next-hop ATM switch, which is typically the DSLAM. This command sends management traffic called Operation, Administration, and Maintenance (OAM) packets to the DSLAM. You should receive a normal ping response if the PVC is configured.

2. Debug the events occurring on the interface processor with the **debug atm events** command. This should show no output when everything is working well; when there are problems, however, it can show useful information such as the VPI/VCI number that the DSLAM expects. The ISCW course recommends beginning a continuous ping over the Internet (not over the internal network) to the router's IP address before giving this command.
3. Verify that the router is receiving data by using the **show interfaces atm** *interface_number* command. Look for packets input and output.
4. If the previous procedures show that everything is working, check for PPP problems. PPP should go through three phases: Link Control Protocol (LCP) negotiation, authentication, and Network Control Protocol (NCP) negotiation. The IP address is assigned by IPCP during the NCP phase. Use the commands **debug ppp negotiation** and **debug ppp authentication** to see whether there is a failure at any of these phases.

   When debugging PPP, look first for a lack of response from the aggregation router. If data link parameters cannot be negotiated, LCP will not open. If the authentication parameters are incorrectly configured, CHAP authentication will fail. If IPCP fails, the IP parameters are likely configured incorrectly either on the CPE or on the aggregation router.

CHAPTER 3

Frame Mode MPLS

Multiprotocol Label Switching (MPLS) is a technology that provides any-to-any connectivity between remote sites, using only a single WAN connection per site. The "magic" to MPLS is done in the WAN provider's network where traffic is switched from hop to hop, rather than routed. MPLS tunnels each company's traffic through the provider's network, providing an extra level of separation and security. Some large companies set up their own private MPLS networks, but most rely on the provider. Most companies just connect their WAN edge routers to a provider MPLS edge router and have no MPLS configuration on their own routers at all.

The destination IP network usually determines the path between sites, but MPLS allows other considerations to influence the path, such as the following:

- Virtual private network (VPN) destination
- Quality of service (QoS) settings
- Source address
- Outbound interface
- Layer 2 circuit

Having path-selection options other than IP route enables MPLS to support non-IP protocols. MPLS uses labels that are read and acted upon at Layer 2 to indicate the selected path. MPLS routers remove the received label and insert a new label before the packet is forwarded to the next hop.

Cisco Express Forwarding

MPLS relies on Cisco Express Forwarding (CEF) to indicate the next hop for a packet to use. Cisco routers can use three types of packet switching:

- **Process switching**—The CPU must be interrupted and a route table lookup done for every packet. This is the slowest type of switching.
- **Fast switching**—A route table lookup is done only for the first packet in a flow. The next-hop information, including the Layer 2 header, is cached and used for the remainder of the packets in the flow. Faster than process switching.
- **CEF switching**—The router builds tables of next-hop and Layer 2 information before any traffic is received. This is the fastest type of switching.

CEF takes information from the IP routing table and builds its own table, the Forwarding Information Base (FIB). Because the CEF table is based on the routing table, any route changes are immediately reflected in it. CEF also builds an adjacency table, which contains the Layer 2 header for each next-hop neighbor. When a packet needs to be forwarded through the router, CEF can usually do all the processing in hardware, making it extremely fast. With MPLS, an extra field with label information is added to the FIB.

MPLS Routers

MPLS defines two roles for routers. A *Label Switch Router* (LSR) has all its interfaces within the MPLS network and does its path selection primarily based on labels. An *Edge LSR* has some interfaces in the MPLS network and some in a normal IP network, and so does some routing and some label switching. An LSR is sometimes referred to as a *provider* (P) router, and the edge LSR as a *provider edge* (PE) router.

LSRs function at two planes, the control plane and the data plane. The control plane handles routing protocols and a label-exchange protocol called Label Distribution Protocol (LDP). It contains the routing table and the Label Information Base (LIB). The data plane contains the CEF FIB and adjacency table and the MPLS Label FIB (LFIB); it forwards traffic based on those. Figure 3-1 shows the functions at each plane.

Figure 3-1 Functions of the Control and Data Planes on an LSR

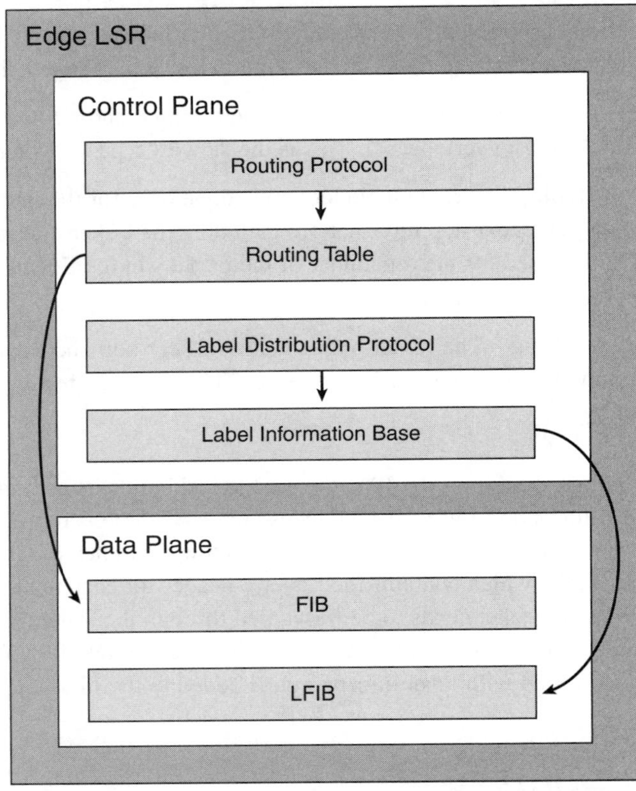

Figure 3-1 shows an edge LSR, which does both routing and label switching. Four forwarding scenarios could occur in this router:

- An unlabeled IP packet is received and is forwarded unlabeled to a next hop in the IP network.
- An unlabeled IP packet is received, a label is imposed, and it is forwarded to a next hop in the MPLS network.
- A labeled packet is received, the label is swapped, and it is forwarded to a next hop in the MPLS network.
- A labeled packet is received, the label is removed, and it is sent as an unlabeled, regular IP packet.

MPLS Labels

MPLS has two modes: Cell mode and Frame mode. Cell mode is used with ATM, and the virtual path identifier / virtual circuit identifier (VPI/VCI) values are used as the MPLS label. Frame mode is used with any Layer 2 protocol that uses frames and inserts a 32-bit label between the Layer 2 and Layer 3 headers. MPLS routers can do one of three things with a label. They can *impose* a label, which means they insert it into the header. They can *swap* a label, which means they remove one label and replace it with another. Or they can *pop* a label, which means they remove the label. Figure 3-2 shows the structure of an MPLS label.

Figure 3-2 MPLS Label

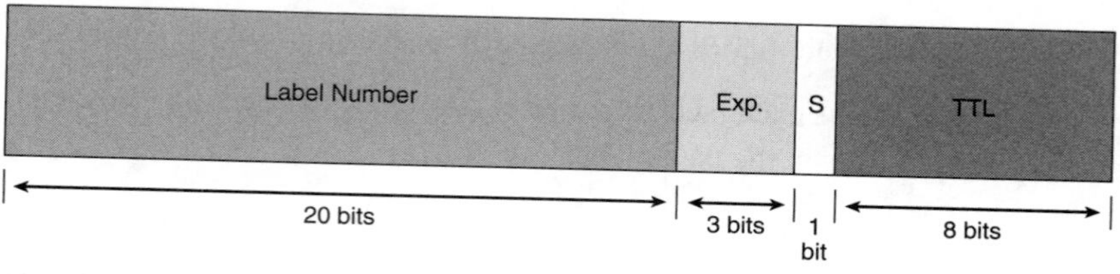

The label's Number field is 20 bits, the 3 Experimental bits are used to indicate IP precedence, the 1-bit Bottom of the Stack field indicates whether this is the last label, and the last 8-bit field indicates a Time to Live value. Multiple labels can be imposed, such as when using an MPLS VPN, MPLS traffic engineering, or a combination of the two. Each LSR only acts based on the top label.

Special Ethertypes are used in an Ethernet header to indicate that an MPLS label follows, including

- **0x8847**—Indicates a unicast labeled IP packet
- **0x8848**—Indicates a multicast labeled IP packet

Label Distribution and Label Tables

Routers send label information to each other using LDP, but they must first have a route to a network before creating a label for it. The process has four steps:

Step 1. Routing protocols distribute route information. The routing table and CEF FIB are built based on this information.

Step 2. The LSR assigns a locally significant label to each destination network. This is recorded in the LIB table. Label values 0 through 15 are reserved for special use.

Step 3. Each LSR sends the local label for each network to its neighbors via LDP. This is done asynchronously—a router does not wait to receive a label from its downstream router before advertising its own label. Labels are advertised to every neighbor, even the one chosen as the next hop for that network.

Step 4. The LSR records label information received from its neighbors in its LIB, FIB, and LFIB.

Each forwarding table is used as follows:

- The LIB lists each IP network, the local label for that network, and any labels received from neighbors for that network. It is in the control plane.
- The FIB is used to forward unlabeled IP packets. It is in the data plane.
- The LFIB lists each label, what label to swap it for, and the next-hop neighbor. It is in the data plane.

Penultimate Hop Popping

The LSR directly connected to a destination network (typically the PE router) is referred to as the *ultimate hop* for that network. The router right before it is the *penultimate hop* for that network. The directly connected LSR can advertise a label value of 3 for that destination network. Label 3 tells the neighbor router to pop the label before forwarding the packet—referred to as *penultimate hop popping* (PHP). This is recorded in the neighbor's FIBs as a null label.

PHP saves time and work for the PE LSR. Without it, the PE router would have to do an LFIB lookup, remove the top label, and then do a FIB lookup. With PHP, it only needs to do the FIB lookup, which helps optimize MPLS performance.

Figure 3-3 puts all these concepts together to show how MPLS routers use labels and each of the tables to forward traffic.

Figure 3-3 MPLS Packet Forwarding

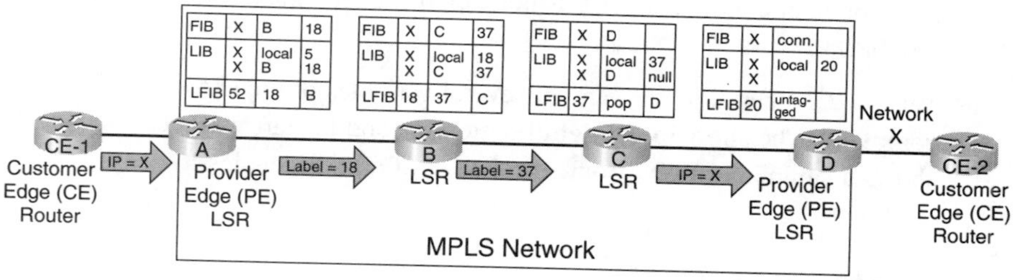

In Figure 3-3, router CE-1 forwards a packet destined for network X, which is directly connected to LSR D. LSR A receives it as an IP packet, does a FIB lookup, and imposes the label of 18. This is the value that LSR B advertised to it for network X. It forwards the labeled packet to LSR B.

LSR B receives the labeled packet, does and an LFIB lookup, and swaps the labels. It forwards the packet to LSR C with a label of 37, the label value advertised by C for network X.

LSR C receives the labeled packet and does an LFIB lookup. It sees that it must pop the label before forwarding the packet to the next hop, router D. When the label is popped, there are no other labels, so the packet is forwarded to LSR D as an IP packet.

The packet is addressed to the WAN interface of CE-2, so LSR D forwards it as an IP packet to CE-2.

Configuring Frame Mode MPLS

Three steps are required to configure a router to run MPLS:

Step 1. Enable CEF.

Step 2. Enable MPLS on the desired interfaces.

Step 3. Optionally adjust the interface maximum transmission units (MTU).

This following subsections examine each of these steps more closely.

Enabling CEF

CEF can be enabled either for all interfaces or on individual interfaces only. If it is not already enabled by default, use the global command **ip cef** [**distributed**] to enable it on all interface. The **distributed** keyword is used to enable distributed CEF on line cards or processors capable of running it.

To enable CEF on an individual interface, use the **ip route-cache cef** interface command. Note that CEF is not supported on logical interfaces, such as loopbacks.

Verify CEF operation with any of several variables of the **show ip cef** command. The **show ip cef detail** option is good to start with because it shows a summary of CEF routes and a list of all adjacencies.

Enabling MPLS

MPLS is globally enabled by default on Cisco routers. If it has been disabled, enable it with the global command **mpls ip**. It must then be enabled on each interface that will participate in label switching; enable it with the interface command **mpls ip**.

LDP is the default label distribution protocol in Cisco IOS Release 12.4(3) and later. There is an older Cisco prestandard version called Tag Distribution Protocol (TDP.) You might need to enable it if you are connecting to a Cisco router that does not support LDP; if you need to specify the protocol, use the interface command **mpls label protocol** [**tdp** | **ldp** | **both**]. Both protocols can run on the same router, and even on the same interface. In some Cisco IOS versions, MPLS commands show in the running configuration as "tag-switching" commands.

Increasing the MTU Size

The MPLS Frame mode tag adds 4 bytes to every frame. You might need to increase the interface MTU size to accommodate this, to prevent packets from being fragmented. The MTU is automatically increased on WAN interfaces, but must be manually configured on LAN interfaces.

Ethernet uses a default MTU of 1500 bytes. If you are using an MPLS implementation that uses just one label, increase it to 1504 bytes. MPLS VPNs and MPLS traffic engineering (TE) use two labels, so you must increase the MTU size to 1508 bytes if you are using either of these. Increase the MTU to 1512 bytes when using MPLS VPNs with TE, to accommodate three headers.

To manually set MTU size, use the **mpls mtu** *bytes* command in interface configuration mode. You may also need to enable jumbo frame support on the connecting switch.

MPLS VPNs

There are two basic types of VPNs: overlay and peer to peer. In an overlay VPN, the service provider sets up the connections. Frame Relay permanent virtual circuits (PVC) are an example of an overlay VPN. The service provider does not participate in the customer's routing when using an overlay VPN. In a peer-to-peer VPN, the service provider transports the customer's routes across its network. Only one circuit per customer site is required, but the service provider is required to have knowledge of each customer's routes. Customers may be required to re-IP address their networks, depending on whether the provider uses a dedicated or a shared PE router. In addition, there is no separation of customer routes.

MPLS VPNs provide the advantages of both types and minimize their drawbacks. They provide the following:

- The service provider participates in customer routing, thus providing optimum paths through the provider network.
- Each customer's routes are kept separate from other customers' routes.
- Overlapping IP addresses are permitted, so customers do not have to renumber.

MPLS VPNs use a two-label stack. In a traditional VPN, the IP header is hidden by a tunnel IP header. In an MPLS VPN, the label identifying the interface to the customer router is hidden by a label identifying the PE router connected to that customer. MPLS switching through the provider network is based on the top label until it reaches the edge (or *egress*) router. The top label is popped, and the egress router reads the second label to learn where to send that traffic. PHP can be used with MPLS VPNs. If so, the PE router can use the second label to identify the VPN customer and do a route lookup based on it. Otherwise, the PE router must do two lookups.

Handling Customer Routes

MPLS PE routers use a separate virtual routing instance for each customer, called a Virtual Routing and Forwarding (VRF) table. Each customer router advertises its routes to its PE router. C routers can use a standard routing protocol to advertise their routes. The PE router looks like any other neighbor to the C router. Because VRFs must be configured on the PE router, the routing protocol needs to support them. EIGRP, OSPF, RIPv2, BGP, and static routing support VRFs.

C routes are then advertised via Multiprotocol BGP (MP-BGP) to other PE routers participating in that VRF. BGP runs only between the edge routers; internal P routers use an Interior Gateway Protocol (IGP) such as OSPF or EIGRP to tell them how to reach the PE routers. P routers have no knowledge of customer routes. Thus, PE routers do the following types of routing:

- IGP, BGP, or static routing with its customer routers to exchange IPv4 routes
- MP-BGP with its peer PE routers to exchange VPNv4 routes
- IGP with its neighboring P routers to exchange core network routes

Route Distinguishers

To support customers with overlapping IP address space, MPLS providers use route distinguishers (RD). An RD is a 64-bit prefix added to each customer's IP address to make it globally unique. The resulting 96-bit IP address is called a *VPNv4 address*.

RDs are used to propagate routes across provider networks in the following way:

Step 1. A C router advertises its normal IPv4 networks to the PE router.

Step 2. The PE router prepends the RD to the C networks to create VPNv4 addresses.

Step 3. The PE router advertises the VPNv4 addresses to its MP-BGP peers.

Step 4. Other PE routers strip the RD from the network address and advertise the route to C routers in the same VRF.

Note
The RD is used only within the MPLS network and only to create a globally unique address. C routers never see the RD and are not aware of their VPNv4 address.

Route Targets

Sometimes, customer sites need to participate in more than one MPLS VPN. Export and import route targets (RT) are attributes attached to BGP routes to indicate which VPNs the route belongs to. This allows the creation of complex topologies with overlapping VPNs:

- **Export RT**—Attached to routes when they are imported into the VRF database to identify the VPNs to which the route belongs. These routes are then advertised to other PE routers.
- **Import RT**—Used by the PE router receiving the routes to identify which VRFs should receive the routes. VRFs with an import RT matching the route's RT will import the route. These networks are then installed in the VRF table and advertised to the appropriate customer routers.

CHAPTER 4

IPsec

IP Security, or IPsec, is a set of rules for securing data communications across a public, untrusted network such as the Internet. It provides the following:

- Data confidentiality by encrypting portions of a packet
- Data integrity by ensuring the packet has not been altered in transit
- Data source authentication to ensure that the data originated with a trusted source
- Anti-replay protection to ensure that packets are not copied and sent

IPsec standards do not specify exactly how packets should be encrypted or authenticated; it relies on other protocols to accomplish those functions. For encryption, it can use Data Encryption Standard (DES), Triple Data Encryption Standard (3DES), and Advanced Encryption Standard (AES). For authentication, it can use Hash-based Message Authentication Codes (HMAC). An HMAC combines a hash function such as Message Digest 5 (MD5) and Secure Hash Algorithm 1 (SHA-1) with a shared secret key. MD5 uses a 128-bit hash, whereas SHA-1 uses a 160-bit hash. Only 96 bits of the SHA-1 hash are used with IPsec, however.

IPsec Headers

IPsec defines two types of headers: Authentication Header and Encapsulating Security Payload.

Authentication Header

Authentication Header (AH) is IP protocol number 51. It authenticates the packet, including the IP header, but does not encrypt the packet payload. AH works by creating an MD5 or SHA-1 hash from the IP header (except any changeable fields such as Time to Live) and the packet payload. It sends this hash in an AH header after the Layer 3 IP header. The receiving host also creates a hash value from the IP header and original payload and compares the two hashes. If they match, the packet was unchanged during transit. A shared key is used to create the hashes, so a match also serves to authenticate the source of the packet. AH is rarely used without ESP.

Encapsulating Security Payload

Encapsulating Security Payload (ESP), IP protocol number 50, encrypts packet payloads and can optionally authenticate and do integrity checks by using it with AH. It adds a header and a trailer to the packet. When used with AH, the packet is encrypted first and then put through the hash mechanism.

IPsec Modes

IPsec can operate in either Transport mode or Tunnel mode. The headers differ based on the mode used:

- Transport mode IPsec uses the original IP header. The data payload can be encrypted, and the packet can be authenticated from the ESP header back. Transport mode is often used with generic routing encapsulation (GRE) tunnels, because GRE hides the original IP address.
- Tunnel mode IPsec replaces the original IP header with a tunnel header. The ESP header is placed after the new header, before the original one. The original IP header can be encrypted along with the data payload, and the packet can be authenticated from the ESP header back. Tunnel mode adds about 20 bytes to the packet.

Figure 4-1 shows the packet headers in the two IPsec modes.

Figure 4-1 Transport Mode Versus Tunnel Mode IPsec

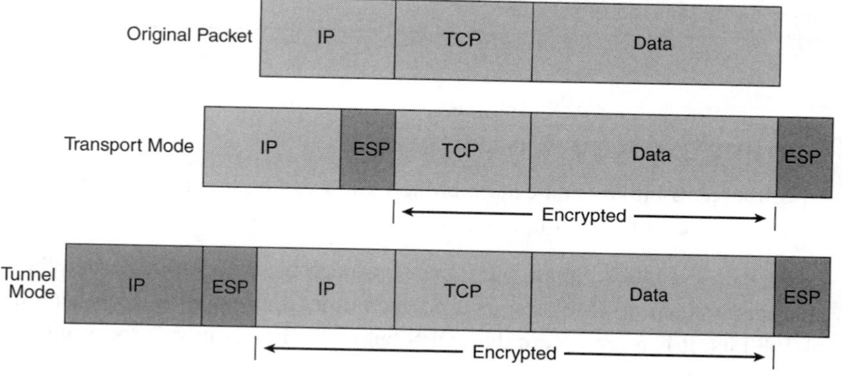

Tunnel mode ESP can cause problems when used with Network Address Translation (NAT). The original TCP or UDP header is encrypted and hidden, so there are no Layer 4 port numbers for NAT to use. *NAT Traversal* detects the existence of a NAT device and adds a UDP header after the tunnel IP header. NAT can then use the port number in that UDP header.

Authentication Methods

Several authentication methods are supported with IPsec virtual private networks (VPN):

- Username and password
- A one-time password
- Biometric features, such as fingerprint
- Preshared key values
- Digital certificates

Encryption Methods

IPsec encryption uses key values to encrypt and decrypt data. Keys can be either symmetric or asymmetric. Symmetric keys use the same value to both encrypt and decrypt the data. These include DES, 3DES, and AES. Asymmetric keys use one value to encrypt the data and another one to decrypt it. Diffie-Hellman and RSA use asymmetric keys.

Note

RSA is not an acronym—it is the initials of the last names of the algorithm's inventors: Ron Rivest, Adi Shamir, and Len Adleman.

Symmetric Key Algorithms

DES uses a 56-bit key and can be broken fairly easily. It is a block cipher—it encrypts 64-bit blocks of data at a time.

3DES is also a block cipher, but it encrypts each block, decrypts it, and then encrypts it again. A 56-bit key is used each time, thus equaling a key length of 168 bits. It is more secure than DES but also requires more processing power.

AES is a stronger block cipher encryption method than DES or 3DES. It uses a 128-bit data block and a key length of 128, 192, or 256 bits. AES has been approved for use with government classified data.

Asymmetric Key Algorithm

RSA uses asymmetric keys and can be used for signing messages and encrypting them. A public key is used to encrypt or sign the data. It can only be decrypted with a private key held by the receiver. RSA is slower than symmetrical key algorithms, but more secure if a large enough key is used. A key length of 2048 bits is recommended.

Diffie-Hellman Key Exchange

The Diffie-Hellman protocol solves the problem of exchanging keys over an insecure network. Each device creates a public key and a private key. They exchange their public keys in the open, unencrypted. They each then use the other device's public key and their own private key to generate a shared secret key that each will use.

Key Management

The Public Key Infrastructure (PKI) manages encryption and identity information such as public keys and certificates. It consists of the following components:

- Peer devices that need to communicate securely.
- Digital certificates that validate the peer's identity and transmit their public key.
- Certificate authorities (CA), also known as *trustpoints*, that grant, manage, and revoke certificates. This could be a third-party CA or an internal one. Cisco has a Cisco IOS Certificate Server.
- Optional registration authorities (RA) that handle certificate enrollment requests.
- A way to distribute Certificate Revocation Lists (CRL), such as HTTP or Lightweight Directory Access Protocol (LDAP).

PKI credentials, such as RSA keys and digital certificates, can be stored in a router's nonvolatile random-access memory (NVRAM). They can also be stored in USB eTokens on routers that support them.

Establishing an IPsec VPN

When IPsec establishes a VPN between two peer hosts, it sets up a security association (SA) between them. SAs are unidirectional, so each bidirectional data session requires two. The Internet Security Association and Key Management Protocol (ISAKMP) defines how SAs are created and deleted. There are five basic steps:

Step 1. Interesting traffic arrives at the router—"Interesting" traffic is that which should be sent over the VPN. This is specified by a crypto access list. Any traffic not identified as "interesting" is sent in the clear, unprotected.

Step 2. Internet Key Exchange (IKE) Phase 1—Negotiates the algorithms and hashes to use, authenticates the peers, and sets up an ISAKMP SA. Has two modes: Main and Aggressive. Main mode uses three exchanges during Phase 1. Aggressive mode sends all the information in one exchange. The proposed settings are contained in transform sets, which list the proposed encryption algorithm, authentication algorithm, key length, and mode. Multiple transform sets can be specified, but both peers must have at least one matching transform set; otherwise, the session is torn down.

Step 3. IKE Phase 2—Uses the secure communication channel created in Phase 1 to set up the SAs for ESP/AH, negotiating the SA parameters and settings to be used to protect the data transmitted. Periodically renegotiates the SAs. SAs have lifetimes that can be measured in either amount of data transferred or length of time. May do an additional Diffie-Hellman key exchange during Phase 2.

Step 4. Data is transferred along the VPN between the two peers. It is encrypted by one peer and decrypted by the other, according to the transform sets negotiated.

Step 5. Tunnel termination—the IPsec session drops either because of direct termination or timeout.

Configuring a Site-to-Site VPN Using Cisco IOS Commands

Configuring a site-to-site IPsec VPN using Cisco IOS commands requires six steps, as follows:

Step 1. Configure the ISAKMP policy.

Step 2. Configure the IPsec transform set or sets.

Step 3. Configure a crypto access control list (ACL).

Step 4. Configure a crypto map.

Step 5. Apply the crypto map to the outgoing interface.

Step 6. Optionally configure and apply an ACL that permits only IPsec or IKE traffic.

Configuring an ISAKMP Policy

To configure an ISAKMP policy, first create the policy, and then give the parameters. These parameters might include such things as type of encryption, type of hash, type of authentication, SA lifetime, and Diffie-Hellman group. The following example shows an ISAKMP policy configuration, along with the options available with each parameter. Options will vary based on Cisco IOS version:

```
IPSEC_RTR(config)#crypto isakmp policy ?
 <1-10000> Priority of protection suite
IPSEC_RTR(config)#crypto isakmp policy 1
!
IPSEC_RTR(config-isakmp)#encryption ?
 3des Three key triple DES
 aes  AES - Advanced Encryption Standard.
 des  DES - Data Encryption Standard (56 bit keys).
IPSEC_RTR(config-isakmp)#encryption 3des
!
IPSEC_RTR(config-isakmp)#hash ?
 md5 Message Digest 5
 sha Secure Hash Standard
IPSEC_RTR(config-isakmp)#hash sha
!
IPSEC_RTR(config-isakmp)#authentication ?
 pre-share Pre-Shared Key
 rsa-encr  Rivest-Shamir-Adleman Encryption
 rsa-sig  Rivest-Shamir-Adleman Signature
IPSEC_RTR(config-isakmp)#authentication pre-share
!
IPSEC_RTR(config-isakmp)#group ?
 1 Diffie-Hellman group 1
 2 Diffie-Hellman group 2
 5 Diffie-Hellman group 5
IPSEC_RTR(config-isakmp)#group 2
```

CCNP ISCW

```
IPSEC_RTR(config-isakmp)#lifetime ?
 <60-86400> lifetime in seconds
IPSEC_RTR(config-isakmp)#lifetime 300
```

Configuring an IPsec Transform Set

An IPsec transform set defines how VPN data will be protected by specifying the IPsec protocols that will be used. You can specify up to four transforms and the algorithm to use with each. You can also configure either Tunnel or Transport mode (Tunnel is default). Transforms include combinations of the following:

- AH with either MD5 or SHA-1
- ESP encryption using DES, 3DES, AES, or others
- ESP authentication using MD5 or SHA-1
- Compression using the Lempel-Ziv-Stac (LZS) algorithm

The following example shows a transform set with ESP encryption and authentication. Note that these commands are all given as part of the same command:

```
IPSEC_RTR#conf t
Enter configuration commands, one per line. End with CNTL/Z.
IPSEC_RTR(config)#crypto ipsec transform-set TRANSFORM1 esp-aes
  192 esp-md5-hmac
```

Configuring a Crypto ACL

You use a crypto ACL to identify traffic that should be protected by the IPsec VPN. Any traffic permitted in the ACL will be sent over the VPN. Traffic denied by the ACL will not be dropped—it will just be sent normally.

The following example shows a crypto ACL that permits traffic from two internal networks—172.16.1.0 and 172.16.4.0—if it is bound to the server network of 10.6.3.0.

Note
When configuring the crypto ACL on the router at the other end of the tunnel, be sure to reverse the source and destination IP addresses.

```
IPSEC_RTR(config)access-list 172 permit ip 172.16.1.0 0.0.0.255
  10.6.3.0 0.0.0.255
IPSEC_RTR(config)access-list 172 permit ip 172.16.4.0 0.0.0.255
  10.6.3.0 0.0.0.255
```

CCNP ISCW

Configuring a Crypto Map

A crypto map pulls together the transform sets and crypto ACLs and associates them with a remote peer. A sequence number can be used when configuring a crypto map. Multiple crypto maps with the same name but different sequence numbers form a crypto map set. Traffic is evaluated against each crypto map depending on its sequence number to see whether it should be protected. This permits more complex and granular traffic filtering.

The following example shows a crypto map that links the transform set and ACL configured in previous examples:

```
IPSEC_RTR(config)#crypto map TO_SERVERS 10 ipsec-isakmp
% NOTE: This new crypto map will remain disabled until a peer
    and a valid access list have been configured.
IPSEC_RTR(config-crypto-map)#set peer 10.1.1.1
IPSEC_RTR(config-crypto-map)#match address 172
IPSEC_RTR(config-crypto-map)#set transform-set TRANSFORM1
```

Applying the Crypto Map to an Interface

After the crypto map has been configured, it must be applied to an interface for it to take effect. It is applied at the *outgoing* interface—the one that VPN traffic will use to reach the other end of the VPN. You might need to use a static route or otherwise adjust your routing to force traffic bound for the VPN destination networks to use the correct outgoing interface.

The following example shows the crypto map TO_SERVERS applied to interface serial 0/0/0. Note that the router replies with a message that ISAKMP is now enabled:

```
IPSEC_RTR(config)#int s0/0/0
IPSEC_RTR(config-if)#crypto map TO_SERVERS
IPSEC_RTR(config-if)#
01:19:16: %CRYPTO-6-ISAKMP_ON_OFF: ISAKMP is ON
```


Configuring an Optional Interface Access List

You might want to have an interface ACL on the VPN interface. Typically, you would permit only IPsec-related traffic, and perhaps routing protocol traffic, in and out that interface. Keep in mind the following port numbers when configuring the ACL:

- ESP is IP protocol 50.
- AH is IP protocol 51.

- IKE uses UDP port 500.
- NAT Traversal uses UDP port 4500.

The source and destination addresses should be the IP addresses of the outgoing VPN interfaces. The following example shows an ACL that permits IPsec traffic between two hosts:

```
IPSEC_RTR(config)#access-list 101 permit ahp host 10.1.1.2 host
  10.1.1.1
IPSEC_RTR(config)#access-list 101 permit esp host 10.1.1.2 host
  10.1.1.1
IPSEC_RTR(config)#access-list 101 permit udp host 10.1.1.2 eq
  isakmp host 10.1.1.2
IPSEC_RTR(config)#access-list 101 permit udp host 10.1.1.2 host
  10.1.1.2 eq isakmp
!
IPSEC_RTR(config)#interface s 0/0/0
IPSEC_RTR(config-if)#ip address 10.1.1.2 255.255.255.252
IPSEC_RTR(config-if)#ip access-group 101 out
```

Configuring a Site-to-Site VPN Using SDM

Cisco Security Device Manager (SDM) provides a graphical user interface (GUI) for configuring and monitoring your routers. It has wizards to simplify common tasks and is designed to allow small to medium-size businesses to easily deploy their routers. It comes with 800 to 3800 series routers at no extra charge. You can use the SDM to configure site-to-site VPNs, among other things.

The VPN Wizard comes with two IKE policies and an IPsec transform set. It also has a way for you to enter information manually and edit configurations created by the wizard.

The Quick Setup Wizard requires just one screen. On it, you enter the following information:

- Outgoing interface
- Peer IP address
- Authentication information
- What traffic to encrypt

SDM then shows you a recap of the configuration. You click the **Finish** button to apply it.

You can also use the Step-by-step Setup Wizard, which leads you through each of the tasks separately, letting you have more control over the settings. It also lets you review the completed configuration before applying it.

When the configuration is complete for one side of the tunnel, you can click the **Generate Mirror** button to generate a configuration for the router on the other side of the tunnel. When both routers are configured, the **Test Tunnel** button lets you verify that it is working. There is also a tab to monitor the VPN tunnel status.

Monitoring and Troubleshooting IPsec VPNs

Some useful Cisco IOS commands for monitoring your IPsec VPNs include the following:

- **show crypto isakmp sa**—This command shows all the IKE SAs currently active on the router. Look for a status of QM_IDLE to verify that the SA is active.
- **show crypto ipsec sa**—This command shows the parameters used by each SA and shows traffic flow. Look for the count of packets being encrypted and decrypted, to verify the VPNs operation.

To troubleshoot VPN problems, first verify IP connectivity. If that exists, review your configuration one more time. If the configuration looks correct on both peers, you can view detailed information about the IKE negotiations by using the command **debug crypto isakmp**.

Using GRE with IPsec

GRE is a tunneling protocol that can support multiple Layer 3 protocols, such as IP, IPX, and AppleTalk. It also allows the use of multicast routing protocols across the tunnel. It adds a 20-byte IP header and a 4-byte GRE header, hiding the existing packet headers. The GRE header contains a Flag field, and a Protocol Type field to identify the Layer 3 protocol being transported. It may optionally contain a tunnel checksum, tunnel key, and tunnel sequence number. GRE does not encrypt traffic or use any strong security measures to protect the traffic.

GRE can be used along with IPsec to provide data source authentication, data confidentiality, and assurance of data integrity. GRE over IPsec tunnels are typically configured in a hub-and-spoke topology over an untrusted WAN to minimize the number of tunnels that each router must maintain.

Figure 4-2 shows how the GRE and IPsec headers work together.

Figure 4-2 GRE over IPsec Headers

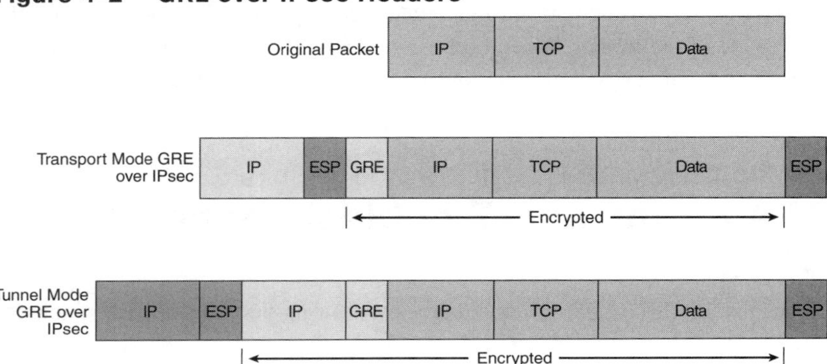

Configuring a GRE Tunnel Using Cisco IOS Commands

To configure GRE using Cisco IOS commands, you must first configure a logical tunnel interface. GRE commands are then given under that interface. You must specify a source and destination for the tunnel; the source is a local outgoing interface. You may also give the tunnel interface an IP address and specify the Tunnel mode. GRE is the default mode.

The following example shows a tunnel interface configured for GRE. The **mode** command is shown only as a reference—because it is the default, it would not normally appear in the configuration:

```
interface Tunnel1
 ip address 172.16.5.2 255.255.255.0
 tunnel source Serial0/0
 tunnel destination 10.1.1.1
 tunnel mode gre ip
```

Configuring a GRE over IPsec Tunnel Using the SDM

The Site-to-Site VPN Wizard has an option for configuring a GRE over IPsec VPN. It leads you through creating the tunnel interface and specifying the parameters such as tunnel source and destination and interface IP address. The wizard also leads you through creating an optional backup GRE tunnel in case the primary one goes down.

Next, the IPsec parameters are presented. The wizard walks you through creating an IKE policy and transform set. You can either use the ones included with SDM or create new ones through the wizard.

You then have the option of configuring either static routing or the dynamic routing protocols Enhanced Interior Gateway Routing Protocol (EIGRP) or Open Shortest Path First (OSPF).

As before, the wizard shows a summary of the VPN configuration so that you can review it before applying it by clicking **Finish**. You can test the tunnel and monitor its status through SDM. Use the same **show crypto** and **debug** commands shown earlier to verify and troubleshoot the VPN. In addition, the **show interfaces** command shows the status of the logical tunnel interface as the physical outgoing interface.

High-Availability VPNs

Four typical types of failures that affect a VPN, and ways to mitigate them, are as follows:

- **Failure of an access link**—Use multiple links to mitigate an access link failure.
- **Failure of a remote IPsec peer**—Use multiple peers to mitigate a remote peer failure.
- **Failure of a VPN device**—Use multiple devices in critical locations to mitigate a device failure.
- **Failure someplace along the Internet path**—Provide multiple independent paths to mitigate a path failure.

Routers can use a routing protocol or IPsec's Dead Peer Detection (DPD) to detect a failure across a VPN. Hot Standby Routing Protocol (HSRP), Virtual Router Redundancy Protocol (VRRP), and Gateway Load Balancing Protocol (GLBP) can detect local failures.

Detecting a Failure Using DPD

DPD sends periodic keepalives to its remote peer (similar to an older proprietary Cisco IOS method called IKE Keepalives). Periodic keepalives help routers quickly detect the failure of a remote peer, but they also mean more packets to encrypt and decrypt. DPD has an on-demand option. If the router needs to send traffic and has not received anything from the peer recently, it sends a DPD message to verify the peer's status. No messages are sent if there is no traffic.

You can configure multiple peers in a crypto map. Then, if DPD discovers that the primary peer (designated by the **default** keyword) is down, IPsec removes any SAs associated with that peer. It can then fail over to the backup peer listed in the crypto map. Configure the router to use DPD with the command **crypto isakmp keepalive** *seconds* [*retries*] [**periodic** | **on-demand**]. The **periodic** option causes the router to use keepalives, whereas the **on-demand** option causes it to use on-demand DPD. If neither option is specified, the IPsec peers negotiate the type of DPD.

Detecting a Failure Using HSRP

HSRP, VRRP, and GLBP are all protocols that allow multiple routers to share a single IP address. They are typically used for default gateway redundancy on a local LAN. You can also use these protocols on a WAN-facing interface. They use the shared, or virtual, IP address as the peer address for IPsec. Then, if the physical router fails, one of the other routers in the group takes over. The IPsec tunnel drops and is then reestablished using the same peer IP address but a new physical router.

HSRP defines an *active* and a *standby* router, which form a *standby group*. The active router answers traffic to the virtual IP address. If it fails, the standby router takes over. HSRP routers share a virtual MAC address, too. Determining the return path to a remote site can be a problem when using HSRP at the headend. Either additionally configure HSRP on the internal interfaces of the routers, or use Reverse Path Injection (RRI). RRI injects remote networks into the internal routing protocol and is enabled with the command **reverse-route** in a crypto map.

Using IPsec Stateful Failover

DPD, routing protocols, and HSRP provide stateless failover—the tunnel drops and must be re-created if a peer fails. Stateful failover maintains SA information between an active and a failover device. It depends on two protocols:

- **HSRP**—Tracks both the inside and outside interfaces. If either goes down, it removes the router from active status, and ownership of the IPsec and IKE SAs passes to the standby router.

- **Stateful Switchover (SSO)**—Synchronizes IPsec state information between the active and standby HSRP routers using Stream Control Transmission Protocol (SCTP) and Inter-Process Communication (IPC) protocol.

For stateful failover to work, you must configure HSRP, use the virtual IP address in the IPsec peering, and configure SSO. The following example shows this configuration on one router. The configuration must be duplicated exactly on the other router; both routers must use the same Cisco IOS version and must be connected via a switch or hub:

```
Crypto map configuration
crypto dynamic-map VPN1 10
 set peer 10.1.1.1
 set transform-set TRANSFORM1
 match address 172
 reverse-route
!
crypto map HAVPN 10 ipsec-isakmp dynamic VPN1
!
HSRP Configuration--must be done on both inside and outside
interfaces
interface FastEthernet0/0
 ip address 10.3.7.3 255.255.255.0
 standby 1 ip 10.3.7.1
 standby 1 preempt
 standby 1 name IPSEC1
 standby 1 track FastEthernet0/1
 crypto map HAVPN redundancy IPSEC1 stateful
!
SSO Configuration
redundancy inter-device
 scheme standby IPSEC1
!
IPC Configuration
ipc zone default
 association 1
 protocol sctp
 local-port 5555
  local-ip 10.3.7.3
  retransmit-timeout 300 10000
  path-retransmit 10
  assoc-retransmit 10
 remote-port 5555
  remote-ip 10.1.1.1
```

Using an IPsec Tunnel as a Backup WAN Link

You can configure an IPsec VPN tunnel over the Internet as a backup to your primary WAN link. Switchover can use either an IGP or HSRP. Ensure that the primary WAN link is used when it is available by either adjusting the routing protocol metric or using floating static routes.

Cisco Easy VPN

Easy VPN allows a server to push down VPN configuration to a client. It is a way to create site-to-site VPNs without manually configuring each remote router. Therefore, it is good for remote sites without technical support. It can also be used with software clients for remote users.

Cisco Easy VPN dynamically handles the following items:

- Negotiating VPN tunnel parameters
- Establishing the VPN tunnel based on those parameters
- NAT, PAT, or ACL configuration
- User authentication
- Managing encryption and decryption keys
- Authenticating, encrypting, and decrypting traffic

Cisco Easy VPN has two components: a server and a remote client. The *Easy VPN Server* can be a Cisco router, PIX firewall, or Cisco VPN concentrator. It contains security policies and pushes those to remote clients. The *Easy VPN Remote* can be a Cisco router, PIX or ASA firewall, or a hardware client or a software client. It contacts the server and receives policies from it to establish the tunnel.

Establishing an Easy VPN IPsec Session

The steps in establishing an IPsec session differ slightly when using Easy VPN. They are as follows:

Step 1. The remote client contacts the server and begins IKE Phase 1. If preshared keys are used, the client initiates Aggressive mode. If digital certificates are used, the client initiates Main mode.

Step 2. The remote client attempts to establish an ISAKMP SA with the server. It sends proposals with various combinations of hashes, authentication types, and Diffie-Hellman groups.

Step 3. The server finds a match to one of the client's proposals, accepts it, and establishes an ISAKMP SA. The device is now authenticated.

Step 4. When using Extended Authentication (XAuth), the server issues a username and password challenge. It checks the remote client's response against a RADIUS or TACACS+ authentication, authorization, and accounting (AAA) server, or uses tokens. The user is now authenticated.

Step 5. The server pushes configuration parameters to the device. At a minimum, this must include an IP address.

Step 6. RRI creates a static route to the remote client.

Step 7. IPsec Quick mode is used to negotiate an IPsec SA. When this is complete, the VPN is established.

Using SDM to Configure the Easy VPN Server

You can use SDM to create and configure an Easy VPN Server. Before beginning, decide on the IKE authentication method, the user authentication method, and the IP addressing scheme you will use. In addition, set up AAA servers or certification authority information, any needed DNS resolution for the Easy VPN servers, and Network Time Protocol if needed for key exchange. The tasks to create an Easy VPN server include the following:

- Create a privileged user.
- Configure an enable secret password.
- Enable the router to use the AAA server's database.
- Use the SDM's Easy VPN Wizard to configure the following:
  - The tunnel interface
  - IKE policies
  - RADIUS or TACACS+ policy lookup
  - User authentication
  - Local group policies
  - IPsec transform set

SDM enables you to test the configuration. In addition to crypto **show** commands mentioned earlier in this chapter, the following Cisco IOS commands help in verifying and troubleshooting your configuration:

- **debug crypto isakmp**—Shows IKE messages
- **debug aaa authentication**—Shows user authentication messages
- **debug aaa authorization**—Shows messages relating to group policy configuration
- **debug radius**—Shows RADIUS messages

Configuring the Cisco VPN Client

The Cisco VPN Client runs on a computer and communicates with an Easy VPN Server to create a VPN between the user and the server. Installing and configuring the Cisco VPN Client on a remote user's computer requires the following steps:

Step 1. Install the Cisco VPN Client software on the computer.

Step 2. Create at least one client connection entry. This includes configuring the IP address of the server and preshared keys or certificates. You can configure multiple connection entries, but only one can be used at a time.

Step 3. Configure authentication parameters such as group authentication, mutual group authentication, or certificate authentication.

Step 4. Configure transparent tunneling, which allows the tunnel to work through a router or firewall doing NAT or PAT. Access to local LAN resources, and the use of IPsec over UDP or TCP, can also be enabled here.

Step 5. Optionally add backup VPN servers.

Step 6. Configure the Internet connection. This can be either through a home LAN, or through dialup using Microsoft Dial-Up Networking or a local ISP.

CHAPTER 5

Cisco Device Hardening

Because of their important role in packet forwarding, Cisco routers make attractive targets for network attacks. This chapter reviews how to harden Cisco devices against the most common types of attacks.

Mitigating Network Attacks

Before starting to harden Cisco devices against attack, you need to understand the types of attacks that are in common use today.

Cisco Self-Defending Network

The Cisco Self-Defending Network strategy consists of three interrelated components:

- **Secure connectivity**—Virtual private network (VPN) solutions, including VPN-enabled routers, VPN concentrators, and VPN-enabled firewalls
- **Threat defense**—Cisco IOS-based and appliance-based firewalls
- **Trust and identity**—Network Access Control (NAC), Cisco Secure Access Control Server (ACS), and 802.1x

Types of Network Attacks

There are three major categories of network attacks:

- **Reconnaissance attacks**—In reconnaissance attacks, the intruder attempts to gain information about a network, typically in preparation for a more aggressive attack later. Methods used in reconnaissance attacks include ping sweeps, installation of packet sniffers to gather passwords and other sensitive information, port scans to discover vulnerable services, and Internet information queries (Domain Name System [DNS] records, Internet Assigned Numbers Authority [IANA] records, search engine queries, and so on).

- **Access attacks**—In access attacks, the intruder attempts to gain unauthorized access to a network. Methods used in access attacks include password cracking or guessing, trust exploitation, port redirection, man-in-the-middle (MitM) attacks, buffer overflows, and attacks against network applications
- **Denial-of-service (DoS) attacks**—In DoS attacks, the attacker tries to deny legitimate users access to a network resource. This might involve destruction of a compromised network system (such as erasing hard drives or operating system files) or just flooding the resource with more traffic than it can process. A DoS attack that is launched from a large number of hosts simultaneously is called a distributed DoS (DDoS) attack. These types of attacks are usually the most difficult to mitigate.

Mitigating Reconnaissance Attacks

You can mitigate reconnaissance attacks in several ways:

- **Firewall and intrusion prevention system (IPS)**—A firewall (either Cisco IOS based or appliance based) is an effective way to stop ping sweeps, port scans, and other network probes. An IPS can detect and sometimes take countermeasures against these probes.
- **Authentication**—Strong authentication is an effective way to defeat password sniffers. Use of two-factor authentication such as token cards makes it extremely difficult for an attacker to gather passwords with a packet sniffer because the password hashes expire continually.
- **Cryptography**—Even with strong authentication, an attacker with a packet sniffer could still gather other sensitive information on the network. Encrypting traffic with standards-based encryption protocols prevents this.
- **Antisniffer tools**—Several manufacturers offer tools designed to detect the presence of packet sniffers on a network.
- **Switched infrastructure**—By isolating collision domains to individual ports, switches make it more difficult for packet sniffers to find sensitive information. Advanced switch security tools such as DHCP inspection and dynamic Address Resolution Protocol (ARP) inspection add to this functionality.

Mitigating Access Attacks

You can mitigate access attacks as follows:

- **Strong password security**—A surprising number of access attacks are carried out through simple password-guessing or brute-force dictionary attacks against passwords. The use of encrypted or hashed authentication protocols (for instance, Secure Shell [SSH] for terminal access, TACACS+ for authentication, authorization, and accounting [AAA]) along with a strong password policy (requiring different passwords on different systems, locking out accounts after a string of unsuccessful attempts, and complex password requirements) greatly reduce the probability of password access attacks.
- **Principle of minimum trust**—Systems should not trust one another unnecessarily. A common trust exploitation attack occurs when an inside network host trusts a device in the demilitarized zone (DMZ). If an attacker is able to compromise the DMZ system, the DMZ system can be used as a stepping-stone to access and compromise the trusted internal system. Secure network designs take this into account by ensuring that inside systems do not trust DMZ systems unconditionally.
- **Cryptography**—The MitM attack, in which an attacker inserts himself between two trusted hosts and impersonates both to gather sensitive information, can be thwarted only by using cryptography in the communications channel between the trusted hosts.

Mitigating Denial-of-Service Attacks

DoS attacks are difficult to stop. Companies with a high-profile Internet presence should plan in advance their responses to potential DoS attacks. Historically, many DoS attacks were sourced from spoofed source addresses. These types of attacks can be thwarted through use of antispoofing access lists on border routers and firewalls. Today, however, many DoS attacks are carried out by distributed networks of real hosts that have been compromised for the purpose of building attack networks. Mitigating a large DoS or DDoS attack typically requires careful diagnostics, planning, and cooperation from Internet service providers (ISP).

Disabling Unused Cisco Router Network Services and Interfaces

In any network security strategy, you need to identify and deactivate services that are on by default but not actually used. This section discusses deactivating these services on Cisco routers.

Unused Router Interfaces

Attacks can exploit active, unused router interfaces to gain access to a router or to gather information about it. Disable unused router interfaces with the **shutdown** command.

Vulnerable Router Services

The following services have the potential to be exploited by attackers under certain conditions. If they are not required on a particular router, ensure that they are disabled. Remember, however, that many of these services perform important functions in some networks; they should only be disabled after considering the potential drawbacks of doing so:

- **BOOTP server**—Enabled by default. Disable with the **no ip bootp server** command.
- **Cisco Discovery Protocol (CDP)**—Enabled by default for most interface types. Disable on interfaces where not needed with the **no cdp enable** command.
- **Configuration auto-loading**—Disabled by default.
- **FTP/TFTP servers**—Disabled by default.
- **Network Time Protocol (NTP)**—Disabled by default, but necessary for many security features.
- **Packet assembler/disassembler (PAD) Service**—Enabled by default. Disable with the **no service pad** command.
- **TCP and UDP small servers**—For example, Echo, Chargen, Discard, Daytime. Disabled by default.
- **Maintenance Operations Protocol (MOP) service**—Enabled for some Ethernet interfaces by default.
- **Simple Network Management Protocol (SNMP)**—Disabled by default, but widely used.

- **HTTP**—Enabled by default. Disable with the **no ip http server** global command if not needed.
- **DNS**—Disabled by default.
- **Internet Control Message Protocol (ICMP) redirects**—Enabled by default. Disable with the **no ip redirects** command if not needed.
- **IP source routing**—Enabled by default. Disable with the **no ip source-route** command.
- **Finger service**—Disabled by default.
- **ICMP unreachables**—Enabled by default. Disable with the **no ip unreachables** command if not needed.
- **ICMP mask reply**—Disabled by default.
- **TCP keepalives**—Disabled by default. Enable with the **service tcp-keepalives** command.
- **Proxy ARP**—Enabled by default. Disable with the **no ip proxy-arp** command if unneeded.
- **IP directed broadcasts**—Disabled by default.

Hardening with AutoSecure

AutoSecure is a feature found in Cisco IOS Release 12.3T and later that automates many of the tasks involved in hardening a router. It can be operated in either Interactive mode or in Noninteractive mode. Interactive mode prompts the user with questions regarding security features such as enabling and disabling services. Noninteractive mode automatically hardens the router according to Cisco-recommended guidelines.

AutoSecure can selectively lock down the router with the following features:

- Management plane features, including disabling unneeded services
- Forwarding plane features, such as Cisco Express Forwarding (CEF) and basic access control lists (ACL)
- Cisco IOS Firewall services
- Login and password security
- NTP
- SSH
- TCP Intercept

Configuring AutoSecure

In Cisco IOS Release 12.3(8)T and later, AutoSecure retains the pre-lockdown configuration in Flash under the name *pre_autosec.cfg*. If AutoSecure configuration fails, you can revert to the pre-lockdown configuration with the command **configure replace flash:pre_autosec.cfg**.

AutoSecure is initiated from the command-line interface (CLI) with the **auto secure** command. The **management**, **forwarding**, **ntp**, **ssh**, **firewall**, and **tcp-intercept** arguments activate the features described in the preceding list. By default, the AutoSecure script interactively prompts the user with questions about each feature that it configures. To switch to Noninteractive mode, add the **no-interact** keyword to the **auto secure** command.

Security Device Manager

The Security Device Manager (SDM) is a web-based security configuration tool that runs on Cisco routers. You can use it to lock down a router in a way similar to the AutoSecure script. You can also use it to audit an existing configuration for compliance with Cisco security recommendations.

Securing Cisco Router Installations and Administrative Access

Password-Creation Rules

Cisco router passwords are subject to the following restrictions:

- 1 to 25 characters in length
- Can include any alphanumeric characters, symbols, and spaces
- Cannot have a number as the first character
- Leading spaces ignored, but subsequent spaces (including trailing spaces) not ignored

Types of Router Passwords

Many different types of passwords are used for Cisco IOS routers. The most common ones are described here:

- **Enable secret**—The enable secret controls access to privileged EXEC mode on the router. The password is stored in a nonreversible one-way Message Digest 5 (MD5) hash. If the enable secret is present in the configuration, it overrides the enable password. To configure the enable secret password, use the **enable secret** *password* command.
- **Enable password**—The enable password controls access to privileged EXEC mode on the router if the **enable secret** command is not present. The enable password is stored in clear text in the configuration, unless the **service password-encryption** command is present. To configure the enable password, use the **enable password** *password* command.
- **Line passwords**—Access to a router's tty lines can be controlled either with AAA or with individual passwords applied to the lines. AAA configuration is discussed later. To configure individual passwords on a TTY line, use the **password** *password* command in line configuration mode. Line passwords are stored in clear text in the configuration, unless the **service password-encryption** command is present. tty lines include the console port, vty lines for Telnet/SSH access, the AUX port, as well as regular tty lines. The **login** command must also be present in the line configuration for password prompts to be displayed.

Password-Length Enforcement

You can globally set a minimum length for all router passwords with the **security passwords min-length** *length* command.

Password Encryption

Many types of passwords are stored in clear text in the configuration, by default. To prevent casual discovery of these passwords, use the **service password-encryption** command. Software to decrypt passwords that are ciphered with this command is widely available on the Internet, so it should not be relied on to protect highly sensitive passwords.

Enhanced Username Password Security

When configuring a local username/password database on a router, use the **username** *username* **secret** *password* command. This protects the password with a MD5 hash rather than plain text or weak Type 7 encryption.

Password Example

Example 5-1 shows a configuration that incorporates all the password features previously discussed.

Example 5-1 Configuring Router Passwords

```
service password-encryption

security passwords min-length 6
enable secret 5 $1$jSlS$QbQmCuRx0UfOgQiMkxbHk0
enable password 7 053B0A2F70427A5A0111

username admin secret 5 $1$zltV$9tNP0xX4ehfQ0pKceNG6A/

line con 0
  password 7 053B0A2F70427A5A0111
  login
  stopbits 1
line aux 0
  password 7 01230A240A05325C3958
  login
  stopbits 1
line vty 0 4
  password 7 046B07265E2F781D110D
      login
```

Securing ROMMON

By default, Cisco routers allow a user connected to the console port to execute a keyboard break sequence to enter the ROM Monitor (ROMMON). From ROMMON, it is possible to perform a password override sequence to reset the enable secret while retaining the configuration file. To prevent unauthorized users with physical access to the router from doing this, you can use the **no service password-recovery** command. After this command has been configured, it is impossible to reset any router passwords without completely erasing the configuration.

Rate-Limiting Authentication Attempts

Cisco IOS commands offer several ways to rate-limit authentication attempts:

- The **security authentication failure rate** *threshold-rate* **log** command enables you to set a number of failures after which a 15-second delay is imposed and a syslog message triggered.

- The **login block-for** *seconds* **attempts** *tries within seconds* command enables you to block login attempts for *seconds* if the number of login attempts exceeds *tries* within *seconds*. You can exclude a list of addresses from blocking by configuring the **login quiet-mode access-class** {*acl-name* | *acl-number*} command.
- The **login delay** *seconds* command enforces a minimum delay of *seconds* between successive login attempts. This helps mitigate dictionary attacks against the router.

Setting Timeouts

CLI sessions stay logged in for 10 minutes by default. You can change this with the **exec-timeout** *minutes seconds* command, in line configuration mode.

Privilege Levels

Cisco routers enable you to define up to 16 privilege levels with different command sets assigned to each. Normal user-level privileges are level 0. Standard privileged mode (access to all commands) is level 15. Example 5-2 shows how to assign the **traceroute** command to level 2, with a separate enable secret of cat. After applying this configuration, users at level 0 can no longer execute traceroutes.

Example 5-2 Configuring Privilege Levels

```
R2(config)#privilege exec level 2 traceroute
R2(config)#enable secret level 2 cat
```

Configuring Banner Messages

Example 5-3 shows how to configure a banner message that displays every time a user logs in to the router CLI. Note that the character used to begin and end the message is the percentage sign (%) in the example, but it can be any character that does not appear in the text of the message. The other type of banner commonly used in Cisco IOS configurations is the "message-of-the-day" banner, which is configured with the **banner motd** command.

Example 5-3   Configuring a Login Banner

```
R2(config)#banner login %
Enter TEXT message.  End with the character %.
You are entering the Test Network. Unauthorized access is pro-
hibited.
All activity is logged.
%
R2(config)#
```

Role-Based CLI

Role-based CLI is a relatively new method of limiting access to CLI commands in a much more flexible way than privilege levels. Cisco IOS commands are grouped into "views," which can then be assigned to users (or interfaces) in a variety of ways. The "root view" has access to all commands and can be used to create up to 15 additional views. Views can be offloaded to AAA servers for even more flexibility. "Superviews" enables you to group together multiple views, allowing you to assign multiple views to users with less configuration complexity. Example 5-4 shows a basic role-based CLI configuration similar to Example 5-2.

Example 5-4   Configuring Role-Based CLI

```
R2(config)#aaa new-model
R2(config)#exit
R2#enable view
Password:[enter level 15 password]
*Dec 16 19:44:39.411: %PARSER-6-VIEW_SWITCH: successfully set to
  view 'root'.
R2#conf t
R2(config)#parser view TRACEROUTE_VIEW
*Dec 16 19:45:16.403: %PARSER-6-VIEW_CREATED: view
'TRACEROUTE_VIEW' successfully created.
R2(config-view)#password 5 cat
R2(config-view)#commands exec include traceroute
R2(config-view)#exit
```

You can verify role-based CLI configuration with command **show parser view** [**all**] command.

Cisco IOS Resilient Configuration

The Cisco IOS Resilient Configuration feature allows for faster recovery in situations in which an attacker has compromised a router and erased its Cisco IOS image / configuration file. This feature is available only on platforms with PCMCIA ATA Flash drives. When enabled, this feature saves nonerasable copies of the running Cisco IOS image and running configuration to the Flash drive. If the configuration / Cisco IOS image is then erased, the secure backup copy of the Cisco IOS image can be booted from ROMMON. After the boot, you can restore the secure backup copy of the configuration from the Flash drive.

Mitigating Threats and Attacks with Access Lists

ACL Review

Standard access lists (standard ACLs) allow filtering based on source IP address only. Extended access lists (extended ACLs) allow filtering based on source or destination address and most other fields in the IP packet header (Layer 4 protocol type, source/destination port number, IP options, Differentiated Services Code Point [DSCP] values, fragmentation parameters, and so on).

Access lists can be either numbered or named. Numbered standard ACLs have numbers from 1 to 99 or 1300 to 1999. Numbered extended ACLs have numbers from 100 to 199 or 2000 to 2699.

You can apply access lists either inbound or outbound on an interface. Inbound ACLs affect traffic moving toward the interface. Outbound ACLs affect traffic leaving the interface.

Access lists are used extensively in router security configurations for permitting or denying access to services, mitigating address spoofing, mitigating various attack types, and more.

Mitigating Spoofed Addresses (Inbound)

You can use access lists to prevent packets with spoofed source addresses from entering your network. When configuring inbound antispoof ACLs, you should deny packets from, at a minimum, the following:

- Any internal address space
- Internal loopback addresses
- RFC 1918 reserved addresses
- Multicast addresses

Mitigating Spoofed Addresses (Outbound)

In addition to dropping inbound packets with spoofed source addresses, you should also configure ACLs to prevent packets from leaving your network with spoofed source addresses. No packets should leave your network that do not have source addresses inside your network.

Mitigating SYN Attacks

One common type of network attack is the half-open SYN attack. This is a DoS attack in which the attacker sends a large quantity of TCP SYN messages to a host without ever completing the three-way TCP handshake. This attack can result in the depletion of memory resources on the host. The most flexible way to mitigate this attack is to use the Cisco IOS Firewall feature set. The following subsections identify two other ways to mitigate half-open SYN attacks.

Using the **established** Keyword in ACLs

The **established** keyword in a TCP-based ACL entry permits only packets that have the TCP ACK bit set to pass the ACL entry. Example 5-5 demonstrates this.

Example 5-5 Using the established Keyword

```
R2(config)#access-list 150 permit tcp any any established
R2(config)#interface serial 1/0/0
R2(config-if)#ip access-group 150 in
```

Using TCP Intercept

The TCP Intercept feature permits half-open SYN connections only within configurable thresholds. Half-open SYN connections outside these thresholds are dropped. Example 5-6 demonstrates this.

Example 5-6 Using TCP Intercept

```
R2(config)#ip tcp intercept list 150
R2(config)#access-list 150 permit tcp any 10.1.1.0 255.255.255.0
R2(config)#interface serial 2/0/0
R2(config-if)#ip access-group 150 in
```

ACL Caveats

Remember the following caveats when configuring ACLs:

- **Implicit deny any**—All ACLs have an implicit **deny any** statement at the end. It is not displayed in the configuration. Any traffic not explicitly permitted is implicitly denied.
- **Evaluation order**—ACLs are evaluated from the top down, in order. Be sure not to place a statement at the top of the ACL that negates a later statement. Place the most specific statements at the top of the ACL.
- **ACL direction**—Inbound ACLs affect packets that are moving toward the interface. Outbound ACLs affect packets that are moving away from the interface. It can be easy to confuse these, especially on VLAN interfaces.

Securing Management and Reporting Features

In addition to securing the router itself, it is also important to secure the traffic used to manage the device and collect statistical information from it.

Types of Management Traffic

In-band management traffic flows inside the production network and is intermixed with production traffic. Although common in most networks, the risk of in-band management is that an attacker who compromises a system on the production network could interfere with management traffic, capture sensitive information from management packets, or mount further attacks against network management protocols. With in-band management, you should use encrypted protocols such as IPsec, SSH, or Secure Sockets Layer (SSL) rather than clear text protocols such as Telnet.

Out-of-band management traffic flows on an independent, purpose-built network and is kept totally separate from production traffic. Completely out-of-band management networks are most common in large networks.

With both types of management, you should ensure that the managed devices have synchronized clocks and that configuration archives and change logs are available.

Configuring Secure Shell

Traditionally, network administrators have used Telnet to manage routers and switches. The problem with Telnet, of course, is that it sends all traffic in clear text, allowing attackers with access to the network to sniff passwords and other sensitive information. You should use the encrypted SSH protocol to manage network devices wherever possible. To configure SSH, complete the following steps:

Step 1. Configure the domain name.

Step 2. Generate RSA keys.

Step 3. Optionally configure an SSH timeout interval and retry count.

Step 4. Disable Telnet.

Step 5. Enable SSH.

Example 5-7 demonstrates SSH configuration.

Example 5-7 Configuring SSH

```
R2(config)#ip domain-name test.com
R2(config)#crypto key generate rsa general-keys modulus 1024
The name for the keys will be: R2.test.com
% The key modulus size is 1024 bits
% Generating 1024 bit RSA keys, keys will be non-
exportable...[OK]
*Dec 18 19:16:26.275: %SSH-5-ENABLED: SSH 1.99 has been enabled
R2(config)#ip ssh time-out 10
R2(config)#ip ssh authentication-retries 3
R2(config-line)#line vty 0 4
R2(config-line)#transport input none
R2(config-line)#transport input ssh
```

Configuring Syslog

Syslog is the most common way to archive router events for security monitoring. A router acts as a syslog client that sends messages to a syslog server. Syslog severities range from 0 (critical) to 7 (debugging). Example 5-8 demonstrates how to configure syslog.

Example 5-8 Configuring Syslog

```
R1(config)#logging 10.1.2.1
R1(config)#logging trap informational
R1(config)#logging source-interface loopback 0
R1(config)#logging on
```

Simple Network Management Protocol

SNMP is widely used to gather information from network nodes. SNMP is an application layer protocol that runs on top of TCP/IP, typically on UDP port 161. SNMP is most often used in read-only mode, in which information is read from the node, but no changes can be made. SNMP also supports read-write mode, which allows changes to be made to the node's configuration. SNMP information can be read passively or sent based on triggered events. When used passively, a network management host reads the SNMP Management Information Bases (MIB) on the router to gather information on a periodic basis. The router can also send event-triggered SNMP traps to a network management host when a particular event occurs.

SNMP exists in Versions 1, 2, and 3. SNMPv1 and SNMPv2 lack strong security mechanisms. Read-only or read-write access is controlled via a community string, which is sent across the network in clear text. Using SNMP read-write with clear text community strings is particularly dangerous.

SNMPv3 supports strong security by enabling the use of MD5 or SHA hashed authentication and DES encryption with SNMP messages.

Example 5-9 shows a basic SNMPv3 configuration allowing a management host to read MIBs on the router.

Example 5-9 Configuring SNMPv3

```
R2(config)#snmp-server group SNMP_GROUP v3 auth
R2(config)#snmp-server user SNMP_USER SNMP_GROUP v3 auth md5
  my_password
```

Network Time Protocol

NTP is used to synchronize device clocks in the network. Clock synchronization is important for correlating syslog messages and other security features such as certificate-based encryption, routing protocol authentication key expiration, time-based ACLs, and more. NTP runs over UDP port 123. Time is tracked internally using universal coordinated time (UTC). You can configure a time zone on the router to display the correct local time. Cisco routers allow you to configure NTP to act as either a peer association or a server association. In a peer association, the local system is able to either synchronize to the other system, or the other system can synchronize to it. In a server association, the local system can *only* synchronize to the remote system.

Because time synchronization is a security-related feature, it is wise to configure a router to authenticate NTP information coming from a peer or server. This prevents an attacker from spoofing NTP packets to corrupt the system clock. For added security, you can use an ACL to restrict the IP address(es) with which the router can synchronize time.

Example 5-10 demonstrates configuration of an authenticated NTP server with an NTP ACL. In this example, the router is only allowed to synchronize with a server at 10.1.1.1 that shares the MD5 hashed key value my_ntp_key.

Example 5-10 Configuring Authenticated NTP

```
R2(config)#ntp authenticate
R2(config)#ntp authentication-key 1 md5 my_ntp_key
R2(config)#ntp trusted-key 1
R2(config)#ntp server 10.1.1.1 key 1
R2(config)#access-list 1 permit host 10.1.1.1
R2(config)#ntp access-group peer 1
```


Configuring AAA on Cisco Routers

AAA stands for authentication, authorization, and accounting:

- **Authentication**—Proves the identity of the person logging in to the router via a username and password, token card, biometrics, and so forth
- **Authorization**—Decides what actions the user is allowed to perform, such as accessing privileged mode or running certain commands
- **Accounting**—Maintains records of what the user did during the session, such as login/logout times and commands executed

AAA Services

Cisco routers support AAA either through local databases (using the **username/password** command) or through external security servers. External security servers can use one of two protocols:

- **TACACS+**—Runs over TCP port 49. Includes authentication and encryption of messages between the client and server.
- **RADIUS**—Widely supported, standardized in RFC 2865. Cisco allows the use of proprietary TACACS+ attributes via a vendor-specific attribute (VSA). Runs over UDP. Does not encrypt entire message; passwords are sent as an MD5 hash, but the rest of the message is sent in clear text.

Router Access Modes

You can use AAA in either character mode or packet mode. Character mode is used when logging in to the CLI on the router via a vty or tty line, the AUX port, or the console port. Packet mode is used when authenticating a user on a dialup or serial interface (for example, a PPP-authenticated ISDN dialup session).

Configuring AAA

Example 5-11 shows how to configure communications with the AAA security server using TACACS+. In this example, the TACACS+ server is located at 10.2.2.2 and is configured to use a single TCP socket for all connections, rather than a separate socket for each. This saves processing resources on both the router and server. The server must also be configured with the key T@C_key1.

Example 5-11 Configuring a TACACS+ Server

```
R2(config)#aaa new-model
R2(config)#tacacs-server host 10.2.2.2 single-connection
R2(config)#tacacs-server key T@C_key1
```

Example 5-12 shows how to configure communications with the AAA security server using RADIUS:

Example 5-12   Configuring a RADIUS Server

```
R2(config)#aaa new-model
R2(config)#radius-server host 10.3.3.3
R2(config)#radius-server key R@D_key1
```

Configuring CLI Authentication on a Cisco Router

Example 5-13 shows how to configure character mode AAA to authenticate a CLI session on a router's console and vty ports. In this example, a user on the console port will be authenticated using the AAA list called CUSTOM_LIST. The user will be authenticated against the TACACS+ server if it is available. If it is unavailable, the enable secret or enable password will be accepted instead. A user on one of the vty lines, on the other hand, will be authenticated using the default list. The default list authenticates first against the TACACS+ server (if it is available). If the server is unavailable, the vty user will be authenticated against the local username/password database. If a security server is the sole authentication method, you could get locked out of the router in the event that the security server is unavailable. For this reason, it is important to use either local authentication or enable password authentication as a fallback method.

Example 5-13   Configuring AAA CLI Authentication

```
R2(config)#aaa new-model
R2(config)#aaa authentication login default group tacacs+ local
R2(config)#aaa authentication login CUSTOM_LIST group tacacs+
  enable
R2(config)#line con 0
R2(config-line)#login authentication CUSTOM_LIST
R2(config-line)#exit
R2(config)#line vty 0 4
R2(config-line)#login authentication default
```


Configuring Authorization

Example 5-14 shows how to configure basic command authorization using a TACACS+ security server. In this example, the user must be authorized to use the EXEC shell, and access to commands at privilege levels 1 and 15 must also be authorized. Authorization is performed against the TACACS+ server if it is available, and against the local username/password database if it is unavailable.

Example 5-14 Configuring AAA Authorization

```
R2(config)#aaa new-model
R2(config)#aaa authorization exec default group tacacs+ local
R2(config)#aaa authorization commands 1 default group tacacs+
  local
R2(config)#aaa authorization commands 15 default group tacacs+
  local
```

Configuring Accounting

Example 5-15 shows how to configure basic accounting using a TACACS+ security server. In this example, accounting of EXEC commands is sent to the TACACS+ server.

Example 5-15 Configuring AAA Accounting

```
R2(config)#aaa new-model
R2(config)#aaa accounting exec default start-stop group tacacs+
```

Troubleshooting AAA

The following commands are the most useful for troubleshooting AAA:

- **debug aaa authentication**
- **debug aaa authorization**
- **debug aaa accounting**

CHAPTER 6

Cisco IOS Threat Defenses

The router-hardening techniques discussed in Chapter 5, "Cisco Device Hardening," help to protect the router against many types of infrastructure attacks. The Cisco IOS Firewall feature set enables you to integrate a stateful firewall and an intrusion prevention system (IPS) to protect end stations located behind the router.

DMZ Design Review

A demilitarized zone (DMZ) is an intermediate network between an organization's "inside" network and the "outside" world. Most organizations use a DMZ to host their Internet-accessible devices, such as web servers or mail servers. Some type of security system (for example, stateful firewall, filtering router, application layer gateway) filters packets traveling between the outside world and the systems in the DMZ, and between the DMZ and the inside network. Depending on the design, there can be one filtering device that performs both functions or two separate devices.

Traffic initiated from the outside world should be filtered so that all traffic to nonessential services is dropped. If possible, the systems in the DMZ should not be allowed to initiate conversations with systems on the inside; all communications between the inside and the DMZ should be initiated from the inside. This reduces the probability of a trust exploitation attack in the event that an attacker compromises a DMZ system.

Firewall Technologies

A variety of firewall technologies exist:

- **Packet filtering**—A packet filter (such as an access list on a router) permits or denies packets based in information in the Layer 3 or Layer 4 packet headers.
- **Application layer gateway**—An application layer gateway (ALG) is a piece of software that intercepts application layer requests between the endpoints of a network conversation. The ALG typically passes requests from a client to a server and vice versa after inspecting the

application layer packets to ensure that they pass configured security criteria. In some circumstances, the ALG may change the contents of packets moving in either direction.

- **Stateful packet filtering**—A stateful packet filter combines aspects of a packet filter and an ALG. The attributes of each communications session are maintained in a state table. Only packets whose attributes match the rules of the state table are permitted to pass. For example, an HTTP response packet would typically only be allowed to pass if it is a response to a query packet that was previously permitted by the firewall. Modern stateful packet filters are also capable of tracking complex information about application sessions. For example, a Voice over IP (VoIP)-aware stateful firewall would typically be able to "know" that it should dynamically open UDP ports for a Real-time Transport Protocol (RTP) session based on information gained from examining the call setup traffic that takes place inside various call-control protocols.

Cisco IOS Firewall

The Cisco IOS Firewall is a stateful packet filter that is built in to Cisco IOS security images. Some of its features include the ability to dynamically alter router access control lists (ACL) to permit return traffic for sessions originated on the inside, the ability to track TCP sequence numbers and permit only expected TCP traffic, and the ability to mitigate some types of TCP-based and IP fragmentation-based denial-of-service (DoS) attacks.

TCP Handling in the Cisco IOS Firewall

When a router running the Cisco IOS Firewall detects an outbound TCP packet, it tracks the source and destination IP addresses, source and destination TCP port numbers, the TCP flags, and the SYN/ACK numbers associated with the session. Only inbound packets whose packet headers match the expected parameters for a legitimate response to the session are permitted.

UDP Handling in the Cisco IOS Firewall

Because UDP packets do not have the same kind of state information as TCP packets (that is, there are no TCP flags or SYN/ACK numbers), UDP return packets are permitted based on matching source/destination IP addresses and port numbers and a configurable timeout interval. If the UDP return packet arrives outside the timeout window, or with unexpected packet headers, it is dropped.

Alerts and Audit Trails

The Cisco IOS Firewall can trigger, based on configurable parameters, syslog alerts and log audit information about firewall sessions to a syslog server.

Cisco IOS Authentication Proxy

The Cisco IOS Firewall can authenticate HTTP, HTTPS, Telnet, and FTP sessions against local username/password databases or against TACACS+ or RADIUS security servers. Therefore, an administrator can define specific access policies for each user rather than generic policies for entire subnets or interfaces.

Configuring Cisco IOS Firewalls

To configure the Cisco IOS Firewall, follow these five steps:

Step 1. Define external and internal interfaces.

Step 2. Configure access lists on the interfaces.

Step 3. Define inspection rules.

Step 4. Apply inspection rules to interfaces.

Step 5. Test and verify the configuration.

Defining External and Internal Interfaces

The external interface is the one connected to the "outside" network, whereas the internal interface is the one connected to the inside, protected network. For example, the external address might be connected to an Internet service provider (ISP), whereas the internal interface might be connected to your corporate LAN. Traffic arriving on the external interface is considered less trusted than traffic arriving on the internal interface. The most common type of firewall configuration is to allow outside traffic to pass the external interface only if it is a response to a legitimate session that was originated from the inside.

Configuring Access Lists on the Interfaces

Consider the following guidelines when configuring ACLs in association with the Cisco IOS Firewall:

- Extended ACLs (as opposed to standard ACLs) are required if you want to dynamically allow return traffic for sessions originated from the inside.
- Consider implementing antispoofing ACLs, as discussed in Chapter 5.
- If you want to enable application layer inspection for a protocol that is permitted through the firewall, that protocol must also be permitted by the relevant extended ACLs. For example, if you want to perform H.323 inspection, your extended ACLs must permit H.323.

Defining Inspection Rules

Inspection rules determine which application layer protocols are inspected at the firewall interface. Typically, only one inspection rule is defined, and all the protocols you want to inspect are added to it. The exception to this scenario is where you want to inspect different protocols in different directions. You define inspection rules with the **ip inspect** command. Example 6-1 demonstrates how to configure basic protocol inspection.

Example 6-1 Basic Protocol Inspection

```
R2(config)#ip inspect name FW tcp alert on audit-trail on
  timeout 300
R2(config)#ip inspect name FW ftp alert on audit-trail on
  timeout 300
R2(config)#ip inspect name FW h323 alert on audit-trail on
  timeout 300
R2(config)#ip inspect name FW udp alert on audit-trail on
  timeout 300
```

Example 6-1 defines an inspection rule named FW with four protocols that will be inspected: generic TCP, FTP, H.323, and generic UDP. When a packet initiated from the inside interface exits the router, the inspection rule allows replies to that session to pass through the external interface's ACL, provided that the reply packet does not violate any parameters of the protocol. The **alert** and **audit-trail** keywords configure syslog alerting and auditing for the protocol. The **timeout** keyword sets the period (in seconds) after which the dynamic "hole" in the external ACL will be closed if there is no activity.

The **alert** and **audit-trail** keywords produce log messages only if the global commands **ip inspect audit-trail** and **no ip inspect alert-off** are also configured. The following output shows sample representative sample messages that the router sends when the alert and audit-trail features are active:

```
%FW-6-SESS_AUDIT_TRAIL: tcp session initiator (10.1.1.2:5590)
sent 22 bytes -- responder (10.1.1.3:23) sent 88 bytes
%FW-4-ALERT_ON: getting aggressive, count (550/500) current
  1-min rate: 250
%FW-4-ALERT_OFF: calming down, count (0/400) current 1-min
  rate: 0
```

Applying Inspection Rules to Interfaces

After you have created an inspection rule, you must apply it to an interface. The most common configuration is to have the inspection rule applied inbound on the inside interface. This configuration allows the router to dynamically create holes in the ACLs applied to other interfaces that allow replies to sessions initiated by hosts on the inside interface. Example 6-2 demonstrates this.

Example 6-2 Applying Inspection Rule Inbound on Inside Interface

```
interface FastEthernet0/0
 description inside interface
 ip address 10.1.1.1 255.255.255.0
 ip inspect FW in
```


Verifying Inspection

The following commands are useful for verifying Cisco IOS Firewall configurations:

- **show ip inspect** *inspection-name*
- **show ip inspect config**
- **show ip inspect interfaces**
- **show ip inspect session** [**detail**]
- **show ip inspect statistics**
- **show ip inspect all**
- **debug ip inspect detail**
- **debug ip inspect events**
- **debug ip inspect** *protocol*

Introducing Cisco IOS IPS

The Cisco IOS Intrusion Prevention System can help detect and mitigate attacks against routers and hosts. This section reviews the components and configuration of the IOS IPS.

Defining IDS/IPS Terms

The following terms are important to an understanding of intrusion detection systems (IDS) and intrusion prevention systems (IPS):

- **Intrusion detection system**—An IDS is a device that listens passively to network traffic and produces alerts when suspicious activity is detected. An IDS is often located outside the traffic forwarding path and monitors traffic that is copied to a Switched Port Analyzer (SPAN) port on a switch.
- **Intrusion prevention system**—An IPS is a device that not only alerts on suspicious activity, but that can also be configured to actively block it. An IPS is typically located in the forwarding path. The Cisco IOS IPS is a feature offered in Cisco IOS security images that allows the router to detect and respond to possible network attacks.
- **Signature-based approach**—Signature-based IDS/IPS devices detect possible attacks by matching preconfigured patterns (that is, "signatures") in network traffic.
- **Policy-based approach**—Policy-based IDS/IPS devices detect attacks based on thresholds or other policies, such as a number of half-open TCP SYN sessions.
- **Anomaly-based approach**—Anomaly-based IDS/IPS devices profile network traffic and build up a set of patterns that is considered "normal." Traffic that falls outside of normal parameters triggers alerts or other actions.
- **Honeypot approach**—"Honeypots" are systems that are deliberately left vulnerable to network attacks so that security researchers can analyze an attack methodology. The network design must prevent a compromised honeypot from ever having access to legitimate systems.
- **Host-based IDS/IPS**—A host-based IDS/IPS (HIDS/HIPS) resides on end-system hosts. It is typically written to prevent attacks against a particularly operating system, such as the installation of unauthorized software.

- **Network-based IDS/IPS**—A network-based IDS/IPS (NIDS/NIPS) resides on the transport network. It may be a passive IDS located on a switch SPAN port or an active IPS colocated on a firewall or router.

Cisco IOS IPS Signatures

A Cisco router running the IPS module comes with 100 attack signatures preloaded in the Cisco IOS Software. Many additional signatures can be loaded by installing Signature Definition Files (SDF) on the router.

Cisco IOS IPS Alarms

When an attack signature is detected, the router can take any of the following configurable actions:

- Send an alarm
- Drop the packet
- Reset the TCP connection
- Block the source IP address of the packet for a configurable amount of time
- Block the connection for a configurable amount of time

Configuring Cisco IOS IPS

Example 6-3 demonstrates how to configure the most common Cisco IOS IPS features.

Example 6-3 Configuring Cisco IOS IPS

```
ip ips sdf location flash:sig.sdf
ip ips signature 1107 0 disable
ip ips signature 6190 0 list 199
ip ips name MY_IPS list 100
!
interface serial 1/0
 ip ips MY_IPS in
!
access-list 100 deny   ip host 10.1.1.1 any
access-list 100 permit ip any any
```

```
!
access-list 199 deny   ip host 172.16.1.1 any
access-list 199 permit ip any any
```

The commands in Example 6-3 function as follows:

- **ip ips sdf location**—Specifies the location of the signature definition file.
- **ip ips signature 1107 0 disable**—Disables signature 1107, subsignature 0.
- **ip ips signature 6190 0 list 199**—Specifies that signature 6190, subsignature 0 will be filtered against access list 199. Packets matching a **deny** statement in the ACL bypass the IPS engine, whereas packets matching a permit statement are scanned with the IPS engine.
- **ip ips name MY_IPS list 100**—Creates an IPS rule named MY_IPS and filters it against access list 100. Packets matching a **deny** statement in the ACL bypass the IPS engine, whereas packets matching a permit statement are scanned with the IPS engine.
- **ip ips MY_IPS in**—Specifies that packets inbound to the interface are scanned with the IPS rule MY_IPS.

PART IV

ONT

CHAPTER 1

Network Architecture

Modern converged networks include different traffic types, each with unique requirements for security, Quality of Service (QoS), transmission capacity, and delay. Some examples include:

- Voice signaling and bearer
- Core application traffic, such as Enterprise Resource Planning (ERP) or Customer Relationship Management (CRM)
- Database transactions
- Multicast multimedia
- Network management
- "Other" traffic, such as web pages, e-mail, and file transfer

Cisco routers are able to implement filtering, compression, prioritization, and policing (dedicating network capacity). Except for filtering, these capabilities are referred to collectively as QoS.

Although QoS is wonderful, it is not the only way to address bandwidth shortage. Cisco espouses an idea called the Intelligent Information Network (IIN). IIN builds on standard network design models to enable these new services to be reliable and layered on top of traditional data delivery.

SONA and IIN

IIN describes an evolutionary vision of a network that integrates network and application functionality cooperatively and allows the network to be smart about how it handles traffic to minimize the footprint of applications. IIN is built on top of the Enterprise Composite Model and describes structures overlaid on to the Composite design as needed in three phases.

Phase 1, "Integrated Transport," describes a converged network, which is built along the lines of the Composite model and based on open standards. This is the phase that the industry has been transitioning. The Cisco Integrated Services Routers (ISR) are an example of this trend.

Phase 2, "Integrated Services," attempts to virtualize resources, such as servers, storage, and network access. It is a move to an "on-demand" model.

By "virtualize," Cisco means that the services are not associated with a particular device or location. Instead, many services can reside in one device to ease management, or many devices can provide one service that is more reliable.

An ISR brings together routing, switching, voice, security, and wireless It is an example of many services existing on one device. A load balancer, which makes many servers look like one, is an example of one service residing on many devices.

VRFs are an example of taking one resource and making it look like many. Some versions of IOS are capable of having a router present itself as many virtual router (VRF) instances, allowing your company to deliver different logical topologies on the same physical infrastructure. Server virtualization is another example. The classic example of taking one resource and making it appear to be many resources is the use of a virtual LAN (VLAN) and a virtual storage area network (VSAN).

Virtualization provides flexibility in configuration and management.

Phase 3, "Integrated Applications," uses application-oriented networking (AON) to make the network application-aware and to allow the network to actively participate in service delivery.

An example of this Phase 3 IIN systems approach to service delivery is Network Admission Control (NAC). Before NAC, authentication, VLAN assignment, and anti-virus updates were separately managed. With NAC in place, the network is able to check the policy stance of a client and admit, deny, or remediate based on policies.

IIN allows the network to deconstruct packets, parse fields, and take actions based on the values it finds. An ISR equipped with an AON blade might be set up to route traffic from a business partner. The AON blade can examine traffic, recognize the application, and rebuild XML files in memory. Corrupted XML fields might represent an attack (called *schema poisoning*), so the AON blade can react by blocking that source from further communication. In this example, routing, an awareness of the application data flow, and security are combined to allow the network to contribute to the success of the application.

Services-Oriented Network Architecture (SONA) applies the IIN ideal to Enterprise networks. SONA breaks down the IIN functions into three layers:

- Network Infrastructure—Hierarchical converged network and attached end systems.
- Interactive Services—Resources allocated to applications.
- Applications—Includes business policy and logic

IOS features, such as Survivable Remote Site Telephony (SRST) and AutoQoS, cooperate with centralized services to increase the resiliency of the network by easily distributing network application logic to the edges of the enterprise, so that the entire network participates in operations instead of just the core.

Figure 1-1 shows how IIN and SONA more specifically compare.

Figure 1-1 IIN and SONA

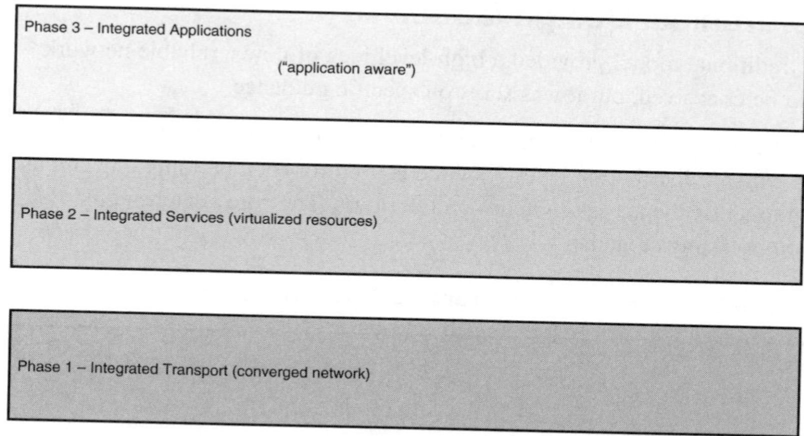

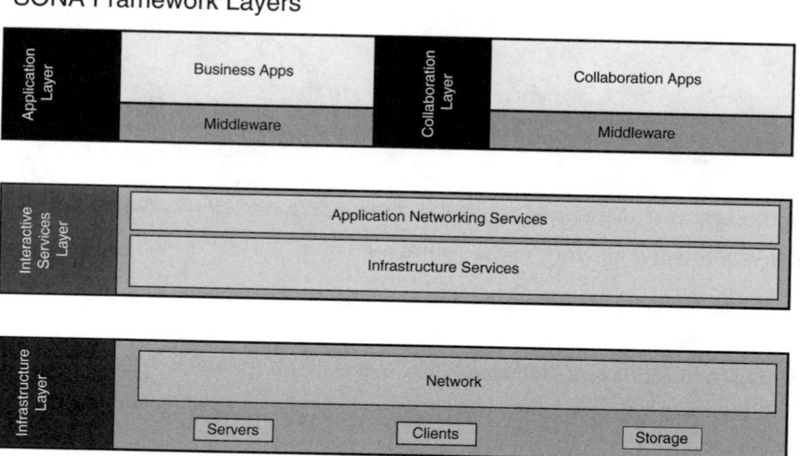

Network Models

Cisco has developed specific architecture recommendations for Campus, Data Center, WAN, branches, and telecommuting. These recommendations add specific ideas about how current technologies and capabilities match the network roles within an enterprise.

Each of these designs builds on a traditional hierarchical design and adds features such as security, QoS, caching, and convergence.

Hierarchical Design Model

The traditional model provided a high-level idea of how a reliable network could be conceived, but it was short on specific guidance.

Figure 1-2 is a simple drawing of how the three-layer model might have been built. A distribution layer-3 switch is used for each building on campus, tying together the access switches on the floors. The core switches link the various buildings together.

Figure 1-2 Three-Layer Hierarchical Design

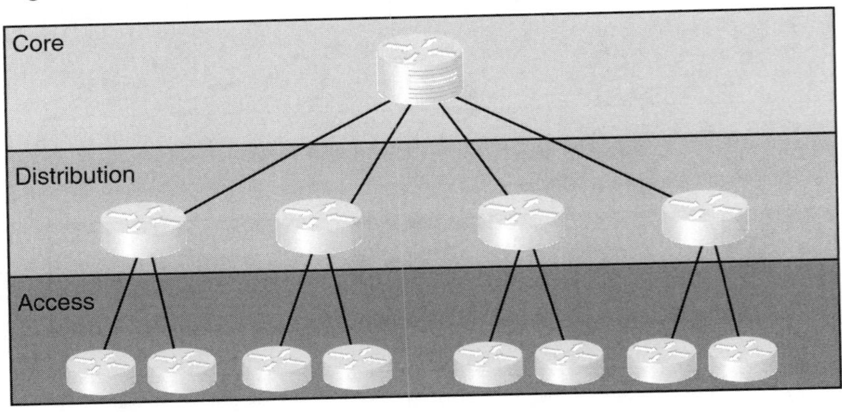

The layers break a network in the following way:

- Access layer—End stations attach to the network using low-cost devices.
- Distribution layer—Intermediate devices apply policies.
  - — Route summarization
  - — Policies applied, such as:
    - Route selection
    - Access lists
    - Quality of Service (QoS)

- Core layer—The backbone that provides a high-speed path between distribution elements.
  - Distribution devices are interconnected.
  - High speed (there is a lot of traffic).
  - No policies (it is tough enough to keep up).

Enterprise Composite Network Model

The newer Cisco model—the Enterprise Composite Model—is significantly more complex and attempts to address the shortcomings of the Hierarchical Design Model by expanding the older version and making specific recommendations about how and where certain network functions should be implemented. This model is based on the principles described in the Cisco Architecture for Voice, Video, and Integrated Data (AVVID).

The Enterprise Composite Model is broken into three large sections:

- Enterprise Campus
- Enterprise Edge
- Service Provider Edge

The first section, the Enterprise Campus, looks like the old Hierarchical Design Model with added details. It features six sections:

- Campus Backbone
- Building Distribution
- Building Access
- Management
- Edge Distribution—A distribution layer out to the WAN
- Server Farm—For Enterprise services

The Enterprise Edge details the connections from the campus to the Wide Area Network and includes:

- E-commerce
- Internet connectivity
- Remote access
- WAN

The Service Provider Edge is just a list of the public networks that facilitate wide-area connectivity. These include:

- Internet service providers (ISP)
- Analog phone dialup
- Frame Relay, ATM, and PPP, which have private connectivity

Figure 1-3 shows the Campus, Enterprise Edge, and Service Provider Edge modules assembled. Security implemented on this model is described in the Cisco SAFE (Security Architecture for Enterprise) blueprint.

Figure 1-3 Enterprise Design

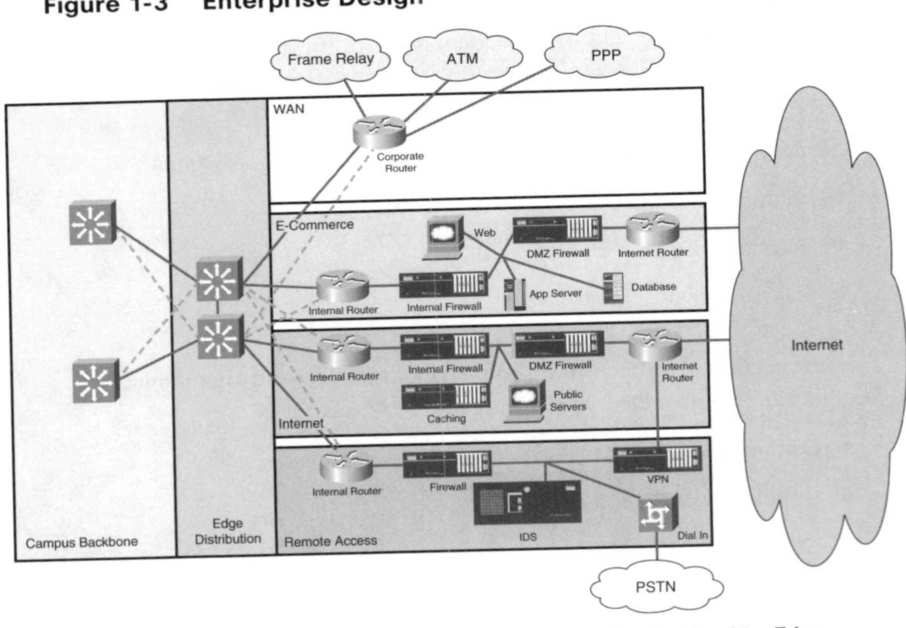

CHAPTER 2

Cisco VoIP

Voice over IP (VoIP) is a set of technologies that seeks to replace traditional analog voice services. There are three main compelling benefits to VoIP:

- VoIP makes better use of network capacity. Traditional voice uses a 64-kbps circuit, even when it is not active, but VoIP can use much less and no capacity when the line is not in use.
- VoIP allows new and revolutionary features, such as the following:
  - Integration of voice and data systems (so that operators get customer information popped on to the screen when a phone call arrives).
  - Voice CODECs can improve sound quality (at the expense of bandwidth).
  - Integration with new clients. Instead of an analog phone, VoIP clients can include television boxes, Personal Digital Assistants (PDAs), cell phones, laptops, and so on.
- VoIP can save money by avoiding toll calls.

IP telephony solutions include many pieces:

- Internet Protocol (IP) phones
- Analog phones connected to IP by a Gateway
- Control and number resolution by a Gatekeeper
- Conferencing capabilities provided by a multipoint control unit (MCU)
- Applications, such as directories and product information that interface with smart IP phones

Transmission

Figure 2-1 shows a VoIP transmission scenario.

Figure 2-1 Passing Voice Packets

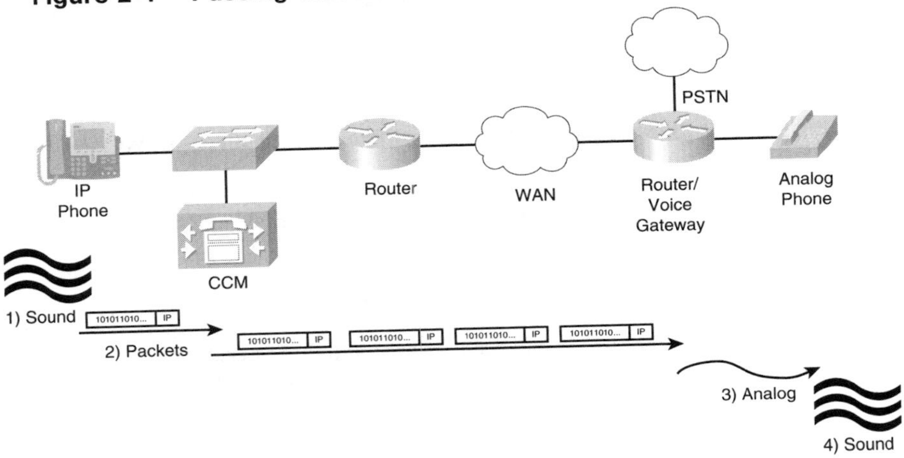

Voice is passed over an IP network by packetization. Example 2-1 shows an IP phone communicating with an older analog phone, but any combination of the two is supported. The numbered list below matches the steps involved in taking sound and converting it packets and then back to sound:

1. Incoming sounds are grouped into slices of sound (typically 20 ms), sampled, and digitized.
2. Each slice of sound is fitted with headers (data link, IP, User Datagram Proocol [UDP], and Reliable Transport Protocol [RTP]) and transmitted across the IP network.
3. Because the analog phone doesn't understand packets, a gateway (in this case, it is housed in a router) translates the stream of packets into an analog electrical signal.
4. The analog phone receives an analog electrical signal and sends it to a speaker, where the recording is restored to audio.

Cisco routers are commonly deployed as gateways. Three types of analog connections are supported:

- Foreign Exchange Station (FXS)—FXS ports connect analog phones. FXS ports supply line voltage.

- Foreign Exchange Office (FXO)—FXO ports connect to a Private Branch Exchange (PBX) or to the Public Switched Telephone Network (PSTN). FXO ports receive line voltage.
- E&M—E&M (which is alternately said to stand for Ear and Mouth or Earth and Magneto) interfaces supply advanced signaling to a PBX using a separate set of wires.

Three digital phone ports are supported:

1. ISDN—ISDN interfaces support advanced Q.931 signaling.
2. T1/E1 CCS (Common Channel Signaling)—T1/E1 CCS uses a channel for signaling. ISDN PRI uses CCS.
3. T1/E1 CAS (Channel Associated Signaling)—Robs bits from the analog waveform for signaling and is not as full-featured.

Although Figure 2-1 focused on the flow of voice records, signaling is equally important to understand. Signaling is what tells the system which phone to ring and when the line is hung up. Phone companies, in particular, are interested in this (and might write it $signaling) because signaling is used in billing. Figure 2-2 shows the types of signaling that are expected.

Figure 2-2 Signaling

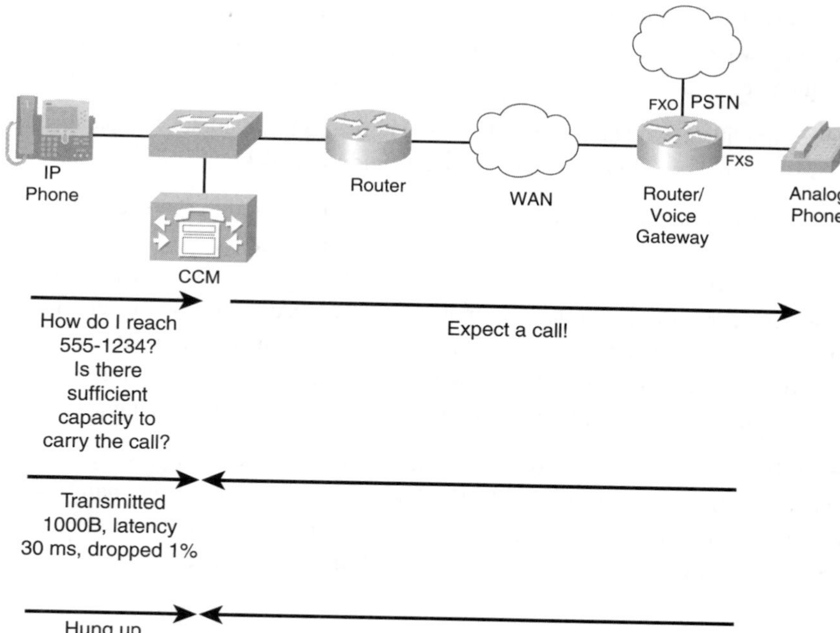

CCNP ONT

Signaling plays several important roles:

- Information about the receiver is obtained.
- Capacity is checked before starting; otherwise, call quality suffers.
- Call quality is monitored so that adjustments may be made to maintain call quality.
- Connect and disconnect times are kept for billing.

In Figure 2-2, a Call Manager is shown receiving the signaling. A Call Manager allows centralized call control, which provides oversight of the call and records of connections and quality. Voice trunking may be accomplished without such supervision (called distributed call control), but care must be taken to not overburden links and quality must be manually maintained.

Packetization

Before voice may be transmitted over a network, sound has to be captured from a microphone and digitized. The digital recording is then chopped into sections (each is typically 20 ms), which are sent sequentially and replayed in order out a speaker.

Sound is captured at a microphone by sampling (periodically taking a power reading). The Nyquist theorem says that to reproduce a signal, sampling must occur at twice the maximum frequency. The phone system is designed to capture frequencies less than 4 kHz, which are samples of 8,000 times per second.

Pulse Amplitude Modulation (PAM) is used in the PSTN. Samples are quantized to 8-bit numbers 8,000 times per second (yielding a 64-kbps DS0).

Two forms of quantization are used. A linear scale is used in the U.S., while abroad, a logarithmic scale is used. The U.S. system (called µ-law) was developed earlier, and it suffered from lower-powered sampling systems. A-law (logarithmic sampling) was developed later to be different and give domestic opportunities to European companies that were still recovering from World War II. A-law benefits from greater computing resources, and the logarithmic scale does a better job of reproducing sound.

After being captured, Pulse Amplitude Modulation (PAM) samples are encoded using a coder/decoder (CODEC). Coders work using two main techniques: PCM, which encodes the signal straight to bits, and CELP, which matches the waveform to a predefined library and sends a code.

G.711 and G.726 use PCM. G.711 uses 8 bits per sample, whereas G.726 uses 7, 6, or 5, depending on the desired quality. G.728 and 729 use CELP. Resulting voice quality is shown in Table 2-1. Remember that the figures for bandwidth do not include headers.

Table 2-1 Details of Five CODECs

CODEC	Technique	Bandwidth	20 ms Sample Size	Quality
G.711	PCM	64	160	4.10
G.726	ADPCM	32, 24, 16	80, 40, 20	3.85
G.728	LDCELP	16	40	3.61
G.729	CS-ACELP	8	20	3.92
G.729A	CS-ACELP	8	20	3.90

Voice quality is measured on a scale called Mean Opinion Score (MOS). MOS has been scored by averaging judges' scores: a MOS of 5 is perfect, whereas 4 is toll quality, and anything less gets less and less acceptable. Perceptual Speech Quality Measurement (PSQM) is a newer technique that compares wave forms pre- and post-transmission and grades on a scale of 0 to 6.5. PSQM is repeatable and less arbitrary, but the non-traditional scale made it hard to compare to MOS, so Perceptual Evaluation of Speech Quality (PESQ) is a version of PSQM that uses an MOS scale.

All the ideas discussed in this section—sampling, quantization, encoding, and compression—depend on specialized processors called Digital Signal Processors (DSP). DSPs are also used for translating CODECs (transcoding) and for conferencing.

Transmitting

VoIP depends on three pillars:

- Signaling is used for call setup and teardown. Common protocols include H.323, SIP, and MGCP.
- Packetization sends voice samples inside IP packets.
- QoS prioritizes VoIP traffic.

There are three reasons users will throw new VoIP phones at you and beg for old analog headsets: packet loss, delay, and echo. The biggest reason for packet loss is tail-drop in queues, which is solved through QoS. The biggest issue with delay is variation in delay (called jitter), which causes large de-jitter buffers to be used and causes more delay. The solution to jitter is QoS. Echo is solved through a technique called echo-cancellation (G.168), which is on by default and compensates for delay.

Voice samples are encapsulated in Real Time Protocol (RTP) packets. Voice does not need the reliability provided by TCP; by the time a retransmission happened, the moment to play the sound would have passed. Voice does need a way to order samples and recognize the time between samples, which UDP by itself doesn't allow. RTP is a protocol within UDP that adds the necessary features.

A complete VoIP packet needs to include a data link header (Ethernet has a 14 byte header and 4 bytes CRC), an IP header (20 Bytes), an 8 byte UDP header, and 12 bytes for RTP. Each 20 ms sample therefore includes 58 bytes of overhead. G.711 sends 8000 bytes per second (20 ms would therefore need 160 bytes), so about a quarter of the transmission is headers!

Figure 2-3 shows the header overhead graphically and Table 2-1 shows the bandwidth consumed by the various CODECs, including headers. If the phone uses 20 ms samples (50 samples per second), then there will be 50 headers. G.711, instead of being 64 kbps, turns out to be:

(Headers + Sample) * 50/s=

(14B + 20B + 8B + 12B + 160B + 4B) * 50/s =

218 B * 50/s= 10900 B/s = 87,200 b/s = 87.2 kbps

Figure 2-3 Protocol Layout for Voice Transmission over IP

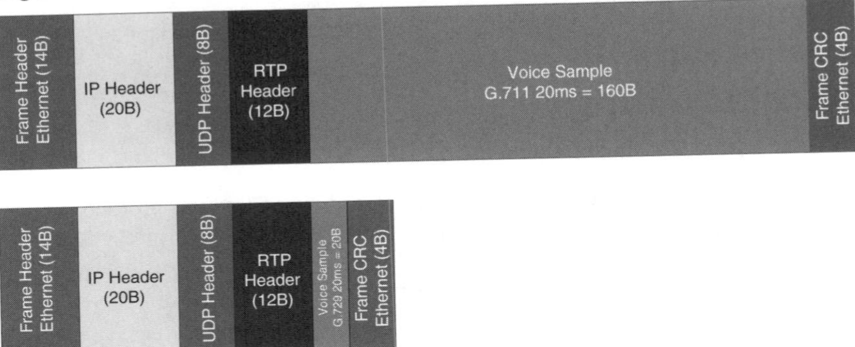

Note that G.729 uses 20-byte samples, so it needs only 31.2 kbps.

At this point, you may have sticker shock. If G.729 is billed as 8 kbps per conversation, 31.2 kbps seems extreme. There are ways to mitigate the difference, although the techniques do not completely erase the need for headers.

One way is to use RTP header compression. Header compression is configured per link and remembers previous IP, UDP, and RTP headers, substituting 2B- or 4B-labels subsequently. By taking the header set from 40B to 4B, cRTP delivers G.729 using 22-B headers and a consumption of 16.8 kbps!

Voice Activity Detection (VAD) is a technology that recognizes when you are not talking and ceases transmission, thus saving bandwidth. In normal speech, one person or the other is talking less than 65 percent of the time (there are those long, uncomfortable silences right after you say, "*You did what?*"). VAD can therefore dramatically reduce demands for bandwidth.

The bad news with VAD is that it doesn't help with music (such as hold music) and that it creates "dead air," which can be mistaken for disconnection. Some phones, in fact, will play soft static to reinforce that the line is still live (this is called comfort noise).

Bandwidth Requirements

Various tradeoffs go into selecting the parameters for a VoIP implementation, each of which affect voice quality and bandwidth. These include:

- Sample period—Each packet represents a period of time. Longer periods mean that fewer headers have to be sent, but add delay while accumulating samples. Shorter periods mean more header overhead, but less delay.
- Packets per second—One second divided by the sample period.
- CODEC—Each coding protocol uses more or less bandwidth and offers more or less quality. See Table 2-1 for details.
- IP/UDP/RTP overhead—40 B, or 4 B if using cRTP with checksum, or 2B if using cRTP without checksum.
- Data Link overhead—Ethernet uses 18 B. This varies by protocol.

A Worksheet for Calculating VoIP Bandwidth

Sample period = _____	*Packets per second =*	_____
CODEC = _____	Sample size =	_____
Header size (40 B without cRTP, 4 B with) =		_____
Data Link overhead =		_____
Total packet = sample + header + data link =		_____
**Packets per second =*	×	_____
		_____
Multiply by 8 to get b/s	×	8
		_____
Divide by 1000 to get kbps	/	1000
		_____

An Example for G.711, No Compression over Ethernet, 20 ms Samples

Sample period = 20 ms	*Packets per second =*	*50/s*
CODEC = G.711	Sample size =	160 B
Header size (40 B w/o cRTP, 4 B with) =	+	40 B
Data Link overhead =	+	18 B
Total packet = sample + header + data link =		**218 B**
** Packets per second =*	×	*50/s*
		10900 B/s
Multiply by 8 to get b/s	×	8 b/B
		87200 b/s
Divide by 1000 to get kbps	/	1000 kb/b
		87.2 kbps

Additionally, allot 30–73 bytes for IPSec headers if used.

Implementing IP Telephony

In the enterprise, IP telephony is deployed to replace a PBX. A typical PBX contains a switching function (the "brains") and cards that attach extensions (station cards) and connect to the outside world (line cards). Figure 2-4 shows the evolution from an old PBX to a modern distributed IP telephony solution.

Figure 2-4 Evolution from PBX to IP Telephony

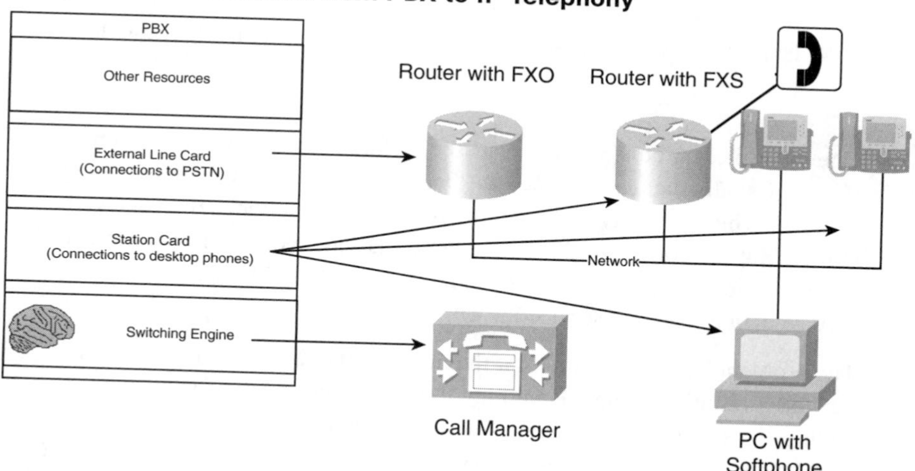

A Cisco Call Manager takes the place of the "brains" and helps end stations understand how to reach each other. CCM also oversees the dial plan, produces utilization reports, and determines functionality. CCM is typically deployed in a cluster, so that the system does not rely on one machine.

Note

Cisco Call Manager Express runs on a router and can be used for small offices. Routers are also deployed as backup call managers (this is called Survivable Remote Site Telephony or SRST), so being disconnected from a remote CCM does not disable a branch phone system.

IP phones and soft phones connect directly to the network, whereas legacy phones connect to the network through FXS ports on routers. Routers operating this way are called gateways. Think of the network and gateways as being equivalent to the station cards in an old PBX.

Routers with external connections, such as FXO ports, are also called gateways. In this scenario, however, the router takes the place of an external line card.

Telephony deployments follow one of four models:

- Single Site—One office uses a CCM cluster to handle local phones.
- Multisite with centralized call processing—One CCM cluster at headquarters handles local and remote phones. Branch offices typically are set up with SRST.
- Multisite with distributed call processing—Each site has a CCM cluster.
- Clustering over WAN—The CCM cluster is distributed between locations.

One other piece, not shown or discussed so far, is Call Admission Control (CAC). Usually data is described as "better to degrade service than to deny service," which is to say that when more users need service, everyone goes slower. But the voice world has never said that one more user would cause quality to go down. In fact, voice engineers would say "It's better to deny service than to degrade service."

The problem is, how do you limit the number of calls going across a VoIP network? Intuitively, there is nothing to prevent one more person from calling. This is where CAC comes in. CAC is a tool that tracks the number of calls and—when it reaches a threshold value—prevents another call. CAC is an important part of an IP telephony solution.

Configuring Cisco Routers to Support VoIP

Consider Figure 2-5 as a precursor to reading about the configuration of a router with FXO, FXS, and VoIP neighbors.

Figure 2-5 Voice over IP Network Topology

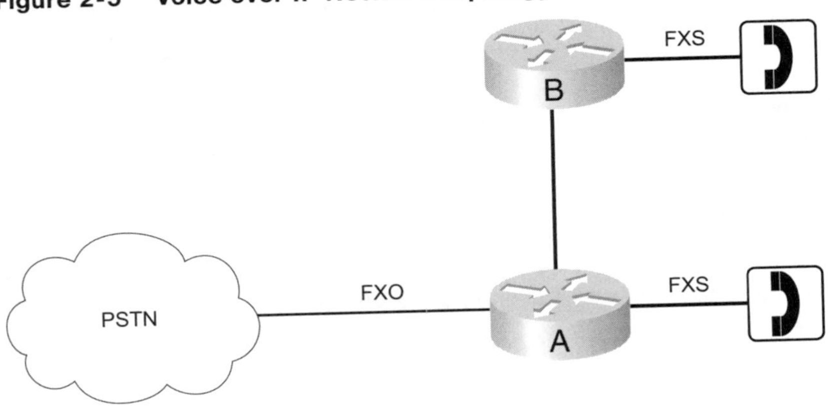

The configuration is shown in Example 2-1.

Example 2-1 Configuration of Router A

```
hostname router_A
interface s0/0
 ip address 172.21.77.1 255.255.255.0

dial-peer voice 1 voip
 destination-pattern 720
 session-target ipv4:172.21.77.2

dial-peer voice 2 pots
 destination-pattern 721
 port 1/0/0

dial-peer voice 3 pots
 destination-pattern 9
 port 2/0/0
```

In Example 2-1, the dial plan consists of three patterns: Dialing 9 gets an outside line, dialing 720 rings the phone on the other router, and 721 rings the pots line on the local router.

All patterns need a destination-pattern statement to configure the dial plan. Phones reached over IP also need a session target, whereas directly attached analog phones are referenced by port.

CHAPTER 3

QoS Overview

Quality of service (QoS) configurations give special treatment to certain traffic at the expense of others. This helps make your network performance more deterministic and predictable for this traffic. Using QoS in the network addresses the following problems:

- Lack of bandwidth for important applications
- Delay of sensitive data, such as voice and video
- Jitter (variable delay)
- Packet loss due to data being dropped at a congested interface

Bandwidth

In a network with several hops, the available bandwidth is only as much as the smallest link. When multiple applications and multiple flows use the same links, the available bandwidth per application is even smaller—it equals the smallest link bandwidth divided by the number of flows. Insufficient bandwidth especially affects time-sensitive and interactive traffic, and traffic with large flows.

You can increase link speeds to get more bandwidth—that can be expensive, time-consuming, and introduce technological difficulties. Alternatively, QoS mechanisms can guarantee bandwidth to specific applications.

Compressing the traffic on slower links creates more useable bandwidth; because each frame is smaller, there are fewer bits to transmit. However, compressing data uses processor and memory resources and introduces some latency while the compression is being done. Because of this, use compression only on T1 links or less. You can compress the whole payload or just compress the protocol headers with TCP or Real-time Protocol (RTP) header compression (cRTP). Cisco supports three payload compression algorithms:

- Stacker
- Predictor
- Microsoft Point-to-Point Compression (MPPC)

For voice, use Low Latency Queuing (LLQ) and cRTP compression, and for data, use Class-Based Weighted Fair Queuing (CBWFQ) and TCP compression. LLQ and CBWFQ are discussed later in this chapter.

Delay and Jitter

Network traffic experiences four types of delay:

- Processing delay—The time it takes a packet to move from the input interface of a router or Layer 3 switch, to the output interface. Processing delay depends on switching mode, CPU speed and utilization, the router's architecture, and interface configuration. This is a variable delay.
- Queuing delay—The length of time a packet waits in the interface queue before being sent to the transmit ring. Queuing delay depends on the number and size of packets in the queue, and the queuing methods in place. This is a variable delay.
- Serialization delay—The length of time it take to place the bits from the interface transmit ring onto the wire. Serialization delay depends on the bandwidth of the interface—higher bandwidth equals smaller serialization delay. This is a fixed delay.
- Propagation delay—The length of time it takes the packet to move from one end of the link to the other. Propagation delay depends on the type of media, such as fiber or satellite links. This is a fixed delay.

The total delay is the sum of all four delays on every link along the path. Because processing and queuing delay times can vary, end-to-end delay can vary from packet to packet. This variation is called *jitter*.

To decrease delay, you can increase the link bandwidth, prioritize important packets (note that this increases the delay for non-priority traffic), or compress the packet headers or the payloads. On links under T1 speed, you can fragment large packets and interleave smaller, interactive, packets between them—this is called Link Fragmentation and Interleave (LFI).

When your traffic traverses an ISP network, you might need to reprioritize it to match the provider's standards.

Packet Loss Issues

Packet loss can cause jerky transmission of voice or video, slow application performance, or corrupt data. By default, when a software queue is full (congested), the switch or router drops all other traffic bound for that queue. This is called *tail drop*. It can cause some problems:

- TCP global synchronization.
- TCP buffer starvation.
- Delay and jitter.
- High-priority traffic is dropped, whereas low-priority traffic is sent.

Congestion avoidance attempts to prevent tail drop. To accomplish this, increase link bandwidth, use queuing to guarantee a certain amount of traffic to each application, or use Weighted Random Early Detection (WRED). WRED drops lower-priority traffic (based on Differentiated Services Code Point [DSCP] or IP Precedence values) as a queue starts to fill and drops high-priority traffic only when the queue is almost full. If the queue fills completely, however, tail drop is used. The drop thresholds and the drop ratios are configurable. WRED works best with TCP traffic, because TCP dynamically adjusts its sending rate when packets are dropped. Do not use WRED for voice traffic. The "Congestion Avoidance" section describes this more completely.

Four other causes of packet drop are: frame errors, lack of buffer space (called an *ignore*), a CPU that is unable to assign a free buffer to it (called an *overrun*), or a CPU that is too busy to process inbound packets so the inbound queue fills.

Defining QoS Requirements for Network Traffic

To implement QoS, you need to identify the types of network traffic, determine the requirements for each, divide the traffic into classes, and then set policies for those classes.

A network audit helps identify the types of traffic on the network.

The relative importance of each application is a business decision, accomplished by a business audit. Applications should be grouped into classes that have about the same QoS requirements. Some common classes include: Voice, Interactive, Mission-critical, Transactional, Best-effort, and Scavenger.

A QoS policy then can be created for each class of traffic. You need to decide such things as allocated bandwidth (minimum and/or maximum), prioritization, and congestion avoidance.

QoS Models

There are three QoS models:

- Best effort—Traffic is sent with no guarantees of bandwidth or priority.
- Integrated Services (IntServ)—The QoS parameters are signaled throughout the path and guaranteed for the length of the session.
- Differentiated Services (DiffServ)—QoS parameters are applied to traffic classes at each hop along the path.

Best Effort

Best-effort delivery is the default method—traffic is sent out in the order it arrives with no differentiation between types of traffic and no guarantee of delivery. Benefits of best effort include its scalability (the Internet is based on best-effort delivery), and its ease of deployment. Drawbacks include the fact that all traffic is given the same service level.

IntServ

IntServ is a QoS model that guarantees a specific level of service to each flow of identified traffic, throughout the entire network, for the length of the session. This is done using Resource Reservation Protocol (RSVP). An RSVP-aware application, or a router or CallManager acting in proxy for a nonRSVP-aware device, requests a specific level of service from its next-hop router. A check is made along the path between the two endpoints, and each RSVP-enabled router along the way reserves bandwidth for that flow. If the network cannot provide the required bandwidth, the session is not allowed or its service level is downgraded.

RSVP works for any type of traffic, but it is usually used for real-time applications that are either rate-sensitive or delay-sensitive, such as voice and video. Figure 3-1 shows a call between two IP phones.

Figure 3-1 Using RSVP for Voice Calls

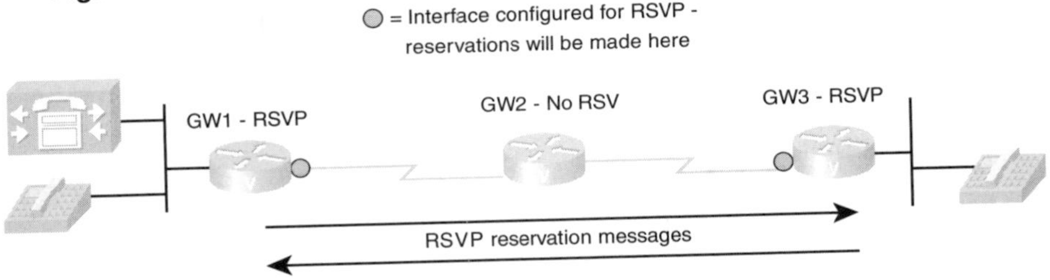

Two of the routers in the path—GW1 and GW3—are configured with RSVP; however, GW2 is not. When GW1 and GW3 receive the RSVP messages requesting a service level, they reserve that amount of bandwidth on their WAN interface. There must be some sort of QoS configured on the routers to implement the reservation. When GW2 receives the RSVP messages, it merely passes them on to the next hop router unchanged. Note that reservations are made in both directions becuase this is a voice call.

All routers in the path are not required to be configured with RSVP, but reservations are made only on those routers and those interfaces with it enabled. To ensure end-to-end service, configure RSVP on all router interfaces in the data path.

The path between endpoints is determined by the routing protocol, not by RSVP. If there is a network change, and the routing protocol changes the path, then RSVP reconverges also.

Current applications use DiffServ to enact IntServ QoS policies, such as guaranteed rate, and controlled load. One of the biggest benefits of IntServ is that it provides per-flow admission control. This can help with VoIP calls. RSVP supports applications that use dynamic port numbers and static ones. Some drawbacks include its overhead—signaling is exchanged at the beginning of a flow, so there can be some delay. It must continue to cross the network for the length of the flow to adjust for changes in path due to network changes, thus causing extra overhead. Additionally, because you need to track each flow, it is not scalable in a large enterprise.

For more information on using RSVP with VoIP, see the Cisco Press book *Cisco Voice Gateways and Gatekeepers* by David Mallory, Ken Salhoff, and Denise Donohue.

DiffServ

DiffServ groups network traffic into *classes* comprised of traffic needing the same type of QoS treatment. For instance, voice traffic is separated from email traffic. However, e-mail might be placed in the same class as web traffic. The exact classes, traffic, and QoS policies used are a business decision.

These classes are distinguished from each other based on the value of certain bits in the IP or ISL header or the 802.1Q tag. Each hop along the way must be configured to treat the marked traffic the way you want—this is called per-hop behavior (PHB).

- In the Layer 3 IP header, you use the 8-bit Type of Service (ToS) field. You can set either IP Precedence, using the top 3 bits, or DSCP using the top 6 bits of the field. The bottom 2 bits are not used for setting priority. The default DSCP value is zero, which corresponds to best-effort delivery.
- At Layer 2, with ISL, you can set 3 of the 4 bits in the ISL priority field to reflect the class of service (CoS). With 802.1Q, you set the 3 802.1p bits to the CoS. The values of these 3 bits correspond to the IP Precedence values.

Benefits of DiffServ include the many classes of service possible, and its scalability. As a drawback, it can be complex to configure. It also does not absolutely guarantee a level of service.

QoS Implementation Methods

The legacy method of configuring QoS was at each interface, on each router, using the Command Line Interface (CLI). The current recommended method is to use the Modular QoS CLI (MQC), which allows you to create one configuration that can then be applied to many interfaces. Common QoS settings have been automated with AutoQoS. For those who prefer a GUI interface, there is the Cisco Router and Security Device Manager (SDM).

Legacy CLI

The traditional QoS configuration using legacy CLI involves accessing the router via Telnet or console port. Traffic classification and policy enforcement are combined in the configuration at each interface, which is time-consuming and can lead to errors.

The types of QoS possible are limited, also. For example, you can do simple priority queuing, custom queuing, and compression. Legacy CLI QoS might be used to tweak AutoQoS settings.

MQC

Modular QoS CLI (MQC) is a method of classifying traffic, marking the traffic, and setting policies for that traffic that can be used on most devices with most kinds of policies. It's most important contribution is the separation of traffic classification from policy implementation. Here are general steps for implementing MQC:

Step 1. Create the necessary access control lists, if classifying traffic by ACL, or configure network-based application recognition (NBAR).

Step 2. Create class maps that specify matching such items as ACLs, protocol, DSCP, or IP Precedence values.

Step 3. Create a policy map that links to each class map and defines the policy for each.

Step 4. Apply the policy map to the appropriate interfaces.

When access control lists (ACL) are used to classify traffic, the way a router or switch reacts to specific access control entries (ACE) is different in a QoS context than with security-based ACLs. In a QoS access list:

- If the traffic matches a *permit* statement, the designated QoS action is taken.
- If the traffic matches a *deny* statement, the rest of the ACEs in that ACL are skipped and the switch goes to the next ACL.
- If there are multiple ACLs in a policy applied to an interface, the switch stops reading them as soon as a permit statement match is found for the traffic.
- If the traffic does not match any ACL entry, the switch just gives best-effort delivery to the traffic.

MQC Configuration

First, configure the ACLs if using them to identify traffic.

Second, configure a class map for each classification of traffic. Class map names are case-sensitive.

```
(config)#class-map [match-any ¦ match-all] name
(config-cmap)#match {match options, such as ACL}
```

Third, configure a policy map that calls the class maps and sets policies or types of treatment for each class. Policy map names are also case sensitive.

```
(config)#policy-map name
(config-pmap)#class class-map-name
(config-pmap-c)#policy options, such as set DSCP or bandwidth
```

Finally, apply the MQC policy to the desired interface(s), either inbound or outbound:

```
(config-if)#service-policy {output | input} name
```

Verifying QoS Configuration

Use the following commands to verify your QoS configurations and actions:

- **show class-map** [*name*]—Displays the configured class maps or just the one named.
- **show policy-map** [*name*]—Displays the configured policy maps or just the one named.
- **show policy-map** [**interface** [*interface-number* [**input** | **output**]] | [**class** *class-name*]—Displays the policy maps and statistics by interface or class.
- **show queueing** [**interface** *interface-number*]—Shows the queuing strategy and statistics for any queues configured on the interface.
- **show policy interface** *interface-number*—Displays the policies for all classes applied to the interface, along with statistics.
- **debug ip rsvp**—If using RSVP for voice, shows information about packets received and sent.

AutoQoS

AutoQoS is a utility that automates and simplifies QoS configuration, giving a consistent configuration across the network. It discovers the applications traversing the router or switch and configures standard best practice QoS policies for them. It can be used with both LAN and WAN interfaces. Automatic configurations can be tuned if necessary by using the MQC or with legacy CLI. AutoQoS was originally only for VoIP applications, but recent versions can be used with data applications also.

When configured on a WAN interface, AutoQoS:

- Detects and classifies VoIP and data traffic (typically using NBAR).
- Builds appropriate services policies, including placing Real-Time Protocol (RTP) traffic into a low-latency queue (LLQ) and guaranteeing bandwidth to VoIP control traffic.
- Sets up traffic shaping, fragmentation, or compression where needed.
- Enables SNMP traps and syslog alerting for VoIP events.

When configured on a LAN interface, AutoQoS:

- Sets up priority/expedited queuing on the switch interface.
- Configures the COS mapping to queues, and adjusts queue size and weights.
- Sets up trust boundaries on user access ports and links between switches. Trusts the incoming CoS only when an IP phone is present.

To use AutoQoS, CEF must be enabled, and the correct bandwidth configured on each interface, then AutoQos is enabled as follows. This example enables AutoQoS for VoIP only. Notice that after the commands are given, the router has created a policy map (not shown) and applied it to the interface:

```
Router(config)#int s1/0/0:1
Router(config-if)#bandwidth 1544
Router(config-if)#auto qos voip
!
Router#show auto qos int s1/0/0:1

Serial1/0/0:1 -
 !
 interface Serial1/0/0:1
  service-policy output AutoQoS-Policy-UnTrust
```

SDM QoS Wizard

SDM allows GUI configuration of router interfaces, firewall, ACL features, VPNs, routing, Network Address Translation (NAT), Intrusion Prevention, Network Access Control (NAC), and QoS. It helps nonexpert users to configure these router functions. SDM comes preinstalled on the ISR routers, but to use the SDM Wizard, the router's HTTP server function must be enabled.

With the SDM's QoS Wizard, you can configure, monitor, and troubleshoot QoS configurations. Browse to http://10.10.10.1—the default IP address for SDM. From the "Configure" menu, choose to configure QoS. This launches the QoS Wizard, shown in Figure 3-2.

Figure 3-2 SDM QoS Wizard

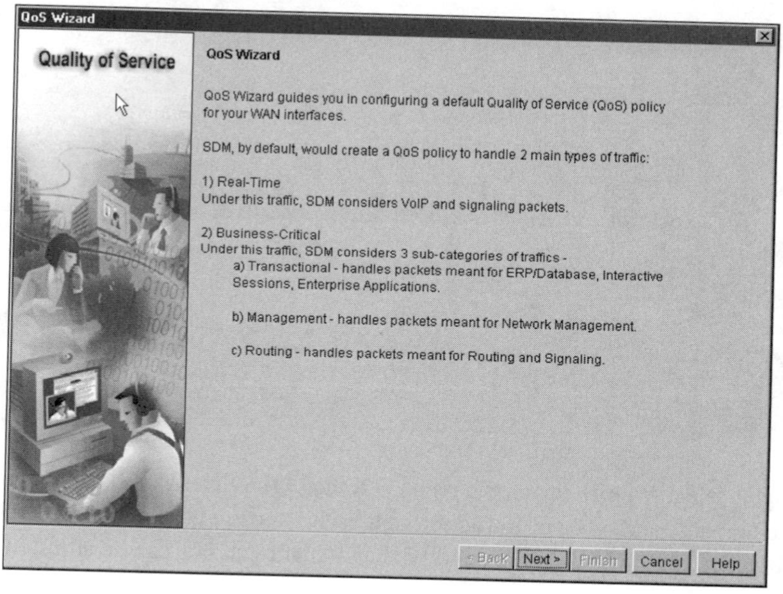

Notice that the wizard creates policies for two types of traffic:

- Real-Time—VoIP and signaling packets
- Business-Critical—This has three subcategories:
  - — Transactional—Database, interactive sessions, and enterprise applications
  - — Management—Network management applications
  - — Routing—Routing protocols

You can specify bandwidth allocation for these classes or use the wizard's recommendations. After the wizard is done, it shows you the policies and loads them into the router's configuration. You can edit them later, as shown in Figure 3-3.

Figure 3-3 Editing the QoS Wizard Policies

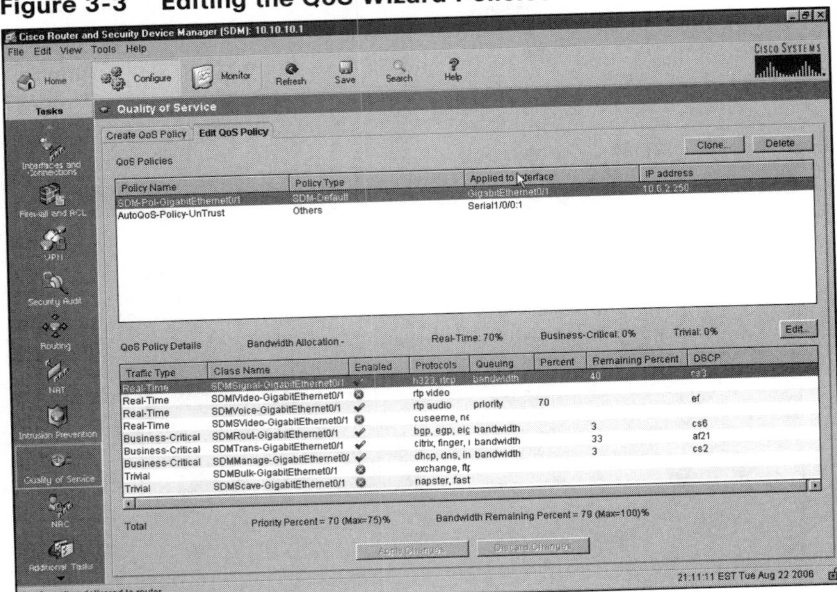

If you select **Monitor** from the menu and then **QoS Status**, you can monitor the amounts and types of traffic through each interface configured for QoS. The interval, traffic direction, and type of statistics shown can be adjusted.

QoS Methods Comparison

Thus, Cisco provides four ways for you to configure QoS in your network. They each have their strengths and weaknesses.

- Legacy CLI—Hardest to use, little capability to fine-tune, takes the longest to implement, and is not modular.
- MQC—Easier to use and takes less time to implement on multiple interfaces than does legacy CLI. Has excellent capability to fine-tune configurations, and it is modular.
- AutoQoS—Easy to use, but it has limited inherent fine-tuning, takes the least time to implement, and has excellent modularity.
- SDM QoS Wizard—Simple to use, can do some limited fine-tuning, is fast to implement, and has good modularity.

CHAPTER 4

QoS Details

This chapter explores, in detail, ways of choosing and configuring quality of service. The way you classify and mark traffic, and the type of QoS policies you implement, will depend on the policy location and types of network traffic present.

Classification and Marking

Classification is the most basic Quality of Service (QoS) step—until traffic is identified, it cannot be provided a unique level of service. Traffic is often classified by application, source or destination IP address, or inbound interface.

After traffic is classified, an appropriate marking can be applied to it. The location where traffic is marked defines a *trust boundary*. If the device that marked the traffic is trusted, then that marking is passed through the network and honored by each device. If that device is untrusted, then some trusted network entity must re-mark the traffic.

Classification and marking should be done as close to the traffic source as possible because they can be resource intensive. Marking at the end device, such as an IP phone, is ideal. Otherwise, mark (or re-mark) traffic at the access switch or distribution switch if necessary.

Layer 2 markings include 802.1Q Class of Service (CoS) and Multiprotocol Label Switching (MPLS) experimental bits. Frame relay markings are different—they include setting the Backward Explicit Congestion Notification (BECN) bit, the Forward Explicit Congestion Notification (FECN) bit, or the Discard Eligible (DE) bit in the frame relay header. Layer 3 markings include Differentiated Services Code Point (DSCP) and IP precedence. After traffic is classified and marked, other routers and switches in the network can be configured to provide QoS to it.

Using NBAR for Classifying Traffic

There are several ways to identify traffic so that it can be classified. Access lists are commonly used to identify application data, but Cisco has an IOS-based tool that provides more granularity and goes beyond static port numbers. Network-Based Application Recognition (NBAR) is an IOS protocol discovery and classification mechanism. It monitors the traffic going in and out of an interface, identifies it by protocol, port number, or payload contents (up to 400 bytes), and provides traffic statistics. NBAR recognizes common applications, even those that use dynamic ports. For instance, Real-Time Protocol (RTP) carries voice and video traffic and uses dynamic port numbers within a large range. An access list can match traffic within that range of port numbers, but NBAR can match on the following RTP characteristics:

- Audio traffic (using payload types 0–23)
- Video traffic (using payload types 24–33)
- Payload type for a specific payload type value

Note
NBAR does not identify RTP control traffic, just RTP bearer traffic.

You can additionally configure NBAR to recognize custom applications. Cisco provides downloadable Packet Description Language Modules (PDLM) that also add additional applications.

CEF must be enabled on each interface where NBAR is used. To enable NBAR at an interface, and then view the traffic that it discovers, use the commands:

```
Router(config-if)#ip nbar protocol-discovery
Router#show ip nbar protocol-discovery
```

You can download new PDLMs from the Cisco web site: http://www.cisco.com/cgi-bin/tablebuild.pl/pdlm. You must be a registered user. After the file is downloaded, you should either save it in the router's flash or place it on a TFTP server reachable by the router. Instruct the router to load the PDLM with the following command:

```
Router(config)#ip nbar pdlm pdlm_name
```

The name is in URL format, and points the router either to the file in flash or to the TFTP server. For example, you might use **ip nbar pdlm flash://bittorent.pdlm** to load the PDLM for Bit Torrent from flash memory.

Sometimes users map protocols to different ports than NBAR expects. To tell NBAR to look for a protocol on additional ports and to then verify your configuration, use the commands:

```
Router(config)#ip nbar port-map protocol [tcp | udp] port
Router#show ip nbar port-map
```

To use NBAR for classifying traffic with the MQC, follow these steps:

Step 1. Enable NBAR on all appropriate interfaces.

Step 2. Create a class map that matches against one or more of the NBAR protocols, using the **match protocol** option. Repeat this step for each class desired.

Step 3. Create a policy that links to those class maps, and assigns desired service to it.

Step 4. Apply the policy to an interface.

Example 4-1 shows NBAR enabled on a GigEthernet interface, and class maps created to match three types of traffic discovered by NBAR: RTP, any web traffic that has the word "ccnp" in its URL, and eDonkey. A policy map is created that marks this traffic, and it is applied inbound to the LAN interface.

Example 4-1 Using NBAR with the MQC

```
Router(config)#int gi 0/0
Router(config-if)#ip nbar protocol-discovery
!
Router(config)#class-map VOIP
Router(config-cmap)#match protocol rtp audio
Router(config-cmap)#!
Router(config-cmap)#class-map Exams
Router(config-cmap)#match protocol http url ccnp*
Router(config-cmap)#!
Router(config-cmap)#class-map eDonkey
Router(config-cmap)#match protocol edonkey
!
Router(config)#policy-map NBAR
Router(config-pmap)#class VOIP
Router(config-pmap-c)#set ip dscp ef
Router(config-pmap-c)#class Exams
Router(config-pmap-c)#set ip dscp 31
Router(config-pmap-c)#class eDonkey
Router(config-pmap-c)#set ip dscp 13
!
Router(config-pmap-c)#int gi 0/0
Router(config-if)#service-policy input NBAR
```

This classifies and marks the traffic and uses NBAR to identify it. Classification and marking needs to happen only once—all other devices in the network can just look for the DSCP markings and set policies based on those. Thus, the next part must be to configure some way to treat this classified and marked traffic. An example of this configuration is the section on LLQ and CBWFQ.

For more detailed information on NBAR, including a list of applications it currently is able to recognize, see http://www.cisco.com/en/US/products/ps6616/products_qanda_item09186a00800a3ded.shtml

Marking at Layer 2

CoS uses the three 802.1p bits in the 802.1Q trunking tag to mark traffic. These three bits have eight possible values, ranging between zero and seven. IP Precedence uses three bits in the IP header, so it has the same range of values as does CoS. Table 4-1 lists the values and their standard meanings.

Table 4-1 IP Precedence and CoS Values

IP Precedence/CoS	Name
7	Network
6	Internet
5	Critical
4	Flash-override
3	Flash
2	Immediate
1	Priority
0	Routine

When frames enter a switch, the Layer 2 header is stripped off. The switch maps the CoS value to an internal DSCP value as the packet moves through it. This DSCP value is then translated back to a CoS value if the packet is sent over another trunk link. There are default values for the mappings between and CoS and DSCP, but they can also be configured.

MPLS labels have a three-bit field, called the MPLS experimental (MPLS EXP) field, which has the same eight possible values as CoS and IP Precedence. By default, any IP Precedence value is copied into this field and becomes the Layer 2 marking for MPLS traffic. Service providers alternatively can set these bits independently, thus marking the traffic within their network without changing their customer's Layer 3 marking. The value of MPLS EXP bits is preserved through the MPLS network.

Table 4-2 lists the eight Layer 2 markings, and some suggested applications for them.

Table 4-2 Layer 2 Markings and Applications

CoS Value	Application
7	Reserved
6	Reserved
5	Voice Bearer
4	Video
3	Call Signaling
2	High-Priority Data
1	Medium-Priority Data
0	Best-Effort Data

Marking at Layer 3

The concept behind DiffServ (DS) is to group traffic into classes and mark it once at the edge of the network. DiffServ was created to be highly scalable by separating classification from policy creation and by servicing aggregate classes of traffic rather than individual flows.

DiffServ uses Layer 3 markings, setting the eight-bit ToS field in the IP header. Unlike the Layer 2 header, this marking remains with the packet as it traverses the network, and changes only if some device overwrites the value of these bits. You can set either IP Precedence, using the top three bits, or Differentiated Services Code Points (DSCP), using the top six bits of the field. The bottom two bits can be used for congestion notification. The default DSCP value is zero, which corresponds to best-effort delivery. When properly configured, DSCP is backward compatible with IP Precedence.

Each hop in the network is provisioned to treat traffic differently based on its markings; this is called "per-hop behavior" (PHB). RFC 2475 defines PHB as "the externally observable forwarding behavior applied at a DS-compliant node to a DS behavior aggregate." A *behavior aggregate* is a logical grouping of traffic that needs similar service levels. It is also referred to as a *service class*. Four PHBs are defined:

- Default
- Assured forwarding
- Class selector
- Expedited forwarding

Default PHB

All the bits in the TOS byte are set to "0," which gives best-effort delivery. Any unmarked traffic is mapped to this PHB.

Assured Forwarding and Class Selector PHB

Figure 4-1 shows the TOS byte in the IP header.

Figure 4-1 The TOS Byte in the IP Header

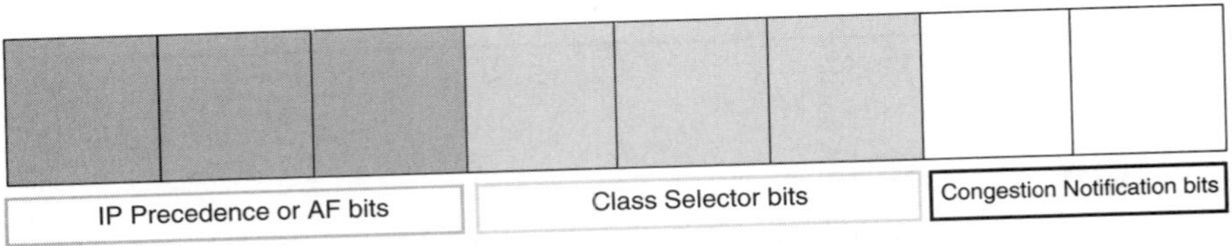

The six DSCP bits can be broken down into two sections: The highest three bits define the DiffServ Assured Forwarding (AF) class (the area in green), and the next three bits are called the "Class Selector (CS)" (the area in yellow). When the three CS bits are all zero, you have a value that is equal to IP Precedence. The lowest two bits (the area in white) are not used in DiffServ marking—they allow the sending of congestion notification information.

Each AF class becomes its own queue at the interface. AF uses the first two CS bits to define the drop probability within that queue. The last bit is always zero and is not used in calculating drop probability values. AF classes 1–4 are defined and within each class, 1 is low drop probability, 2 is medium, and 3 is high (meaning that traffic is more likely to get dropped if there is congestion).

AF guarantees a specified amount of bandwidth to a class. By default, it allows the traffic to burst above that amount if there is extra bandwidth available, although this can be policed.

Table 4-3 lists the classes and their associated AF values.

Table 4-3 Assured Forwarding Values

	Low Drop	Medium Drop	High Drop
Class 1	AF11	AF12	AF13
Class 2	AF21	AF22	AF23
Class 3	AF31	AF32	AF33
Class 4	AF41	AF42	AF43

DiffServ Expedited Forwarding PHB

Another predefined DiffServ classification is Expedited Forwarding (EF), which is DSCP 46. This is equivalent to IP precedence 5. EF traffic becomes a separate queue at the QoS-enabled router interface. You must configure each hop in the network for the type of service you want EF traffic to receive. EF is usually used to put traffic in a low-latency queue, which results in low delay, guarantees a specified amount of bandwidth, and also polices the traffic to prevent it from exceeding that bandwidth.

Classifying and Marking in a VoIP Network

Figure 4-2 shows what happens to the CoS and DSCP settings of a data packet as it moves through a QoS-enabled LAN.

Figure 4-2 CoS and DSCP Changes for a Data Packet

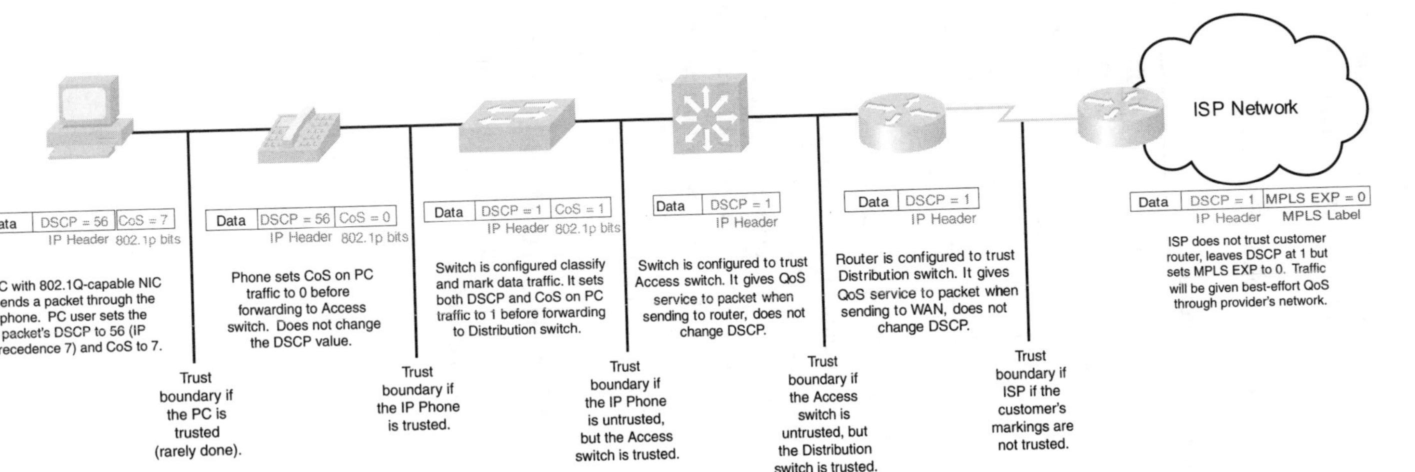

Data | DSCP = 56 | CoS = 7
IP Header 802.1p bits
PC with 802.1Q-capable NIC sends a packet through the phone. PC user sets the packet's DSCP to 56 (IP precedence 7) and CoS to 7.
Trust boundary if the PC is trusted (rarely done).
Data | DSCP = 56 | CoS = 0
IP Header 802.1p bits
Phone sets CoS on PC traffic to 0 before forwarding to Access switch. Does not change the DSCP value.
Trust boundary if the IP Phone is trusted.
Data | DSCP = 1 | CoS = 1
IP Header 802.1p bits
Switch is configured classify and mark data traffic. It sets both DSCP and CoS on PC traffic to 1 before forwarding to Distribution switch.
Trust boundary if the IP Phone is untrusted, but the Access switch is trusted.
Data | DSCP = 1
IP Header
Switch is configured to trust Access switch. It gives QoS service to packet when sending to router, does not change DSCP.
Trust boundary if the Access switch is untrusted, but the Distribution switch is trusted.
Data | DSCP = 1
IP Header
Router is configured to trust Distribution switch. It gives QoS service to packet when sending to WAN, does not change DSCP.
Trust boundary if ISP if the customer's markings are not trusted.
ISP Network
Data | DSCP = 1 | MPLS EXP = 0
IP Header MPLS Label
ISP does not trust customer router, leaves DSCP at 1 but sets MPLS EXP to 0. Traffic will be given best-effort QoS through provider's network.

- In the figure, users with an 802.1Q-enabled Network Interface Card (NIC) on their PC attempts to give their data higher priority within the network. They send a frame with an 802.1Q tag in which they have set the 802.1p bits to CoS of 7. They have also set the DSCP on the packet to 56. This animation shows just the relevant parts of the headers used.
- The IP phone by default creates an 802.1Q trunk between itself and the Access switch. It sets the 802.1p CoS on data traffic to zero, but it does not change any Layer 3 markings.
- The Access switch gets the frame from the phone and strips the Layer 2 header. By default it translates into an internal DSCP of zero as it moves through the switch fabric; however, this switch is configured to classify and mark data traffic. This particular application falls into a class that gets a Layer 3 marking of AF11, or DSCP 10 (binary value 001010). The switch remarks the DSCP value, and then sets the CoS to 1 in the 802.1Q tag when it sends the packet to the Distribution switch.
- The Distribution switch is configured to trust the Access switch's markings. It strips off the Layer 2 header, looks at the DSCP value, and provides the type of QoS service it is configured to provide to AF11 traffic. The switch's interface to the router is a Layer 3 interface, so no trunk tag is used. Instead, it puts on a normal Ethernet frame header and forwards the packet to the router.
- The router is configured to trust the packet's markings. It strips off the Layer 2 header, looks at the DSCP value, and provides the type of QoS service it is configured to provide to AF11 traffic. This might include allocating a certain amount of bandwidth and using Weighted Random Early Detection (WRED) in the queue. The router then forwards the packet to its ISP edge router.
- The ISP is not configured to trust the customer's markings. It could overwrite all DSCP values with zero, but in this case it just sets the MPLS Experimental Bits in the MPLS label to zero. The DSCP stays unchanged. The packet receives only best-effort service as it moves through the ISPs network, but devices in the destination network can use the unchanged DSCP values to provide QoS service to the packet.

Figure 4-3 shows what happens to the CoS and DSCP settings of a voice packet as it moves through a QoS-enabled LAN. In this example, the ISP trusts the customer's markings.

Figure 4-3 CoS and DSCP Changes for a Voice Packet

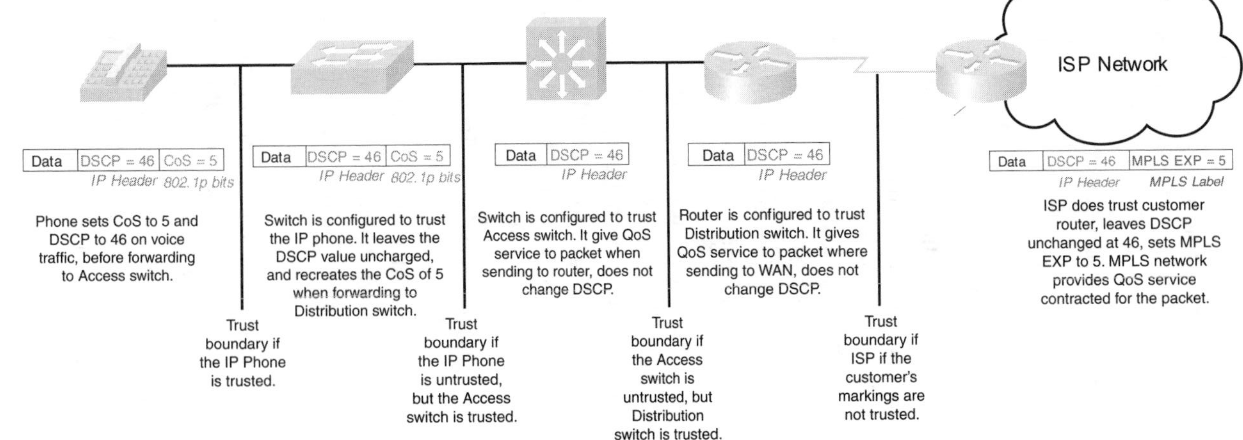

ISP Network
Data | DSCP = 46 | CoS = 5
IP Header 802.1p bits
Phone sets CoS to 5 and DSCP to 46 on voice traffic, before forwarding to Access switch.
Data | DSCP = 46 | CoS = 5
IP Header 802.1p bits
Switch is configured to trust the IP phone. It leaves the DSCP value uncharged, and recreates the CoS of 5 when forwarding to Distribution switch.
Data | DSCP = 46
IP Header
Switch is configured to trust Access switch. It give QoS service to packet when sending to router, does not change DSCP.
Data | DSCP = 46
IP Header
Router is configured to trust Distribution switch. It gives QoS service to packet where sending to WAN, does not change DSCP.
Data | DSCP = 46 | MPLS EXP = 5
IP Header MPLS Label
ISP does trust customer router, leaves DSCP unchanged at 46, sets MPLS EXP to 5. MPLS network provides QoS service contracted for the packet.
Trust boundary if the IP Phone is trusted.
Trust boundary if the IP Phone is untrusted, but the Access switch is trusted.
Trust boundary if the Access switch is untrusted, but Distribution switch is trusted.
Trust boundary if ISP if the customer's markings are not trusted.

- The Cisco IP phone creates an 802.1Q trunk between itself and the Access switch. It sets the 802.1p CoS on its own voice media traffic to 5, and it sets the Layer 3 marking to EF or DSCP 46 (binary value 101110). If this were voice signaling traffic, the phone would set a CoS of 3 and a Layer 3 marking of CS3, or DSCP 24 (binary value 011000).
- The Access switch gets the frame from the phone and strips the Layer 2 header. It is configured to trust the IP phone, so it translates the CoS value into an internal DSCP as the packet moves through the switch fabric. The switch then translates that internal DSCP value back to a CoS of 5 in the 802.1Q tag when it sends the packet to the Distribution switch. The Access switch applies any outbound policies configured for this traffic, such as putting it into a priority interface queue, as it sends it to the outbound interface.
- The Distribution switch is configured to trust the Access switch's markings. It strips off the Layer 2 header, looks at the DSCP value, and provides the type of QoS service it is configured to provide to EF traffic. This typically includes placing the packet in a priority queue at the interface. The switch's interface to the router is a Layer 3 interface, so no trunk tag is used. Instead it puts on a normal Ethernet frame header and forwards the packet to the router.
- The router is configured to trust the packet's markings. It strips off the Layer 2 header, looks at the DSCP value, and provides the type of QoS service it is configured to provide to EF traffic. This typically includes placing the packet in an LLQ and allocating a certain amount of bandwidth to that queue. The router then forwards the packet to its ISP edge router.
- The ISP is configured to trust the customer's markings. It translates the IP precedence value of 5 into an MPLS Experimental Bits value of 5. The DSCP stays unchanged. The packet receives prioritized, real-time service as it moves through the ISPs network, and devices in the destination network can use the unchanged DSCP values to also provide QoS service to the packet.

Queuing Overview

Queuing configuration usually acts on outbound traffic. Each interface has a *hardware queue*, or transmit ring (TxQ), that holds traffic ready to be serialized onto the interface media. This queue is always First In/First Out (FIFO). When outbound traffic arrives at an interface, the interface scheduler sends it to the transmit ring to be placed on the media. If the transmit ring is full, other traffic must wait in some buffer memory space assigned to that interface called a *software queue*. When traffic must be placed into queues, the interface is said to be *congested*.

Causes of congestion include:

- Speed mismatches—Typically LAN traffic needing to go across a much slower WAN link (persistent congestion). It can also be GigEthernet traffic bound out a FastEthernet interface (transient congestion).
- Link aggregation—For WAN links, this occurs when multiple remote sites access a hub site across an oversubscribed link. For LAN links, this typically occurs on a distribution switch with multiple access switches feeding in to it on the uplink port(s) to the core switch.

Hardware Queue

Logical interfaces, such as subinterfaces and tunnel interfaces, use the hardware queue of the physical interface; they do not have their own transmit queues.

The number of packets a TxQ can hold depends on the speed of the interface. It is automatically determined, and that length is typically fine but can be tuned if desired. Most devices use the **tx ring-limit** command for tuning TxQ size.

Lowering the Tx ring size lessens the length of time a packet waits in the FIFO queue, and it increases the chance of a packet hitting the software queue. However, too short of a TxQ results in router resource use, as the CPU must be interrupted each time the Tx ring requests a packet from a software queue. A decrease in ring size means an increase in interrupts.

Increasing the TxQ size is usually not recommended when using QoS, because it decreases the use of the software queue.

Use the **show controllers** *interface* command to find information about the transmit ring size.

Software Queue

The software queuing strategy is configurable, and the next sections deal with various techniques to do this. This is where you can influence the order in which packets are scheduled into the TxQ and the number of packets sent. When using queuing mechanisms, several different logical queues are created, and traffic is placed into the appropriate software queue when it arrives at the interface. Each software queue has size limits, and packets above that limit are dropped.

Remember that fast-switched or CEF-switched traffic enters the software queue only if the hardware queue is congested. Process-switched traffic always goes into the software queue.

Legacy Queuing Techniques

Queuing mechanisms allow you to control the way congested traffic is buffered and send out the interface by placing each type of traffic in its own queue. The router or switch then services each queue, scheduling transmittal of its traffic, according to a configured policy.

FIFO Queuing

By default, most interfaces use FIFO queuing—there is just one software queue, and traffic is buffered and then scheduled onto the interface in the order it is received.

Note

Serial interfaces of E1 speed and below use weighted fair queuing by default, rather than FIFO queuing.

Priority Queuing

With Priority queuing, queues are assigned different priority values and placed in one of four queues. The high-priority queue is a strict priority queue, which means that it gets serviced before anything else until it is empty. After that, each queue is serviced in turn, as long as the priority queue remains empty. The lower-priority queues may never be serviced if there is sufficient traffic in higher-priority queues (a condition called "starvation").

Round Robin Queuing

Round Robin queuing takes one packet from each queue and then starts over. Each queue is serviced, none starve, but there is no way to prioritize any of the traffic or apply any sort of differential treatment to it.

During times of interface congestion, Weighted Round Robin (WRR) queuing weights queues, and more packets are sent from higher weighted queues, thus giving them more bandwidth. However, the bandwidth allocations are done in a way that might lead to more bytes being sent from some queues than desired, which causes other packets to be delayed.

Weighted Fair Queuing

Weighted Fair Queuing (WFQ) attempts to address some of the failing of FIFO and Priority queuing by allowing all traffic some access to the interface. Some characteristics of WFQ include:

- Queues traffic by flow or conversation.
- Flows are identified by header information, such as source and destination IP address, protocol, source and destination ports, and type of service field value. These are used by a hash algorithm to create a queue index number.
- Each interface has a limited number of WFQ queues. Default for most interfaces is 256; it can be configured from 16–4096.
- If the number of flows exceeds the number of queues, multiple flows are placed in the same queue, resulting in less bandwidth per flow.
- Provides queues for system traffic and RSVP traffic separate from the WFQ queues.
- Traffic is weighted by flow, based on IP precedence.
- WFQ schedules small interactive flows before high-bandwidth flows.
- Allows lower-weighted flows relatively more bandwidth than higher-weighted conversations.
- Drops packets from high-volume flows more aggressively than those of low-volume flows.
- The *hold-queue limit* determines how many packets can be held in the WFQ system before all new packets are dropped (tail drop). The default is 1000.

- The *congestive discard threshold (CDT)* determines how many packets can be held by the WFQ before it begins dropping packets from high-volume flows. Packets are dropped from the queues with the most packets first. Packets are not dropped from low-volume conversations. The default CDT is 64.

Advantages of WFQ include simplicity of configuration, support on most platforms and IOS versions, allowing some bandwidth to all traffic, and dropping more packets from higher-bandwidth flows.

Disadvantages of WFQ include lack of support for tunneling or encryption, lack of manual control over traffic classification, lack of minimum or fixed bandwidth guarantees, and chance of multiple flows placed in the same queue.

Configuring WFQ

WFQ is enabled by default on physical interfaces with a bandwidth less than 2.048 Mbps. If it has been disabled, or to enable it on another interface, use the interface command **fair-queue** [*congestive-discard-threshold* [*dynamic-queues* [*reservable-queues*]]]. For example, the following commands enable WFQ on the serial interface, set a CDT of 100, increase the number of flow queues to 512, and reserve 10 queues for RSVP to use.

```
Router(config)#int s1/0/0:0
Router(config-if)#fair-queue 100 512 10
```

To change the size of the hold queue, use the **hold-queue** *number* {**in** | **out**} interface command, as shown:

```
Router(config-if)#hold-queue 2000 out
```

To monitor the interface queues, use either **show interface** *interface* or **show queue** *interface*:

```
Router#show interface s1/0/0:0
[output omitted]
  Input queue: 0/75/0/0 (size/max/drops/flushes); Total output
 drops: 0
  Queueing strategy: weighted fair
  Output queue: 0/2000/100/0 (size/max total/threshold/drops)
     Conversations  0/0/512 (active/max active/max total)
     Reserved Conversations 0/0 (allocated/max allocated)
     Available Bandwidth 2250 kilobits/sec
 [output omitted]
```

```
Router#show queue s1/0/0:0
  Input queue: 0/75/0/0 (size/max/drops/flushes); Total output
 drops: 0
  Queueing strategy: weighted fair
  Output queue: 0/1000/100/0 (size/max total/threshold/drops)
     Conversations  0/0/512 (active/max active/max total)
     Reserved Conversations 0/0 (allocated/max allocated)
     Available Bandwidth 2250 kilobits/sec
```

CBWFQ and LLQ

CBWFQ

Class-Based Weighted Fair Queuing (CBWFQ) addresses some of the problems with WFQ. It allows manual configuration of traffic classification and minimum bandwidth guarantees. It uses the MQC to configure classes and allocate bandwidth. Therefore, you can group traffic into classes based on any of the criteria available through the MQC. Each class becomes its own FIFO queue at the interface. This is still considered Weighted Fair Queuing because each queue is assigned a weight based on the class bandwidth guarantee, and the scheduler takes packets from each queue based on those weights.

There are three ways to designate bandwidth within an MQC policy map. All the CBWFQ classes within a single policy map must use the same method.

- The **bandwidth** *bandwidth-in-kbps* command
- The **bandwidth percent** command
- The **bandwidth remaining percent** command

Each of these methods designates a minimum bandwidth to allocate to the class. Traffic is allowed to burst above that amount if extra bandwidth is available. You can allocate up to 75 percent of the interface bandwidth by default; the rest is reserved for system traffic, such as routing updates. This can be changed using the **max-reserved-bandwidth** interface command.

You can optionally specify the maximum number of packets allowed in each class queue with the policy map command **queue-limit** *number-of-packets*. The default is 64.

Each policy map has a default class that is created automatically. All traffic not identified by one of the other classes is placed in this queue. You can allocate bandwidth to this class or enable WFQ for its traffic, but not both. To enable WFQ, use the **fair-queue** command. If WFQ is enabled, you can also configure the number of dynamic queues with the **fair-queue** *number-of-queues* command.

Benefits of CBWFQ include:

- Control over traffic classification
- Minimum bandwidth guarantees
- Granular control and scalability

Drawbacks of CBWFQ include:

- Voice traffic can be delayed

LLQ

LLQ addresses the needs of real-time traffic for low delay and guaranteed bandwidth. It creates one priority queue (in addition to the CBWFQs) with bandwidth that is both guaranteed and policed. This is a strict priority queue—traffic is sent from it before any other queues. However, when the interface is congested, the priority queue is not allowed to exceed its configured bandwidth to avoid starving the other queues. Voice traffic is typically enqueued into the LLQ. You can place more than one class of traffic in the LLQ. If so, the router still creates just one priority queue but allocates bandwidth to each class, and meters the traffic so that it does not exceed the bandwidth assigned to that class.

Configure LLQ under the class statement in the policy map:

```
(config-pmap-c)#priority {bandwidth [burst] ¦ percent percentage
 [burst]}
```

Bandwidth is configured in kilobits per second, and burst is configured in bytes. These bandwidth amounts include the layer 2 headers.

Example 4-2 shows RTP voice traffic put into an LLQ, then guaranteed and policed to 256K of bandwidth. Traffic bound to URLs that include the string "ccnp" are placed in another queue, guaranteed 128K of bandwidth, and congestion avoidance is applied via WRED. Traffic bound for eDonkey applications is dropped. All other traffic falls into the default class, is placed in its own queue, and WRED is applied. The policy is applied outbound on the serial interface.

Example 4-2 Configuring LLQ and CBQFQ

```
Router(config)#class-map VOIP-Out
Router(config-cmap)#match ip dscp ef
Router(config-cmap)#!
Router(config-cmap)#class-map Exams-Out
Router(config-cmap)#match ip dscp 31
Router(config-cmap)#!
Router(config-cmap)#class-map eDonkey-Out
Router(config-cmap)#match ip dscp 13
Router(config-cmap)#!
Router(config-cmap)#policy-map QOS
Router(config-pmap)#class VOIP-Out
Router(config-pmap-c)#priority 256
Router(config-pmap-c)#class Exams
Router(config-pmap-c)#bandwidth 128
Router(config-pmap-c)#random-detect dscp-based
Router(config-pmap-c)#class eDonkey
Router(config-pmap-c)#drop
Router(config-pmap-c)#class class-default
Router(config-pmap-c)#fair-queue
Router(config-pmap-c)#random-detect dscp-based
!
Router(config)#int s1/0/0:1
Router(config-if)#service-policy output QOS
```

Use the **show policy-map interface** *interface* command to see the service policy configuration and also the effect it has had, as shown in Example 4-3.

Example 4-3 Verifying a Policy Map

```
Router#show policy-map output interface s1/0/0:0

 Serial1/0/0:0

  Service-policy output: TestPolicy

    Class-map: VoIP (match-all)
      0 packets, 0 bytes
      5 minute offered rate 0 bps, drop rate 0 bps
      Match: access-group 100
```

```
      Weighted Fair Queueing
        Strict Priority
        Output Queue: Conversation 264
        Bandwidth 128 (kbps) Burst 3200 (Bytes)
        (pkts matched/bytes matched) 0/0
        (total drops/bytes drops) 0/0
    Class-map: class-default (match-any)
      19 packets, 1990 bytes
  30 seconds offered rate 0 bps, drop rate 0 bps
       Match: any
```

Congestion Avoidance

WRED solves two major problems with TCP and tail drop:

- *TCP Synchronization* occurs when all TCP packets exiting an interface are repeatedly dropped. At each tail drop, each session goes into slow start, and then ramps up its sending rate. When the interface queue fills, all packets are dropped again, and all sessions reduce their sending again. Eventually this results in waves of increased and decreased transmission, causing underutilization of the interface.
- *TCP Starvation* results when large flows, with increased window sizes, fill the interface queue. Packets from smaller or less aggressive flows are then dropped. This can cause jitter for those smaller flows due to a lack of a differentiated dropping strategy.

Random Early Detection (RED) attempts to avoid tail drops by preventing the interface from becoming totally congested. Once the queue fills above a threshold level, it drops random packets from the interface queue, dropping a higher percentage of packets as the queue fills. TCP sessions experience a packet loss at different times, and so they go into slow start at different times, thus preventing TCP synchronization.

You need to understand three RED concepts:

- Minimum threshold—The queue depth at which RED begins dropping packets.
- Maximum threshold—The queue depth at which the maximum number of packets are being dropped.

- Mark probability denominator—Controls how many packets are dropped when the maximum threshold is reached. The probability of a packet being dropped equals 1/*max-prob-denom*.

RED has three packet-dropping modes:

- No drop—When the queue depth is between zero and the minimum threshold.
- Random drop—When the queue depth is between the minimum and the maximum thresholds.
- Tail drop—When the queue depth is above the maximum threshold.

Basic RED does not distinguish between flows or types of traffic. Weighted RED, on the other hand, drops traffic differently depending on its IP precedence or DSCP value. WRED is combined with CBWFQ to implement DiffServ's Assured Forwarding PHB. Each PHB has a unique WRED profile, identifying a minimum threshold, maximum threshold, and mark probability denominator for that profile. There are default profiles for each PHB, but they can also be manually configured.

Configure WRED under a physical interface, a VC, or a class within a policy map with the command **random-detect** [**dscp-based**]. Packet drop decisions are based on IP precedence value unless the **dscp-based** option is configured. To change the default profile for a specific DSCP value, use the **random-detect dscp** *dscp-value min-threshold max-threshold mark-probability-denominator* command.

Traffic Policing and Shaping

Traffic policing and traffic shaping are both ways to control the amount of traffic through an interface. Policing drops traffic, whereas shaping buffers it for sending later. Policing can be used inbound or outbound, but shaping is used only on outbound traffic.

Both mechanisms use a token bucket concept to measure the amount of bandwidth allowed. Enough tokens enter the bucket at regular intervals to allow the interface to send the number of bytes configured for that interval. If a packet enqueued has fewer bytes than are represented by tokens in the bucket, it considered a *conforming* packet. The packet is sent and an equivalent number of tokens are subtracted from the bucket. If it has more bytes than there are tokens to send, it is considered an *exceeding* packet. The router then takes action based on whether policing or shaping is configured.

Some implementations use two token buckets. If a packet exceeds the first bucket, it is checked against the second one. If there are not enough tokens in the second bucket to send the packet, it is considered a *violation*.

If all the tokens are not used within the interval, they can accrue and remain available to future packets if bursting is enabled.

Traffic Policing

By using the QoS policing function, bandwidth use can be controlled on physical interfaces. Policing specifies an amount of bandwidth allowed for a particular type of traffic, and generally drops traffic over that amount. It can also be configured to allow the excess traffic, but it marks it with a different (usually lower) DSCP value.

Some uses for policing include:

- Limiting the bandwidth of a high-speed interface to a lower rate
- Limiting the rate of an application or a traffic class
- Remarking the DSCP of traffic exceeding a specified rate

Class-based policing is configured in a policy map. Its possible conditions are: Conform, Exceed, and Violate. Its possible actions are: Drop, Set (DSCP, for example), and Transmit.

Traffic Shaping

Traffic shaping also controls the amount of traffic sent out an interface, but shaping buffers excess traffic instead of dropping it. Because data is usually bursty, the buffered traffic can be sent out between bursts. Thus, shaping smoothes out the flow of traffic. This also results in fewer packet drops, and thus fewer TCP retransmits. It does, however, introduce some delay for traffic that must be buffered. It does not support remarking traffic.

Some uses for shaping include:

- Making the outgoing traffic rate match the contracted committed information rate (CIR).
- To avoid overrunning remote links in networks, such as ATM, Frame Relay, and Metro Ethernet, that might have different bandwidths on hub and spoke devices.
- Interacting with Frame Relay congestion notifications, causing the router to throttle-back its sending rate.

Class-based traffic shaping is configured under the policy map. It works with any type of interface, not just Frame Relay interfaces.

Link Efficiency Mechanisms

Although QoS mechanisms cannot actually create bandwidth, they can help your network use the available bandwidth more efficiently. Two ways of doing this are compression and fragmentation. These mechanisms are typically applied at the WAN edge, where links are slower than within the LAN.

Compression

Compressing the traffic on a line creates more useable bandwidth; because each frame is smaller, there are fewer bits to transmit. Thus, the serialization delay is reduced, and more frames can be sent. Cisco IOS supports two types of compression: payload and header.

Payload compression can be done at either Layer 2 or Layer 3.

- Layer 2 Payload Compression—The Layer 2 payload compression compresses the Layer 3 and 4 headers and the packet data. Layer 2 payload compression is typically a hop-by-hop mechanism, because the Layer 2 header is removed at each hop. Layer 2 compression done in software is CPU-intensive and might actually add extra delay to the traffic flow. Hardware compression, however, adds little delay. Cisco supports three Layer 2 payload compression algorithms:
  - Stacker
  - Predictor
  - Microsoft Point-to-Point Compression (MPPC)
- Layer 3 Payload Compression—Layer 3 payload compression compresses the Layer 4 header and the packet data. It is generally done session-by-session.

Header compression leaves the payload intact but compresses the headers. TCP header compression compresses the IP and TCP headers. RTP header compression compresses the IP, UDP, and RTP headers. It is most effective when the headers are much larger than the payload, such as with Telnet or VoIP. Headers do not change much over the life of a flow and contain many redundant fields (such as source and destination IP address, protocol, and port). Compression removes the redundant information and sends only the new information and an index pointing to the unchanged information.

Compression configured on a physical interface applies to all flows. For more granular control over which traffic is compressed, configure it in the MQC policy map under the desired classes. Header compression uses fairly few CPU resources.

Link Fragmentation and Interleave (LFI)

A typical network has a range of packet sizes. Small packets can be delayed waiting for a large packet to be sent out the interface. This can happen even if LLQ is configured—a small voice packet might be sent immediately to the hardware queue. However, the hardware queue is FIFO. If a large packet arrived there just before the voice packet, it is serialized out the interface first. The voice packet has to wait. This causes delay and jitter.

LFI breaks large packets into smaller segments and intersperses the smaller packets between the pieces of the big ones. Thus, delay and jitter are reduced for the small packets.

The target serialization delay for voice is 10–15 ms. At 2 Mbps link speed, a 1500 byte packet can be serialized in 10 ms. Thus, there is typically no need for LFI on links over E1 speed.

QoS with VPNs

A Virtual Private Network (VPN) is a way of creating a virtual point-to-point link over a shared network (often over the Internet). It can be used either for user remote access or for intrasite links. Two types of remote access VPNs are:

- Client-initiated—The user has a VPN client application, such as Cisco's VPN Client, on their computer. After they are connected to the Internet, they use the application to connect them to their network.
- Network Access Server (NAS) initiated—Users connect into an access server at their ISP. The NAS then sets up a VPN to the private network.

Two types of intrasite VPNs are:

- Intranet VPN—Links sites within the same company to each other.
- Extranet VPN—Links an external group (such as a customer or supplier) to the company's private network.

VPNs have several advantages, including:

- The ability to encrypt traffic across the public network and keep it confidential.
- The ability to verify that the data was not changed between the source and destination.
- The ability to authenticate the packet sender.

Router-to-router VPN tunnels use a logical tunnel interface that is created on the router. This interface is where you put configuration pertaining to the tunnel itself. Tunnel traffic uses one of the router's physical interfaces, determined by the routing table. Configuration on this interface applies to all traffic, even if several tunnels use that interface.

VPNs create an extra challenge for QoS. A VPN tunnels traffic from one device to another by adding an IP header on top of the original one. Thus, the original header, with its QoS markings, is hidden from routers in the packet's path. If the packet needs any special QoS treatment, the markings must be copied from the original IP header into the tunnel IP header.

GRE Tunnels

Generic Routing Encapsulation (GRE) tunnels add a GRE header and a tunnel IP header to the packet. By default, TOS markings on the original packet are copied into the tunnel IP header. When the packet arrives at the physical interface, classification and queuing are based on the markings in the tunnel IP header.

IPsec Tunnels

IP Security (IPSec) can operate in either tunnel mode or transport mode. In tunnel mode, it creates a tunnel through the underlying network. In transport mode, it provides security over normal physical links or over a tunnel created with a different protocol. IPSec can also provide either authentication alone using Authentication Headers (AH) or encryption and authentication using Encapsulation Security Protocol (ESP). Table 4-4 describes the differences between AH and ESP.

Table 4-4 IPSec AH and ESP

	AH	ESP
Protocol	51	50
Fields Added	Authentication Header	ESP Header, ESP Trailer, ESP Authentication Trailer
IP Header—Tunnel Mode	Creates new tunnel IP header	Creates new tunnel IP header
IP Header—Transport Mode	Uses original IP header	Uses original IP header
TOS Byte—Transport Mode	Copies original TOS markings to new IP header	Copies original TOS markings to new IP header
TOS Byte—Transport Mode	Original TOS byte is available	Original TOS byte is available
Payload Change	None	Encrypts payload
Authentication Protocols Supported	MD5, SHA	MD5, SHA
Encryption Protocols Supported	None	DES, 3DES, AES

MD5 = Message Digest 5

SHA = Secure Hash Algorithm

DES = Data Encryption Standard

AES = Advanced Encryption Standard

Although both GRE and IPSec allow traffic to be classified based on its original TOS markings, there are times when you might want to classify based on other fields, such as port number or original IP address. In that case, packets must be classified before the original IP header is hidden or encrypted. To do this, use the **qos pre-classify** command. This command causes the router to make a copy of the original IP header, and classify the packet based on that information.

qos pre-classify can be given on a tunnel interface, in a crypto map, or on a virtual template interface, and it works only on IP packets. Use it on the tunnel interface for a GRE tunnel, on the virtual interface for a L2TP tunnel, and under both the crypto map and the tunnel interface for an IPSec tunnel—IF classification must be done on non-TOS fields.

Enterprise-Wide QoS Deployment

SLA

A company might use a Service Level Agreement (SLA) to contract with their ISP for certain levels of service. This typically provides levels of throughput, delay, jitter, packet loss, and link availability, along with penalties for missing the SLA. With Layer 2 links (such as frame relay), the service provider is not involved in providing QoS through its network. With Layer 3 links (such as MPLS), the service provider can contract for QoS SLAs through its network.

Service providers use a set number of classes, and your marking must conform to their guidelines to use QoS SLAs. When calculating the amount of delay (or latency), jitter, and packet loss for your SLA, remember to take into account your internal network performance. For example, voice is best with an end-to-end delay of 150 ms or less. If the latency in the LAN at each site is 25 ms, then your latency SLA with the ISP should be no more than 100 ms.

Enterprise QoS

Each block within an enterprise network has its own QoS needs and considerations. In general, you should:

- Classify and mark traffic as close to the access edge as possible. Switches that can accomplish this in hardware are more efficient than routers that must do it in software.
- Establish the correct trust boundaries.
- Prioritize real-time traffic (such as voice and video).
- Configure the appropriate queues on outbound interfaces.

At the Access switch level:

- Set the trust boundary appropriately.
- Classify and mark non-VoIP traffic.
- Place VoIP traffic in interface priority queue.
- Set speed and duplex.
- Can use multiple queues, especially on uplink ports.

At the Distribution switch level:

- Set the trust boundary appropriately.
- Place VoIP traffic in interface priority queue.
- Set speed and duplex.
- Can use multiple queues, especially on uplink ports.
- Might use Layer 3 policing and marking.
- Use WRED in data queues.

At the WAN edge:

- Determine SLA.
- Might need to reclassify and remark traffic.
- Use LLQ for real-time traffic.
- Use WRED in data queues.
- Might need to use shaping, compression, or LFI.

Within the service provider's network:

- Have a DiffServ-compliant backbone.
- Use LLQ or modified deficit round robin (MDRR).
- Plan for adequate capacity.
- Use WRED in data queues.

The actual configuration done on WAN edge routers depends on whether or not the router is managed by the provider. If it is managed, then the provider configures output policies on the customer router and does not need any input policies on the provider edge router. For traffic bound from the provider network to the customer network, the provider edge router has the configuration to enforce SLAs.

If the customer edge router is not managed, then customers must configure their own QoS policies. The service provider likely also configures their edge router to enforce contracted SLAs on traffic from the customer. For traffic bound from the provider network to the customer network, the provider edge router has the configuration to enforce SLAs. The customer might have other types of configuration, such as reclassifying and remarking to fit their internal QoS policies.

CoPP

Control Plane Policing (CoPP) allows QoS to be applied to the router's control plane to avoid overrunning the router's CPU. The control plane consists of high-level processes that run on the route processor, and handles management tasks, such as traffic bound to or from the router or switch itself.

CoPP uses the MQC to control the traffic bound to and from the router or switch's control plane. Two policy options are available—police or drop. To configure CoPP, take the following steps:

Step 1. Configure a class map that identifies traffic to be policed.

Step 2. Configure a policy map that either polices the traffic permitted by the class map or drops it.

Step 3. Enter control plane configuration mode using the global **control-plane** command.

Step 4. Apply the service policy to the control plane.

During a DoS attack, or times of heavy processor use, CoPP can ensure that the network device remains available and critical network traffic can be processed.

CHAPTER 5

AutoQoS

Chapter 3 contained an introduction to AutoQoS. This chapter expands on that and offers some restrictions, caveats, and ways to tune it.

Some benefits of AutoQoS include:

- Classification of applications
- Automatic policy generation
- QoS configuration
- Monitoring and recording via SNMP and Cisco QPM
- Consistent QoS policies

AutoQoS originally supported only VoIP applications. AutoQoS for VoIP is available on all Cisco routers and switches. Implementing it is basically a one-step process, as shown in the example in Chapter 3.

AutoQoS for Switches

To configure AutoQoS on a switch, use the interface command **auto qos voip** {**cisco-phone** | **cisco-softphone** | **trust**}. Use the **cisco-phone** keyword when the interface connects to a phone; QoS markings are trusted when a Cisco IP phone is detected. Use the **cisco-softphone** keyword when the interface connects to a computer using the Cisco' SoftPhone. Use the **trust** keyword when the interface links to a trusted switch or a router. Giving this command automatically enables global QoS support (**mls qos**). Use **show auto qos** or **show mls qos interface** *interface-id* to view the AutoQoS configuration and the QoS actions.

AutoQos for Routers

Routers can also use AutoQoS; recent IOS versions support AutoQos for Enterprise applications. AutoQoS for Enterprise is currently supported only on routers, and is a two-step process. The configuration can be manually tuned after it is automatically generated.

Step 1. **Application discovery and policy generation**—The first step is to enable application discovery on interfaces where QoS is configured. NBAR is typically used for this. The router then collects application data for the desired number of days, analyzes the data, and creates QoS templates. You can review these configurations before applying them to the interface.

Use the interface command **auto discovery qos** [**trust**] to enable application discovery. Without the optional **trust** keyword, the router uses NBAR. With it, the router classifies traffic by DSCP markings. Use **show auto discovery qos** to view the traffic discovered and the configuration that is implemented.

Step 2. **Implement the AutoQoS policies**—Apply the policies generated by AutoQoS to the interface(s). Use the interface command **auto qos** [**voip** [**trust**] **fr-atm**]. The optional **voip** keywork enables only AutoQoS for VoIP. If you use this, you can then optionally choose to trust the existing DSCP markings with the keyword **trust**, or enable AutoQoS for frame-relay to ATM with the optional keyword **fr-atm**. Use **show auto qos** to view the AutoQoS configuration.

AutoQoS Restrictions and Caveats

CEF must be enabled for AutoQoS to work. The interface must not have an existing QoS policy configured. Bandwidth should be configured on each interface. If you change the bandwidth after enabling AutoQoS, the router does not change its QoS policies to reflect the new bandwidth. It classifies links as slow or fast, with slow being 768 kbps or less. An IP address must be configured on slow speed links prior to enabling AutoQoS because the router uses Multilink PPP and transfers the IP address to the multilink interface by default. On access switches, CDP must be enabled for the switch to detect a Cisco IP phone.

SNMP support and an SNMP server address must be configured on the router for SNMP traps to work. The SNMP string "AutoQoS" needs to have write permissions.

AutoQoS supports the following WAN interfaces:

- Frame Relay point-to-point subinterfaces. The PVC must not have a map class or virtual template already assigned to it. If LFI is needed, AutoQoS configures it for G.729 codec use. Manual tuning is needed for G.711 use.
- ATM point-to-point PVCs. The PVC must not have a virtual template already assigned to it. Configure it as VBR-NRT.
- Serial interfaces using PPP or HDLC. AutoQoS must be configured on both sides of the link, and both sides must use the same bandwidth.

Tuning AutoQoS

AutoQoS might need tuning for three common reasons. First, it can configure too many classes for your network needs. Second, it does not adapt to changing network conditions. Third, it just might not include the types of policies you want.

Some questions to ask as you evaluate the policies generated by AutoQoS include:

- How many classes were created using class maps?
- What classification criterion was used to place traffic into each class?
- What DSCP and COS markings were configured for each traffic class?
- What types of queuing or other QoS mechanisms were implemented?
- Was the policy applied to the interface, PVC, or subinterface?

AutoQoS Classes

AutoQoS uses up to ten different traffic classes, as shown in Table 5-1. The table also shows the type of traffic included in each class, along with its DSCP and COS markings.

Table 5-1 AutoQoS Traffic Classes

Traffic Class	Traffic Type	DSCP	COS
IP Routing	Network control traffic (for example, routing protocols)	CS6	6
Interactive Voice	Voice bearer traffic	EF	5
Interactive Video	Interactive video data traffic (for example, videoconferencing)	AF41	4
Streaming Video	Streaming media traffic	CS4	4
Telephony Signaling	Voice signaling and control traffic	CS3	3
Transactional and Interactive Data	Transactional database applications such as SQL	AF21	2
Network Management	Network management traffic such as telnet	CS2	2
Bulk Data	Email traffic, general data traffic, bulk data transfers	AF11	1
Scavenger	Traffic needing less-than-best-effort treatment	CS1	1
Best Effort	Default class, includes all other traffic	0	0

Too many classes might be generated for your needs. Most companies use between three and six classes. You might want to manually consolidate some classes with similar QoS needs after AutoQoS has finished its configuration.

AutoQoS and Changing Network Conditions

AutoQoS creates its configuration based on the traffic it discovered during the initial discovery phase with NBAR. If conditions change, you might need to disable it, run autodiscovery again, and then re-enable AutoQoS.

Manually Tuning AutoQoS Configurations

The **show auto qos** command shows the class maps that AutoQoS created, along with their match criteria and any access lists it created. It shows the policy maps, and the policy configured for each class. It shows where the policy was applied and any monitoring that was implemented. This can help you determine what changes are needed to the configuration.

You can modify AutoQoS configuration in two ways:

- Using Cisco QPM
- Manually with the MQC

To modify using the MQC, allow the router/switch to apply its AutoQoS configuration. Copy the relevant portions to a text editor and make the desired changes. This might include changing the classification criteria, combining classes, or altering the policy for a particular class, for instance. Then replace the old configuration with the new one.

CHAPTER 6

Wireless Scalability

Wireless LANs (WLAN) are an extension to wired networks using wireless standards, such as 802.11A/B/G. The 802.11 standards take the place of the Ethernet standard, but both data-links support the same types of services. The benefit of WLANs is that it allows users to relocate within the workspace, closer to machinery or conference rooms, for instance.

WLAN QoS

802.11 wireless uses carrier sense multiple access/collision avoidance (CSMA/CA), meaning transmissions are pre-announced, because systems may not be able to hear each other or recognize collisions later. CA uses a Distributed Coordination Function (DCF) to implement timers and delays to ensure cooperation.

Unfortunately, DCF timers interfere with low-latency applications, such as voice and video. Wi-Fi Multimedia (WMM or 802.11e) is an attempt to shorten timers—proportional to Differentiated Services Code Point (DSCP) priority—and prioritize important traffic. WMM replaces DCF with enhanced DCF (EDCF) that creates four categories (platinum, gold, silver, and bronze) and forces longer interframe waits on lower-priority traffic.

LWAP

Cisco introduced Lightweight Access Points (LWAP) that use the concept of "split MAC," which separates the real-time communication and management functions. An LWAP controls beaconing, buffering, and encryption and uses a controller for 802.1x, Extensible Authentication Protocol (EAP), key management, and bridging functions.

In the LWAP scenario, QoS is handled at the controller. QoS is marked at Layer 2 using 802.11e. 802.11e, like 802.1p, will not pass through a router, so it has to be converted to DSCP if used end-to-end in a large network. Similarly, .1p and DSCP fields must be mapped back to WMM when traffic goes to the client.

Controllers host profiles that describe traffic handling. At the controller, an administrator can specify:

- Average and burst "best-effort" data rate
- Average and burst "real-time" data rate
- Maximum RF usage (set to 100%)
- Queue depth, which is the number of packets that will be in the queu if the line is busy
- WMM-to-802.1p mapping

Furthermore, the controller may be set up to ignore, allow, or require 802.11e.

802.1x and WLAN Security

WLAN security is important because wireless systems are designed to allow easy access and may extend beyond the physical perimeter of your building. Many WLAN implementations do not have encryption or authentication. Small wonder then that "war driving," or the act of randomly wondering in search of an open AP, is so easy to perform.

The number-one problem is that most APs are insecure by default and few have any security added to them. When present, security for WLANs is accomplished through authenticating users and encrypting traffic. Old forms of authentication and encryption have been found vulnerable, so APs must be kept current. Types of wireless security include:

- Service Set Identifier (SSID)
- Authentication by MAC
- Static Wired Equivalent Privacy (WEP) keys
- One-way authentication

Network administrators must not only ensure their APs are secure, they must always look for rogue APs (access points put up by users to accomplish a narrow goal without regard to corporate security).

Note

LWAPs and their controllers help with AP security and rogue AP detection. LWAPs, because they are controlled from a central point, are more scalable because administration is much easier. Cisco LWAP/Controller model also has rogue detection baked in.

Figure 6-1 shows a timeline of WLAN security.

Figure 6-1 WLAN Security over Time

WEP	WPA	WPA2
Weak authentication Static keys Weak broken encryption	Mutual authentication Dynamic keys Better encryption	Mutual authentication Dynamic keys Good encryption (AES) Includes intrusion detection

WLAN Security Development →

802.11 WEP supports open and shared key authentication. Open authentication means that no authentication is used and any user is allowed to associate with an AP. Shared key authentication expects a cryptographic key to be known before accessing the AP; this key is subsequently used to encrypt the payload. To authenticate using a shared key, an AP sends a plain-text challenge, which the PC encrypts and sends back. If it is encrypted correctly, the PC is authenticated. More detail is provided in Figure 6-2, which shows the entire authentication process.

Figure 6-2 WLAN Authentication

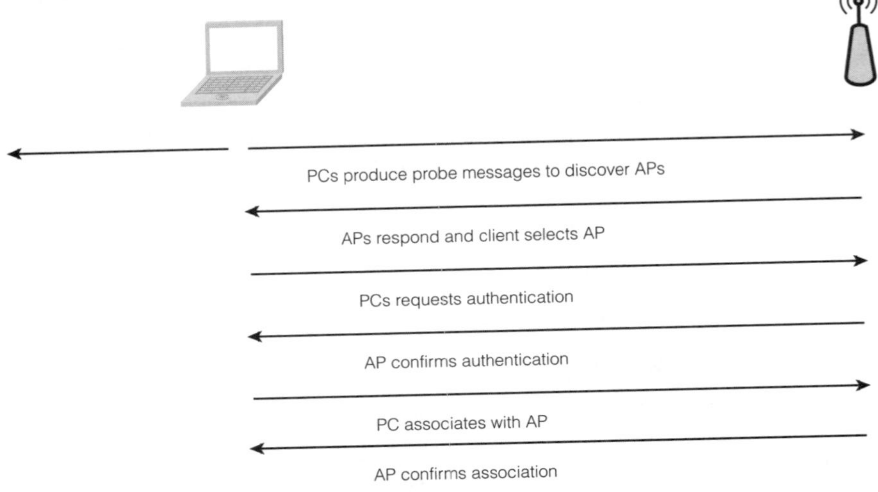
PCs produce probe messages to discover APs
APs respond and client selects AP
PCs requests authentication
AP confirms authentication
PC associates with AP
AP confirms association

Enhanced WEP was a Cisco proprietary fix to WEP that added two improvements:

- 802.1x for authentication
- Cisco Key Integrity Protocol (CKIP) to protect the key

WPA (Wi-Fi Protected Access), the pre-standard version of 802.11i, mirrored the Cisco Enhanced WEP by enhancing encryption and authentication in much the same way. Encryption is improved by incorporating Temporal Key Integrity Protocol (TKIP). WPA2 (standard 802.11i) added Advanced Encryption Standard (AES) encryption. Authentication was improved to support 802.1x and the Extensible Authentication Protocol (EAP).

Key improvements in WPA/WPA2 include the following:

- Per-session keys allow users a different key each time the user accesses the AP.
- TKIP changes the way the key is applied to consecutive packets.
- Encryption uses a starting number called an Initialization Vector (IV). WPA uses an IV that is harder to guess.
- The cryptographic function is changed to 128-bit AES. AES is a standard that is common in security functions, such as virtual private networks (VPN).
- 802.1x for encrypted RADIUS authentication. RADIUS can be linked back to Active Directory, so users sign in with familiar usernames and passwords.

802.1x requires that the client and AP support EAP and that a RADIUS server is present. There are several methods based on EAP to accomplish authentication:

- Lightweight EAP (LEAP)
- EAP Flexible Authentication via Secure Tunnel (EAP-FAST)
- EAP-Transport Layer Security (EAP-TLS)
- Protected EAP (PEAP)

Configuring WLAN Security on Controller

Open (no authentication) is typically set up on public APs. On a Cisco WLAN controller, choose **WLANs > Edit** and then set Layer 2 Security to None.

Setting Layer 2 Security to Static WEP, WPA, or WPA2 allows control of parameters for a static key. If no WPA static key is entered, then the controller will use EAP 802.1x to RADIUS.

Setting Layer 2 Security to 802.1X supports dynamic WEP keys. Key size may be selected, but remember that Windows XP supports only 40-bit and 104-bit keys.

If Layer 3 Security is selected, then users will enter credentials on a customizable web page, which then checks an internal database or a remote RADIUS server.

WLAN Management

Cisco supports two WLAN models.

- Autonomous APs:
  - Users connect to APs.
  - APs are aggregated by Wireless Domain Services (WDS).
  - WDS is controlled by a Wireless Solution Engine (WLSE), which centralizes control similar to an LW Controller.
- Lightweight APs connected to a controller:
  - Users attach to LWAPs.
  - LWAPs are controlled by controllers.
  - Controllers are managed by Wireless Control System (WCS).

The benefit of LWAPs is centralized control. The problem is that loss of the controller brings the whole campus down, so redundancy is recommended. The lightweight model provides displays of RF coverage, dynamic management of the radio environment, detection of rogue APs, and easier roaming.

WLSE brings many of the benefits of a controller to an existing autonomous deployment. WLSE is offered in two versions, both of which also handle AAA:

- Ciscoworks WLSE for large deployments
- Ciscoworks WLSE Express for fewer than 100 APs

WCS allows management of the entire network as a unit. It runs as a service on Linux or Windows. Three feature sets are supported:

- Base, which detects rogue APs and tracks a device to the closest AP.
- WCS with Location, which adds support for RF fingerprinting and tracks a device to within 10 meters.
- WCS with Location+, which adds the ability to track 1500 clients at the same time and collects historical information.

Location is important to support VoIP calls to 911.

INDEX

NUMBERS

A

B

C

D

E

F

G - H

I

J - K - L

M

N

O

P

Q

R

S

T

U

V

W

X - Y - Z